University of
Hertfordshire

Technological Collaboration

Technological Collaboration

The Dynamics of Cooperation
in Industrial Innovation

Edited by

Rod Coombs

*Professor of Technology Management, Manchester School of
Management, UMIST, UK*

Albert Richards

*Research Associate, CROMTEC, Manchester School of Management,
UMIST, UK*

Pier Paolo Saviotti

University of Grenoble, France

Vivien Walsh

Senior Lecturer, Manchester School of Management, UMIST, UK

Edward Elgar

Cheltenham, UK • Brookfield, US

Published by
Edward Elgar Publishing Limited
8 Lansdown Place
Cheltenham
Glos GL50 2HU
UK

Edward Elgar Publishing Company
Old Post Road
Brookfield
Vermont 05036
US

British Library Cataloguing in Publication Data
Technological Collaboration: Dynamics of
Cooperation in Industrial Innovation
  I. Coombs, Rod
  338.064

Library of Congress Cataloguing in Publication Data
Technological collaboration: the dynamics of cooperation in
  industrial innovation/edited by Rod Coombs ... [et al.].
      p.   cm.
  Includes bibliographical references and index.
  1. Technological innovations—Economic aspects. 2. Industrial
management. 3. Technology and stats. I. Coombs, Rod.
HC79.T4T4297 1996
338'.064—dc20   95–18024
                                                          CIP

ISBN 1 85898 235 9

Printed and bound in Great Britain by
Biddles Limited, Guildford and King's Lynn

Contents

Figures

Tables

Contributors

Christophe Bonazzi, Centre d'étude sur les resources naturelles, École Normale Supérieure des Mines, 62 Boulevard St Michel, 75272 Paris, Cedex 06, France

François Chesnais, Professor of International Economics, Université de Paris Nord-Villetaneuse, Paris, France

Steve Conway, Technology Policy Unit, Aston Business School, University of Aston, Birmingham, B4 7ET, UK

Rod Coombs, Professor of Technology Management, Manchester School of Management, UMIST, PO Box 88, Manchester, M60 1QD, UK

Mark Dodgson, Managing Business in Asia, Australian National University, Research School of Pacific Studies, Canberra, ACT 0200, Australia

Wendy Faulkner, Research Fellow, Science Studies Unit, University of Edinburgh, 56 George Square, Edinburgh, EH8 9JU, UK

Philippe Larédo, Centre de Sociologie de l'Innovation, École Normale Supérieure des Mines, 62 Boulevard St Michel, 75272 Paris, Cedex 06, France

François Leveque, Centre d'étude sur les resources naturelles, École Normale Supérieure des Mines, 62 Boulevard St Michel, 75272 Paris, Cedex 06, France

Vincent Mangematin, INRA-SERD, Sciences Sociales, University of Pierre Mendés-France BP47, 38040 Grenoble, Cedex 9, France

Philippe Mustar, Centre de Sociologie de l'Innovation, École Normale Supérieure des Mines, 62 Boulevard St Michel, 75272 Paris, Cedex 06, France

Jorge Niosi, Professor and Director, CIRST, University of Quebec and Montreal, PO Box 8888, Centre-Ville, Montreal, Quebec, Canada

Christian Quental, Centre d'étude sur les resources naturelles, École Normale Supérieure des Mines, 62 Boulevard St Michel, 75272 Paris, Cedex 06, France

Albert Richards, CROMTEC, Manchester School of Management, UMIST, PO Box 88, Manchester, M60 1QD, UK

Pier Paolo Saviotti, Professor of Economics, INRA-SERD, Sciences Sociales, University of Pierre Mendés-France BP47, 38040 Grenoble, Cedex 9, France

Jacqueline Senker, Research Fellow, SPRU, University of Sussex, Mantell Building, Falmer, Brighton, BN1 9RF, UK

Fred Steward, Technology Policy Unit, Aston Business School, University of Aston, Birmingham, B4 7ET, UK

Andrew Tylecote, Professor of Economics and the Management of Technical Change, Sheffield University Management School, 9 Mappin Street, Sheffield, S1 4DT, UK

Vivien Walsh, Manchester School of Management, UMIST, PO Box 88, Manchester, M60 1QD, UK

Mo Yamin, Manchester School of Management, UMIST, PO Box 88, Manchester, M60 1QD, UK

Preface

A phenomenon which has grown dramatically in recent years, and which has attracted a great deal of attention, is that of technological collaboration between firms, and more generally, networks of interactions between a variety of other actors who influence the innovation process, including public sector researchers, government sponsors and regulators, special interest groups and users, as well as those in different functional roles in firms. These formal and informal inter-actions may lead to the production of specific innovations of intermediate technological outputs. Among the important questions raised by the phenomenon are the following:

- Is it a temporary phenomenon caused by the existence of specific new technologies whose development demands risk and cost sharing? Or is it a symptom of a robust new structural paradigm for the process of innovation?
- Does collaboration imply the need to revise our understanding of processes of competition and wealth creation?
- What changes are necessary to our understanding and theoretical accounts of firms and their management processes in order to accommodate the phenomenon of collaboration?
- Are there differences between countries in terms of the abilities of their companies to engage in successful collaboration?
- Are there differences between countries in terms of their abilities to use the collaborative processes to capture a share of the potential wealth creation?
- What are the implications of technological collaboration for the science policies and industrial policies of nation states?

This book considers these questions, by drawing on the scholarship of con-tributors from a variety of disciplines, who examine collaboration from a number of viewpoints. The volume arises from the second ASEAT Conference, organized by the editors at Manchester in the Spring of 1993. It follows on from the first volume in the series: *Technological Change and Company Strategies* (Academic Press, 1992), which resulted from the first conference, held in 1991.

The contributors have substantially revised their papers in the light of the discussion at the ASEAT Conference, and we are grateful to them for the attention they have given to this task, and to the discussants at the conference who provided such detailed comments.

Rod Coombs, Albert Richards, Pier Paolo Saviotti and Vivien Walsh

1. Introduction: technological collaboration and networks of alliances in the innovation process

Rod Coombs, Albert Richards, Pier Paolo Saviotti and Vivien Walsh

The construction of networks of linkages between actors involved in the innovation process, and the individual linkages between the actors themselves, have received a great deal of attention in the innovation literature in the 1980s and 1990s. This work has been carried out from a number of disciplinary perspectives, each with a different emphasis, a different set of empirical studies, and a different theoretical basis. In this introduction we shall briefly survey these different trends, focusing primarily on the economic and sociological approaches which represent the wider context of the chapters that follow.

While work in this area has been carried out from a number of disciplinary perspectives, the object of investigation itself has also varied between studies, but not necessarily in direct correlation with the different disciplinary frameworks. That is, work from various social science perspectives has focused both on collaborative alliances between institutions, and on networks. These networks might be a collection of inter-institutional collaborative alliances, or they might be a much wider range of linkages, of varying levels of formality, between a large variety of different actors.

In the literature on economics of technological change, the focus has tended to be on *collaborative agreements between institutions*, which may be analysed theoretically in a number of ways, and not necessarily or explicitly in terms of networks. Pisano (1989, 1990), for example, used a transaction cost approach (discussed further below) to analyse a set of individual cases of choices of in-house R&D versus collaboration, and collaboration involving equity linkages versus contract R&D, in biotechnology. Networks of multiple linkages were not considered. In contrast Hagedoorn and Schakenraad (1990, 1992), within a neo-Schumpeterian or evolutionary framework (discussed below), mapped a network of inter-firm collaborative agreements in various high-technology fields, each firm linked to several others at the same time. They showed clusters of interactions of varying intensity, and changes in the web of linkages over time. In addition, they analysed the strategic objectives of the alliances and the motives of the partners in entering into them.

Although work in the economics area is not only concerned with alliances between business firms, but also inter-organizational linkages of all kinds, the focus nevertheless tends to be primarily on *firms*. And, while informal networks between individuals are recognized as important, in which the exchange of tacit knowledge is a significant component, the focus in many economic studies is on *formal* agreements, such as those involving legal contracts between organizations. The reason for this focus is largely that some of the most important empirical sources of information about alliances have been drawn from analyses of databases such as those of MERIT (e.g. Hagedoorn and Schakenraad, 1990) and LAREA-CEREM (e.g. LAREA-CEREM, 1992). The way in which these databanks were assembled (mainly from reports published in the financial and trade press) meant that they are chiefly a collection of information about formal agreements between business firms, with some bias towards North America and Europe in addition (Chesnais, 1988).

Other studies, which include informal agreements, exchanges of tacit knowledge, and linkages of public-sector research and other organizations, and based on questionnaire and interview surveys, are also more likely to be carried out by interdisciplinary groups (e.g. Senker and Faulkner, Chapter 5, this volume) or sociologists (e.g. Vaváková, 1995).

Within an evolutionary economic framework, the trend of increased collaboration is explained mainly as a consequence of escalating R&D costs, the risks of radical technological change in a period of economic and financial instability, the growing pressure of competitiveness within an increasingly globalized economy, and the importance of synergies, complementarities and interactions between a variety of scientific and technological fields.

Sociological approaches to the analysis of technological change are also concerned with institutions, in that they deal with the effect of organizational culture on behaviour, with hierarchical structures and with power relationships. However, where the sociology of innovation literature deals with networks and linkages, the focus has been less on firms or other organizations as such, and more on interactions between *actors*, within and between organizations.[1] The role of the business firm, as the central institution through which innovations are commercialized, does not receive the same emphasis in the sociology as in the economics of innovation literature. On the other hand, details of the nature of linkages, and of the process of their creation and development, receive more attention in the sociology than in the economics literature. It is rather more common for sociologists to approach the question of linkages in the context of a network; mapping, for example, networks of relationships between innovators, users, suppliers of finance, materials and components, public research laboratories, regulatory authorities, economic and technology policy makers, and potentially competing firms with complementary skills. And not just mapping them: their creation and evolution are typically described in some detail, showing, for example, how the establishment and maintenance of such linkages is essential to the success of an innovation, and incomplete networks or weak linkages associated with failure. But sociologists also deal with data sets of individual linkages (rather than networks) surveying, for example, the motivations of the partners; how each sees the benefits and disadvantages in the relationship; the issues involved in working with someone from a business versus public research culture, or a different national culture; how questions of power, control, decision making and hierarchy may be resolved, and so on. Clearly there is some overlap here between economic and sociological surveys, in that some within both disciplines are concerned now with issues of strategy and motivation. Indeed it is not always possible to say that a particular study is clearly sociological or economic, rather than interdisciplinary. There is thus already the beginning of some convergence in the methodology of empirical studies, though less so in the theoretical frameworks within which explanations are proposed.

An interest in networks has also developed among researchers who might broadly be described as being at the interface of marketing and innovation, particularly in Sweden. Two books edited by Håkansson (1982, 1987) can be considered to be representative of work within this framework. Based empirically on case studies of new product development in industrial markets, this literature describes networks, based on a taxonomy along various dimensions, of the bonds established. Håkansson himself (1987) writes about three variables: actors (which can be individuals, groups or companies); activities performed by actors (transformations and transactions); and resources (physical assets, financial assets and human assets, although it is not entirely clear how human assets differ from actors). Each of the three classes of variables form within them a network structure, and at the same time are interwoven in a total network. The inclusion of both actors and resources has some resonances with actor-network theory (discussed further below), but this approach lacks the *dynamics* of the latter, and its notion of *intéressement* or enlistment of new supporters.

Geographers and planners have focused on linkages between individuals and organizations from a spatial perspective, looking, for example, at regional networks of firms and other institutions, industrial districts, and the possibility of urban, regional and national economic regeneration through their promotion. This approach links up with an analysis of the decline of the dominant production paradigm – mass production – in favour of flexible production, encouraging the 'bottom-up' evolution of networks between small and medium-sized enterprises as a positive contribution to regional economic development, in contrast to 'top-down' hierarchical networks between large firms and regional suppliers, now widely believed to hinder regional economic restructuring (Salais and Storper, 1992; Storper and Harrison, 1991; Dankbaar, 1993). Regional networks which cut across nation states raise questions about the importance of the national system of innovation (Nelson, 1993; Lundvall, 1992) versus geographical closeness, and the influence of supranational (e.g. EU) policy instruments which may be promoting cross-border links within a region (e.g. 'Euregion' policies).

Public policy has focused attention on promotion of collaboration as a strategic weapon in the competitiveness of nations and regions. These regions may be within nations, regions which cut across national borders, or regions which include several nations, such as Europe. In addition to Europe, Euregions and intra-EU collaboration, countries of the Southern hemisphere have been interested in the possibility of South–South collaborations by firms and/or other institutions, as a means of promoting economic development independently of the multinationals and the economically advanced countries (Mytelka, 1994). While alliances in this case are considered from a perspective of technology *policy*, they are not necessarily analysed solely within the discipline of political science. There is considerable blurring of the boundaries here between comparative political economy, economics, sociology, socioeconomic geography/planning, management, and other social sciences. For example, ESPRIT and other European technological programmes in which a prominent feature has been the encouragement of alliances between firms, and between firms and public-sector research organizations, have been evaluated by several groups of researchers, including Mytelka (1995), Georgiou et al. (1993), Vavákova (1995) and Larédo and Mustar (Chapter 8, this volume; see also Mustar, 1993 and Larédo, 1993), who between them combine all these disciplines. The four sets of authors have produced evaluations of the EU and other European programmes which are not necessarily incompatible, but are certainly quite different in emphasis and focus one from the other.[2]

We now turn to the disciplinary approaches in more detail. In the rest of this introduction we shall briefly sketch the main theoretical ideas underlying the various chapters, and then bring together the contents of the chapters in a synthesis.

SOCIOLOGICAL APPROACHES TO NETWORKS AND COLLABORATION

Several authors in the area of sociology and organizational behaviour have been independently developing conceptual structures of networks (e.g. Callon, 1992; Barley and Freeman, 1991; Powell, 1990) and at present it is a rather fragmented field. The actor-network perspective of Callon and Latour (1981) represents one of the most developed theoretical approaches, largely within the realm of sociology but with some evolutionary economic inputs (e.g. Callon, 1992). The links with all manner of actors – individuals or institutions – are treated in a similar way, and the importance of non-humans, such as equipment, publications, money, or samples of biological, chemical or geological material, as intermediaries in the network is stressed. The whole concept of 'actor-network' draws attention to the fact that actors do not exist without the network of relationships they create in the course of their social existence (the innovation process being a part of that social existence), and which define who they are and how they function.

This kind of network approach can clearly be used to analyse collaborative alliances between institutions: and indeed Mangematin (Chapter 7) uses it as a basis for his examination of a single innovation by a consortium of firms: a road guidance system. Larédo and Mustar (Chapter 8) use the same starting point for an otherwise rather different kind of study, a survey of the inter-organizational alliances established by the French firms which participated in European technological programmes over a certain period. However, what is being studied is a great deal more than just the linkages between the participants in a consortium, or in a project within the framework of a European programme. Typically, the actor-network approach describes a spiralling process, which widens out as the network of interests expands like ripples on a pond, with each participant drawn in by one or more of the others, and the commitment of one is built on that of each of the others: a variety of individuals with different interests all able to realize their separate aims by the achievement of a common goal, with which all their interests become bound up. This is quite a different sort of network from the kind described earlier, such as those mapped by Hagedoorn and Schakenraad. In the economic literature, the question of *intéressement*[3] is unproblematic – the concept does not exist. Even when looked at from an evolutionary perspective, the starting point is the existence of agreements, and motives and strategy are usually observed with hindsight, although evolutionary economists have recently begun to take an interest in the process of establishing networks. In the actor-network approach the involvement of actors with different goals, orientations, methods and views of what is the problem to be solved, is one of the key moments. How they are selected by the (other) innovators, and persuaded that their interests can be met by supporting the innovation, is a crucial issue.

ECONOMIC APPROACHES TO TECHNOLOGICAL COLLABORATION AND NETWORK RELATIONS

Economic analyses of technological collaboration started to be carried out in the 1980s (Chesnais, 1988; Hagedoorn and Schakenraad, 1990, 1992; Mytelka,

1991). The phenomenon itself has its roots in the trusts of the late nineteenth century, the cartels of the 1930s, and international cross-licensing in chemicals and electrical machinery in the 1920s and 1930s. However, the recent upsurge of collaborative alliances represents a qualitatively new stage, with a much greater *number* of agreements, an increased *range* of industrial sectors involved, and far more *international* collaborations. In particular, the collaboration in the *production of technological knowledge*, with the partners' dependent on each other's complementary skills and assets, is a relatively new phenomenon (Chesnais, 1988) (but see note 5).

The phenomenon is interesting to economists not so much as a result of its novelty, but because it was unexpected according to prevailing theories of industrial organization. According to these theories, transactions should have occurred either in markets or in large, hierarchically structured organizations rather than by means of inter-firm or inter-institutional collaborative agreements (IICAs). The emergence of hierarchical organizations, which is also a relatively modern phenomenon dating from the beginning of this century, was charted empirically and proposed in a general form by Chandler (1962, 1977), and subsequently justified theoretically by Williamson (1975, 1985) in terms of transaction costs. According to these authors, when firms grow large enough and therefore move away from atomistic competition, they are likely to develop first a U-form and then an M-form hierarchical structure and to internalize all functions and stages of production which are subject to high uncertainty and asset specificity. The implication was that an institutional configuration involving inter-firm collaboration would incur higher transaction costs than a hierarchically organized firm. The apparent contradiction between the growing frequency of inter-institutional collaborative agreements (IICAs) and their expected inefficiency can be resolved in at least two ways: first, IICAs are only a temporary deviation from normal behaviour (as represented by markets or by hierarchical organizations) which will soon disappear; second, they represent a new form of industrial organization, which either replaces the previous ones or is added to them. Of course these two 'solutions' are in reality raising a very large number of fundamental questions. Whether IICAs are a temporary deviation from the expected order or are a new form of industrial organization, why have they seen such an upsurge in recent years? Here we could hypothesize, for example, a radical change in the external environment of firms or an intrinsic life cycle for organizational forms. Our understanding of IICAs is at a preliminary stage and our concepts in this area are rather fluid, with a multiplicity of approaches. The chapters in this book represent different attempts to come to grips with the problem of IICAs, and networks of linkages of all kinds in the innovation process. They contain both theoretical analyses, however imperfect, and further empirical results.

Transaction Cost Analysis

Transaction cost theory (see OECD, 1992, p. 86 for a concise summary) tends to predict a low relative efficiency, and therefore a low probability, for IICAs. Williamson's (1975, 1985) analysis of the economic justification for the firm as an entity, and in-house versus external sources of production and supply activities, concludes that transactions take place more efficiently via the market place than hierarchically within the firm, unless bounded rationality, asset specificity and opportunism coexist.[4] Although Williamson does not apply his analysis to the location of R&D, Teece (1988) and Kay (1988) have examined the economic arguments for subcontracted versus in-house R&D, using the concepts of market and hierarchy without explicitly mentioning transaction costs. They conclude that uncertainty, tacit knowledge, cumulative learning processes, the fact that much research may not be product-specific, the difficulty of pricing and the time scales involved, have all tended to encourage in-house rather than subcontracted R&D.

Transaction cost analysis is often invoked as a framework for the discussion of cooperative alliances, although Williamson's work does not in fact deal with them. Pisano (1989, 1990) for example, as already mentioned, has analysed biotechnology alliances within this framework. One of Chesnais's central criticisms (Chapter 2, this volume) of the transaction cost approach as a framework for analysis of co-operative alliances is the way in which it ignores the firm as the central institution in capitalist economies for the transformation and creation of resources, ignores the capacity of firms for strategic behaviour, and presents the firm as an alternative to the market, focusing only on the allocation (and not the creation) of resources, with markets held to be the ideal form in most cases.

However, even economists who are critical of transaction cost analysis from an evolutionary economics perspective use Williamson's idea of the two extremes, market and hierarchy, as a reference point from which to organize a framework for analysis of networks and alliances, the latter being variously described as an intermediate (Hagedoorn and Schakenraad, 1990, Teubal et al., 1991), or hybrid (Foray, 1991) form of organization between the two. Chesnais, however, criticizes both the transaction cost approach in general, and the proposition that alliances represent something 'in between' hierarchical transactions within the firm, and arms-length transactions in the market place. It assumes a continuum between market and hierarchy which is highly unsatisfactory, in his view. Collaborative agreements should be analysed as a phenomenon in their own right, and networks treated as a distinct form of economic organization used for exchanging resources and value-creating assets (see also OECD, 1992, p. 78, Table 9, in which Chesnais lists features of three separate phenomena: markets, hierarchies and networks).

Leveque et al., (Chapter 10) point out that the market versus hierarchy approach, applied to the creation of technology, assumes substitutability between external and internal R&D, thus ignoring the role played by in-house R&D of not only generating innovation but also increasing the firm's absorptive capacity. They suggest that a taxonomy of alliances is needed rather than a spectrum. Yamin (Chapter 9) also argues that strategic alliances are not a feasible substitute for markets or for hierarchical organizations. He maintains that transactions are not the best unit of analysis for a situation in which partners are embedded in a large and complex network of relations/alliances. The formation and dissolution of such networks depends in very important ways on the knowledge both of the partners and in their external environment. Like Chesnais, he argues that strategic alliances are more concerned with creating new knowledge than with using existing knowledge in a situation of much more radical uncertainty than the one envisaged by the transaction cost approach.

Evolutionary Theories

It is hardly surprising that networks have little foundation in neoclassical economics, given the latter's emphasis on the individual and its prediction of perfect competition as the most efficient state of the economy. Atomistic competitors act independently of one another and represent perhaps the only possible network-less state in the economy.

In contrast, evolutionary economic theories, with their emphasis on out-of-equilibrium phenomena, on non-linearity and on open systems, provide, at least in principle, a theoretical explanation for qualitative change and for the formation of structure in systems. In socioeconomic systems such structure is fundamentally constituted by networks (Saviotti, 1996, Chapters 3 and 9). Evolutionary theories are in principle capable of providing a theoretical justification for networks and for their dynamics, although at the moment such justification is not explicit. Cainarca et al. (1992) have developed an evolutionary model which incorporates the idea of technological life cycles and trajectories to analyse IICAs in a way which captures some of the dynamics of evolving collaborative links. This approach is developed by Niosi (Chapter 6). He presents technological alliances as new industrial organization routines emerging from evolutionary technical organization patterns, beginning with purely internal and auxiliary activities and evolving towards more strategic and collaborative research behaviour. This evolution is induced by the emergence of a new technoeconomic paradigm, such as information technology, advanced materials or biotechnology.

Neither neoclassical nor transaction cost economics, with their focus on rational, cost-based decisions, allow for the *strategy* of firms, which is influenced by a range of factors such as firm and national or local culture and history, or individual and group motivation, psychology and behaviour, as well as the calculation of costs and benefits (itself not an unproblematic activity). Strategy is one of the concepts that evolutionary economics takes on board, and in this sense evolutionary economics may be seen as the result of some degree of convergence between economics and other social science disciplines (see also Coombs et al., 1992).

Indeed, evolutionary theories, which are still at a formative stage, can more generally be seen as representing, in their modern form, the convergence of several disciplines and research traditions. Foremost among these are the Schumpeterian tradition, systems theory, out-of-equilibrium thermodynamics, biology, and organization theory (Saviotti and Metcalfe, 1991). It is probably from the last of these that evolutionary theories derive a great emphasis on knowledge in organizations. For example, the concept of routines (Nelson and Winter, 1982) is both very important in explaining firms' behaviour and very closely related to knowledge generation and use. The state of knowledge and its rate of change also turn out to be important variables in attempts to explain IICAs in this book. We discuss the question of knowledge and present a number of generalizations from recent work in this area in the next section.

POTENTIAL FOR CONVERGENCE

Despite the differences in approach which we have outlined, both within and between the disciplines, we believe there is nevertheless some basis for convergence in the future development of an understanding of networks and alliances. Evolutionary economics has already taken several steps towards a *rapprochement* with sociology and other social science disciplines, as mentioned in the last section. Work in the area of knowledge and the learning process has been particularly fruitful in this respect.

Knowledge

The growth in R&D and in the participation of scientists and engineers (see for example Mytelka, 1991) provides evidence that knowledge has been playing a rapidly increasing role in production. Economics has traditionally concentrated on capital goods and on homogeneous labour as important ingredients of production. Knowledge has been given a greater role by philosophers, sociologists and organization scientists. It is only recently that efforts towards the creation of an economics of knowledge have been made. While this cannot in any sense be considered a well developed speciality of economics, a number of generalizations have emerged. For example, knowledge can be *local* (Nelson and Winter, 1982; Saviotti, 1994, 1996); it is *specific* and *cumulative* (Pavitt, 1984); it can be *tacit* or *codified* (Polanyi, 1962; Teece, 1981; Nelson and Winter, 1982). Knowledge accumulation and use occurs by means of search activities, of other learning effects and of routines. R&D contributes not only to the creation of new knowledge but also to the absorptive capacity of firms (Cohen and Levinthal, 1989, 1990). Not all types of knowledge have the same effect on firms. The distinction between radical and incremental innovation and the concept of paradigm is relevant here. For example, radical technological change can be competence-destroying (Tushman and Anderson, 1986). Knowledge creation and accumulation is not a purely individual affair, but it always requires the presence of networks (Lundvall, 1992).

There is considerable potential for mutual influence of the disciplines in discussion of knowledge and learning. The important role played by knowledge in IICAs, and conversely by networks in learning, are covered by several chapters of this book: notably those by Dodgson, Niosi, Senker and Faulkner, Leveque et al. and Yamin. Dodgson treats the firm as a learning institution (a tradition already established in the writings of Arrow, 1962; Cyert and March, 1963; Argyris and Schon, 1978, and more recently Arthur, 1989) and presents an account in which the organizational rationality guiding the evolution of a firm resides at least in part in the intention to acquire and internalize relevant knowledge and expertise. This objective can provide the heuristic which shapes the networking and collaborative behaviour exhibited by firms involved in technological development. In Niosi's view the increased turbulence and complexity determined by the new technological paradigm favours collective learning with respect to other modes of knowledge creation and adoption.

The importance of tacit knowledge in the innovation process is often mentioned, but the chapter by Senker and Faulkner (Chapter 5) is one of the first attempts to collate what is known and analyse the phenomenon systematically (see also Faulkner and Senker, 1995). They point out that even as advances in knowledge and technique codify existing tacit knowledge, they also generate new tacit knowledge. It is a vital element of the knowledge transferred through personal networks, which is integral to innovation in emerging technologies, and which firms make conscious efforts to capture. Yamin argues that strategic alliances seem to be more appropriate for transferring tacit knowledge, which cannot be accurately specified in a contract. Leveque et al. stress the importance of learning as a result of the R&D and the innovation process. Their paper examines the different types of internal structure in firms and particularly the different kinds of in-house R&D, as a basis for understanding and the different forms of cooperative arrangement into which firms enter, and the kind of learning processes that take place as a result.

Analysis of Networks

Chesnais, in his criticism of the transaction cost approach, argues that networks should be analysed as a phenomenon in their own right rather than as an intermediate form of governance between market and hierarchy. Another area of potential for convergence among the disciplines lies in such an analysis of networks as a distinct form of organization, an approach which has been taken by sociologists and some economists (although still with a multiplicity of perspectives). In an analogous way, Imai and Baba (1991) analyse Japanese corporate and industrial networks as a new form of production or technoeconomic system 'transcending markets and hierarchies' (see note 3). In this volume, the aspects of networks which are examined can be usefully categorized into the *formation* of networks, the *content* of networks, and the *consequences* of networks. We now consider each of these aspects in a little more detail.

The formation of networks
When examined from a broadly economic standpoint, it seems clear that network relationships between firms can be theorized to some extent in terms of the incentives that face firms to collaborate with others rather than to be self-sufficient. Such incentives can relate to the availability and costs of technological knowledge, or of other complementary assets (Teece, 1986), or to the opportunity to secure exploitation avenues and markets for existing proprietary technology, or simply to the need to reduce uncertainty and form long-term alliances as alternatives to continuous contracting with suppliers and customers.

In any of these cases, it is plausible to argue that the institutional conditions which shape these incentives will vary with respect to such macro variables as industrial sector and country. In Chapter 3 by Tylecote in this volume an analysis is presented of the influence of the different business cultures in nations such as the UK, Germany and Japan, which tend to generate different predispositions towards collaboration and network formation. Such an analysis points to the multi-layered nature of the sociological factors which mediate the operation and even the perception of economic incentives.

From a sociological point of view it is precisely how the *perceptions* of incentives, technologies and organizational relationships are formed that becomes the focus of interest. In Chapter 7 by Mangematin in this volume, the actor-network approach of Callon and Latour is deployed to analyse a specific case study of collaborations between firms to produce a particular piece of technology. Mangematin argues that it is not possible to see the form of the technology as determined by the form of the collaboration, or vice versa, but that they are joint products of a unified set of social interactions. Each is therefore, in a sense, a condition of existence of the other.

Larédo and Mustar (Chapter 8) argue that the nature and organization of cooperative research may both be understood as new forms. They suggest that the technoeconomic networks, the organizational forms that have evolved to benefit from cooperative research, are a new form of economic actor, which organizes relationships between science, technology and the market, mobilizing various actors, intermediaries and control mechanisms in ways that are not limited to research, but embrace all elements of the innovation process. The basic technological research carried out as a result of cooperation is basic because industrial as well as academic researchers value outputs such as publications in refereed journals and PhD theses; technological because academic as well as industrial researchers expect commercial applications to evolve in due course from the work. The authors consider the nature of the research to be new because it led them to re-think the conventional difference between basic and applied, or industrial and academic research.[5]

Yet another perspective on the processes and motivations underlying the formation of networks can be found in Chapter 4 by Dodgson, treating the firm as a learning institution. Niosi (Chapter 6) relates the evolution of technological alliances to the emergence of new technoeconomic paradigms. Yamin (Chapter 9) links the formation and dissolution of networks to the knowledge of the partners and the knowledge in their environment. Leveque et al. (Chapter 10) relate the establishment of alliances with the nature of in-house R&D in partner firms. They all deal in various ways with the motivations for collaboration, already discussed in the previous section on knowledge.

Summarizing these perspectives on the *formation of networks* we can see that the central issues of concern are:

- Under what circumstances do firms perceive increased incentives to engage in network behaviour, to what extent is this related directly to technological issues and to what extent does it have broader dimensions?
- Is the recent increase in such behaviour transitory and related to special historical conditions, or is it a new phase in the institutional infrastructure of market economies, which is likely to persist for the foreseeable future?
- How do the actual forms of networks and the specific content of the technologies they generate or employ relate to each other? Are there causal relationships between organizational and technological architectures, or is such a way of formulating the question permissible in the context of contemporary approaches to the explanation of technical change?

Finally, it is also clear from the foregoing that the analysis of the formation of networks and collaborations overlaps to a significant extent with the analysis of the *content* of networks. We turn next to this point.

The content of networks and collaborations
The most fundamental point about the content of networks is that they create novelty and variety in the economic system. This is a point made eloquently

by Chesnais (Chapter 2 in this volume) when he argues that networks are not simply alternative ways of deploying existing resources, but that they actually create new economic resources which otherwise would not exist, or whose existence would be delayed. This resonates to some extent with the argument of Dodgson reported above, since the rationality of the firm in attempting to use collaborations to learn is specific and *directed* towards the acquisition of knowledge which will amplify the power of its existing knowledge and potentiate new economic activity. Elsewhere (Coombs, 1994) one of us has presented a similar argument expressed in the terminology of the Prahalad and Hamel (1990) core competence paradigm, by arguing that collaborations can permit the creation of new competences by the assembly of previously separated technological capabilities contributed by different network members.

One of the features of the way these new resources are created by collaboration and networking is that the collaborators contribute not only formal codified knowledge but also tacit knowledge and skills, as we have discussed in the section on knowledge. This is a point investigated by Senker and Faulkner in their chapter, where they reveal from case studies a variety of subtle ways in which networking behaviour creates not simply hard-edged technological projects with specific outcomes, but also intelligence gathering, option-opening technical knowledge, and ideas about the investigative strategies of other scientists and technologists. There is a clear overlap here with the 'learning organization' perspective of Dodgson, and the new forms of organization created as a result of collaboration described by Larédo and Mustar.

The consequences of networks and collaboration
Given that this network behaviour is driven by the types of concerns we have identified, and has the particular technical and resource creating content discussed above, what can be said about the consequences of this behaviour? Steward and Conway (Chapter 11) provide convincing evidence at the micro level that it plays an important role in the dynamics of successful innovation. In that sense this is an early corroboration of Rothwell's (1992) identification of the emergence of a 'fifth generation innovation process' in which collaboration plays an important part.

At the macro level, Chesnais is in no doubt that it is a new and major source of economic growth, in the mainstream of the Schumpeterian interpretation of innovation. However, there are difficulties surrounding the geographical scope of the networks. Do they tend to exist primarily at global or at national and regional levels? It seems that both types can be detected. In the case of regional and national networks, does their existence ensure that the growth potential they create is realized within the nation state which bounds their territory? More problematically, in the case of networks which cut across nation states, are there conditions under which they reinforce or even generate uneven distribution of the growth potential between states, thus complicating the debates about free trade and economic growth in a new way? Alternatively, as Tylecote suggests, can we see the differing character of network behaviour in different nation states as both reflections and reinforcements of the existence of 'national systems of innovation' in the sense proposed by Lundvall, Nelson and others? Clearly, the analysis of networks takes us firmly into the territory of apparent conflict between the 'globalization' thesis and the 'national system of innovation' thesis.

In our view, these two positions may not be as contradictory as first appears. It is perfectly possible to imagine firms with global strategies (or aspirations at least) for the acquisition and deployment of technical knowledge, which happily treat the existence of clear differences between the scientific and technical resources of different nations as happy accidents to be exploited – or – in the language of economics, as positive externalities in the knowledge-generating system which can be systematically valorized. It does not follow that the exploitation of these externalities will, in itself, dilute the potency or self-reproducing power of specific national systems of innovation. (In the case of the UK this may be a case for lamentation!)

Nevertheless, this complex set of issues does raise significant problems in national science and technology policy, and in industrial policy. How can nation states take reasonable measures to ensure that they 'capture' a reasonable proportion of the wealth created by network behaviour, while not at the same time constraining that network behaviour in such a way as to reduce the very resource creation which it generates? It seems clear that one part of the answer to this question is that government support for scientific and technical education and infrastructure is of paramount importance to the processes which localize and intensify technical networking and collaboration within a particular country. However, the simultaneous de-coupling of physical production from conceptual design, characteristic of much current innovation, raises questions over whether capturing the 'front end' of the value chain is a better or worse strategy than capturing the other end, or the whole value chain.

NOTES

1. Although in some approaches, firms may also be considered as actors.
2. Between them they consider both the success of various programmes in meeting their stated objectives, and a range of indirect or unplanned benefits and problems. All the authors found that the programmes strengthened cooperation and enabled researchers in public or academic laboratories or in smaller firms to carry out research or take part in innovative activities that would otherwise have been outside their resources or range of skills. Some found that new organizational forms had been generated, enabling work to be carried out more easily across the traditional frontiers of established disciplines. The performance of European technology programmes using collaboration as a policy instrument to re-establish European competitive ability was either not evaluated or was seen as disappointing.

3. Intéressement is the enlistment or enrolment of new actors. It is a word that is not easily translated into English. In everyday French *intéressement* is used rather specifically to mean the material interest employees might have in a situation of workers' participation, where they share the profits of the firm, in contrast to the more common word *intérêt*, which refers to interest in the cognitive sense, importance, advantage, and indeed any other kind of *material* interest, such as percentage return on investment.
4. Williamson concedes that his framework does not apply to certain cases, mentioning the *zaibatsu* (now *keiretsu*, or Japanese conglomerate or network firm) as an alternative mode of organization, but a culturally specific one which he does not analyse. Japanese corporate and industrial networks have been analysed by several Japanese economists, including Imai and Baba (1991) and Goto (1982), who regard them as an alternative to the market/hierarchy dichotomy, and one with a potentially wide applicability outside the specific culture of Japan.
5. In fact this is not a new phenomenon in the pharmaceutical industry, where research of the kind named 'basic technological research' by Larédo and Mustar, in organizational forms they call technoeconomic networks, and without encouragement from public policy, was noted by one of us twenty years ago (Walsh, 1975).

REFERENCES

Argyris, C. and Schon, D. (1978), *Organisational Learning*, Wokingham: Addison-Wesley.

Arrow, K. (1962), 'The economic implications of learning by doing', *Review of Economic Studies*, June.

Arthur, B. (1989), 'Competing technologies, increasing returns, and lock-in by historical events', *Economic Journal*, **99**, (394), March.

Barley, S.R. and Freeman, J. (1991), 'Niches as networks: the evolution of organizational fields in the biotechnology industry, Cornell University, unpublished conference paper.

Cainarca, G., Colombo, M. and Mariotti, S. (1992), 'Agreements between firms and the technological life cycle model: evidence from information technologies', *Research Policy*, **21**, 45.

Callon, M. (1992), 'The dynamics of techno-economic networks', in R. Coombs, P. Saviotti and V. Walsh (eds), *Technical Change and Company Strategies*, London: Academic Press.

Callon, M. (1993), 'Variety and irreversibility in networks of technique conception and adoption', in D. Foray and C. Freeman (eds) *Technology and the Wealth of Nations*, London: Pinter.

Callon, M. and Latour, B. (1981), 'Unscrewing the big Leviathan: how do actors macrostructure reality?', in K.D. Knorr-Cetina and A.V. Cicourel, *Advances in Social Theory and Methodology*, London: Routledge Kegan Paul.

Chandler, A.D. (1962), *Strategy and Structure*, Cambridge, Mass.: MIT Press.

Chandler, A.D. (1977), *The Visible Hand*, Cambridge, Mass.: Harvard University Press.

Chesnais, F. (1988), 'Technical cooperation agreement between independent firms, novel issues for economic analysis and the formulation of national technological policies', *STI Review*, 4, 51–120.

Cohen, M. and Levinthal, D. (1989), 'Innovating and learning: the two faces of R&D', *Economic Journal*, **99**, 569–96.

Cohen, M. and Levinthal, D. (1990), 'Absorptive capacity: a new perspective on learning and innovation', *Administrative Science Quarterly*, **35**, 128–52.

Coombs, R. (1994), 'Core Competences and the Strategic Management of R&D', Keynote Paper at Conference on R&D Decisions, Keele University, September (mimeo).

Coombs, R., Saviotti, P. and Walsh, V. (eds) (1992), *Technical Change and Company Strategies*, London: Academic Press.

Cyert, R. and March, J. (1963), *A Behavioural Theory of the Firm*, Englewood Cliffs, NJ: Prentice-Hall.

Dankbaar, B. (1993), 'European Commission SAST Project 8; Sub-Report on Euregions', EUR-15431-EN.

Faulkner, W. and Senker, J. (1995), *Public Sector Research and Industrial Innovation in Biotechnology, Engineering Ceramics and Parallel Computing*, Oxford: Oxford University Press.

Foray, D. (1991), 'The secrets of industry are in the air: industrial co-operation and the organizational dynamics of the innovative firm', *Research Policy*, **20**, 393.

Georgiou, L., Cameron, H., Stein, J.A., Nedeva, M., Janes, M., Yates, J., Pifer, M., Boden, M. and Senker, J. (1993), *The Impact of European Community Policies for Research and Development upon Science and Technology in the United Kingdom*, Report prepared for the Commission of the European Communities and the Office of Science and Technology of the UK Cabinet Office, London: HMSO.

Goto, A. (1982), 'Business groups in a market economy', *European Economic Review*, **19**, 2.

Hagedoorn, J. and Schakenraad, J. (1990), 'Inter-firm partnerships and cooperative strategies in core technologies', in C. Freeman and L. Soete (eds), *New Explorations in the Economics of Technological Change*, London: Pinter.

Hagedoorn, J. and Schakenraad, J. (1992), 'Leading companies and networks of strategic alliances in information technologies', *Research Policy*, **21**, 163–90.

Håkansson, H. (ed.) (1982), *International Marketing and Purchasing of Goods*, Chichester: Wiley.

Håkansson, H. (1987), 'Product development in networks', in Håkansson (1987).

Håkansson, H. (ed.) (1987), *Industrial Technological Development: a Network Approach*, London: Croom Helm.

Imai, K. and Baba, Y. (1991), 'Systemic innovation and cross border networks: transcending markets and hierarchies to create a new techno-economic system', in OECD, *Technology and Productivity: the Challenge for Economic Policy*, Paris: OECD.

Kay, N. (1988), 'The R&D function: corporate strategy and structure', in G. Dosi, C. Freeman, R. Nelson, G. Silverberg and L. Soete (eds), *Technological Change and Economic Theory*, London: Pinter.

LAREA-CEREM (1992), *Les Stratégies d 'Accord des Groupes Européens*, Université Paris X Nanterre, Laboratoire de Recherche en Economie Appliquée.

Larédo, P. (1993), 'Les politiques européennes de R&D au milieu du gué', in F. Sachwald (ed.) *Les Défis de la Mondialisation: Innovation et Concurrence*, Paris: Masson-IFRI.

Lundvall, B.A. (1992), *National Systems of Innovation*, London: Pinter.

Mustar, P. (1993), 'La Création d'Entreprise par les Chercheurs', thèse pour le doctorat de Socio-économie de l'École des Mines de Paris.

Mytelka, L.K. (ed.) (1991), *Strategic Partnership and the World Economy*, London: Pinter.

Mytelka, L.K. (ed.) (1994), *South–South Co-operation in a Global Perspective*, Paris: OECD.

Mytelka, L.K. (1995), 'Dancing with Wolves: Global Oligopolies and Strategic Partnerships', in J. Hagedoorn (ed.), *Technical Change and the World Economy*, Aldershot: Edward Elgar.

Nelson, R. (ed.) (1993), *National Innovation Systems*, New York: Oxford University Press.

Nelson, R. and Winter, S. (1982), *An Evolutionary Theory of Economic Change*, Cambridge, Mass.: Harvard University Press.

OECD (1992), *Technology and the Economy: the Key Relationships*, Paris: OECD.

Pavitt, K. (1984), 'Sectoral patterns of technical change: towards a taxonomy and a theory', *Research Policy*, **13**, 343.

Pisano, G. (1989), 'Using equity participation to support exchange: evidence from the biotechnology industry', *Journal of Law, Economics & Organisation*, **5**, 109.

Pisano, G. (1990), 'The R&D boundaries of the firm: an empirical analysis', *Administrative Science Quarterly*, **35**, 153.

Polanyi, M. (1962), *Personal Knowledge: Towards a Post-Critical Philosophy*, New York: Harper Torchbooks.

Powell, W.W.(1990), 'Neither market nor hierarchy: network forms of organizations', *Research in Organizational Behavior*, **12**, 295–336.

Prahalad C.K. and Hamel, G. (1990), 'The Core Competence of the Corporation', *Harvard Business Review*, May.

Rothwell, R. (1992) 'Successful Industrial Innovation: Critical Factors for the 1990s', *R&D Management*, **22** (3),·221–39.

Salais, R. and Storper, M. (1992), 'The four worlds of contemporary industry', *Cambridge Journal of Economics*, **16**, 169.

Saviotti, P.P. (1994), 'Knowledge, information and organizational structures', paper presented at the conference of the Eleventh International Economic History Congress, Milan, 11–16 September.

Saviotti, P.P. (1996), *Technological Evolution, Variety and the Economy*, Aldershot: Edward Elgar (forthcoming).

Saviotti P.P. and Metcalfe, J.S. (eds) (1991), *Evolutionary Theories of Economic and Technological Change: Present State and Future Prospects*, Reading: Harwood.

Storper, M. and Harrison, B. (1991), 'Flexibility, hierarchy and regional development: the changing structures of production systems and their forms of governance in the 1990s, *Research Policy*, **20**.

Teece, D. (1981), 'The market for know-how and the efficient international transfer of technology', *Annals of the American Academy of Political and Social Science*, **458**, 81–96.

Teece, D. (1986), 'Profiting from technological innovation', *Research Policy*, **15**, 6.

Teece, D. (1988), 'Technological change and the nature of the firm', in G. Dosi, C. Freeman, R. Nelson, G. Silverberg and L. Soete (eds), *Technological Change and Economic Theory*, London: Pinter.

Teubal, M., Yinnon, T. and Zuscovitch, E. (1991), 'Networks and market creation', *Research Policy*, **20**, 381.

Tushman, M.L. and Anderson P. (1986), 'Technological discontinuities and organizational environments', *Administrative Science Quarterly*, **31**, 439–65.

Vavákóva, B. (1995), 'Building research–industry partnerships through European programmes', *International Journal of Technology Management* (forthcoming).

Walsh, V. (1975), 'The Relationships and Links between Academic Research in Steroid Chemistry and the Industrial Development of Steroid Drugs', PhD thesis, Manchester University.

Williamson, O.E. (1975), *Markets and Hierarchies: Analysis and Anti-trust Implications*, New York: Free Press.

Williamson, O.E. (1985), *The Economic Institutions of Capitalism*, New York: Free Press.

2. Technological agreements, networks and selected issues in economic theory

François Chesnais

INTRODUCTION

The economics of technological change has long suffered from an excessive tendency towards and/or acceptance of narrow disciplinary specialization. As a result it has almost permanently been threatened by the two parallel and complementary dangers of being marginalized in periods of technological 'normality' and colonized in periods when technological change is perceived to be important. I have always been concerned that economists working on technological change should attempt to put an end to the present situation of unilateral dependence on analytical approaches chosen by the 'nobler' and certainly better organized fields of the profession. In this paper this concern is discussed in relation to 'technoeconomic networks', the bearing that these have on a proper understanding of economic growth and the type of theory of the firm their analysis requires.

The term 'technoeconomic networks' refers to constellations of interactive relationships which are the outcome of linkages established among firms (as well as between them and innovation-related public institutions) through a wide variety of contractual and informal arrangements; and have the property of leading to the formation of innovative and productive capabilities greater than the sum of the technological capabilities of the individual participant firms and institutions.

GROWTH, COMPARATIVE PERFORMANCE AND ACCUMULATION

Since the mid-1980s, considerable effort has been brought to bear by macroeconomic growth theory on the endogenization of technological change and on technology and 'human capital' as sources of increasing returns to investment.

This work is encouraging in so far as it represents a recognition on the part of mainstream economic theory of some of the issues highlighted by the economics of technological change. It remains couched in the neoclassical framework (for a full characterization and critique see Soete in OECD, 1991c) and does not emancipate specialists of technological change from the need to make their own contribution.

Much of this work is still based on highly aggregated production functions and makes an extensive use of the somewhat vague notion of externalities. It offers no explanation of why growth rates differ between countries that are making more or less the same level of investments in 'knowledge'. It fails to offer any characterization of the specific traits of contemporary technology and thus gives no insights into the possible foundations of a new 'accumulation regime', nor on the present situation of structural obstacles to growth. Capital in the usual sense is also absent in most models (the exception being Scott, 1989, who is not really a 'new growth theorist'). As noted by Soete (OECD, 1991c), 'it is either assumed that only investment in knowledge matters, or, in more sophisticated models that there is only an intermediary good which contrary to physical capital does not accumulate'(p. 91).

Work carried out by specialists in the economics of technological change, both on inter-firm cooperation, technoeconomic networks and the working of 'national innovation systems' and on the characteristics of the contemporary 'production regime', has a contribution to make to all these aspects.

Increasing Returns, Externalities and Growth Theory

Let us run quickly over some of the most frequently quoted work. Reference must be made first to Scott's *New View of Economic Growth* (1989). This is a theory of growth strongly concerned with the level, efficiency and spillover effects of investment (both material investment and investment in human capital). It accords considerable attention to the social benefits which stem from a given investment as distinct from those accruing to the investor himself (Scott calls this the 'learning externality'). In many ways this is largely a generalization of the approach found in some of the growth models of the 1960s inspired by Arrow's classic (1962) paper on learning by doing and the non-privately appropriable benefits accruing from the production of new knowledge. Each firm learns as a result of the investment activity of other firms as well as from its own investment, with the result that the very act of increasing the capital stock through investment by a firm raises the level of knowledge elsewhere.

Reference must obviously also be made to the role of externalities and spillovers in the work of the so-called 'new growth' theorists. Two aspects are relevant to the point at hand. The first is the central finding of several Romer models (1986, 1989a, 1989b), that, unlike other factors, in the neoclassical production function scientific and technical knowledge displays, on account of its partially 'non-excludable' nature, increasing marginal productivity or again increasing returns. The second is the emphasis placed by a second parallel set of models by Uzawa (1965), Lucas (1988) and again Romer on R&D and human capital as crucial determinants in the growth process. However as some critics have pointed out (Stern, 1991; Soete, in OECD 1991c), this is done in a way which runs counter to the needs of full 'endogeneity', namely by postulating the existence of a distinct sector specialized in the production of scientific and technical knowledge, which then enters production in ways which differ among models.

In a revealing recognition of the impasse of neoclassical theory, Stiglitz (1991) has come to recognize that 'externalities are pervasive in the economy'. He considers in particular that externalities having to do with 'the *systems* which define the socio-economic environment in which firms and households operate' are important in seeking to understand 'the differences in growth experience across countries'. Such differences do not pertain simply to the level and quality of those areas of public expenditure which affect the socioeconomic environment most strongly. They include quite as importantly the breadth and quality of private-sector institutions capable of 'internalizing externalities', notably in the area of R&D (see e.g. Antonelli, 1988; Weder and Grubel, 1993). These of course are points that economists interested in 'national systems of innovation' (see Freeman, 1987; Lundvall, 1992; Nelson, 1993) have now been making for many years.

The Two Conceptual Pillars of 'National Systems of Innovation'

There are two main conceptual foundations for the existence of such 'systems'. The first concerns the characteristics of the principal education, innovation and investment-related institutions; the degree of coherence between these and the way they link together. These institutions can be viewed as representing the source of *economy-wide* or *systemic externalities*. They are one of the components of what is called 'structural competitiveness' (Mistral, 1983; Chesnais, 1986). At least until recently, governments in most countries have generally quite rightly been considered as the largest purveyors of economy-wide externalities, both because of their role in the organization of education and the provision of basic infrastructures in the form of public services, and because of their responsibility in managing a large public sector. Divergent views on the role of government can be observed, however. Some US authors in particular claim that some of these factors have *at least as much* to do with *sociohistorical factors shaping the attitudes and strategies of private economic agents*, in particular firms, as with the action of governments.

Awareness of the 'systemic' dimensions of competitiveness leads to the recognition that 'the competitiveness of the firm depends not only on its *own* competitive strength, but also on the *interaction* of its capabilities with the capabilities of the external environment in which it operates' (Ostry, 1991, emphasis in the original). Once the focus of the analysis moves from the macro-social institutions which shape the overall 'environment' of corporate activity, to the ones which affect their capacity to innovate, *the need to examine closely the quality of cooperation and linkages between interactions becomes all the more important.*

This is why the second central conceptual building block for the existence of 'national systems' is provided by the economics of technological innovation and concerns the conditions in which the particular returns stemming from successful 'interacting' among innovation-related organizations and firms are captured. This of course is where we enter the area of technology-related inter-firm agreements and networks.

The Interactive Character of Innovation, Cooperation and Networks

A number of advances in the understanding of innovation as an interactive process have been summed in the well-known Kline–Rosenberg (1986) figure of the chain-linked model of innovation. Subsequent work has invariably confirmed the relevance of this approach. But it has also showed that the interactive linkages, which the Kline–Rosenberg model analyses for a *single* representative firm focusing on the internal relationships between different corporate functions and departments and their external relationships with the nation's knowledge base, now have to be approached more broadly and be seen to involve increasingly often the participation of a number of firms and institutions. Successful innovation calls for *cooperation*. It may even depend (as argued by Imai and Itami, 1984), on the degree to which the 'Schumpeterian entrepreneur' is consciously understood to be a 'system' made up of a set of interrelated firms and institutions involved in a complex mix of competition and cooperation.

When one enters the field of technology-related inter-firm agreements, one is in fact moving from the analytical ground of *unplanned* spillovers and related externalities to that of linkages formed in at least a partially conscious manner with the purpose of reaping *partly* predefined or *targeted returns* to technological activity through *cooperation*, e.g. in a collective manner. This is the case in particular when these agreements are sufficiently numerous, dense and frequent to imply the existence of a network.

Since the mid-1970s, the pressure towards inter-institution and inter-firm cooperation in technology, and the premium on success in organizing joint research, alliances and partnerships have increased dramatically. This has been a consequence of sharply rising development costs, the increased risks jointly associated with international macroeconomic, monetary and financial instability and with radical technical change. But it is also related to the generic features of contemporary core technologies and the importance of synergies, complementarities and interfaces both between scientific and technological fields and between previously separate technologies and know-how used in production (see e.g. Chesnais, 1988b; DeBresson and Amesse, 1991). These numerous developments require, at the very least, that the notion of 'complementary inputs' be applied to technology *per se* and not simply to the classical array of corporate inputs other than technology found in the well-known (Teece, 1986) diagram. The new trends are however probably expressed more satisfactorily by the 'techno-fusion' notion proposed by Kodama (1992).The 'technological squeeze' (Fusefeld, 1986) thus created on firms coupled with the other factors leading to soaring R&D costs represents a related financial pressure for cooperation of which firms are highly and easily conscious.

Recognition of the importance of networking and cooperation as a mode of economic coordination leads to further insights about the factors contributing to 'national environments'. American scholars have been particularly active in making this point recently. As argued in two key contributions, while firms may be tempted to view the national environment as something they can take for granted (a 'given' parameter), this environment is in fact strongly affected by the way the business community acts collectively (Ferguson, 1991; Hollingsworth, 1993). Ferguson makes a particularly important remark when he notes that cooperation, when properly recognized and valued by firms, then 'represents *a specific source of increasing returns*'.

A strong case can indeed be made for introducing into growth theory an expression of the resource-creating, value-creating and surplus-creating potentialities which stem from cooperation – in particular when the existence and satisfactory functioning of networks, involving many firms and directed towards technological innovation and/or the production of highly specialized manufacturing or business services, can be established.

The extent to which a given network will effectively exhibit this property depends on the corporate and institutional strategies (see below) of the organizations which have established agreements, as well as on the characteristics of the organizational form displayed by the network. These factors will determine the extent to which mutual advantages are truly conferred by membership in an agreement, thus shaping the level of trust and reciprocity which must to some (significant) degree characterize interfirm and inter-institutional arrangements which are really technology-creating and -sharing.

Contemporary Technology and the Content of Investment

Another broad, extremely important set of reasons for discussing growth as a particular mode of technological, and tangible and intangible capital accumulation, relate to certain features of today's 'production regime', for which Cohendet, Zuscovitch and their colleagues at Strasbourg have already proposed a name, the 'information intensive production system' (see Zuscovitch and Justman, 1993). Here the implications do not concern just the true content of the vague expression 'externalities' and the real nature of technological endogeneity, but some major properties of the investment process itself.

The new *production regime* (which may turn out to be a very weak *accumulation regime*) is increasingly dominated by information technology. It tends to combine a variety of forms of industrial organization pertaining to flexible or differentiated mass production, which are organized and fully controlled by large firms, with situations marked by variety, high specialization and the somewhat more nodal position of small firms, whose long-term viability remains nonetheless problematic in the face of the current institutional set-up, notably regarding finance.

This regime obviously makes numerous and, in some cases, continuous calls on inter-firm and inter-institutional cooperation not simply in technology creation and sharing, but also more broadly in the production and sourcing of specialized inputs. It also requires labour relationships inside firms of a type that is to a large extent in total contradiction with the conditions in which productivity and profits have been sought by management under capitalism. This remark extends to Japanese capitalism where the 'life-long employment' and 'participatory' arrangements offered to the 'high-trust' multi-skilled workforces of the core *keiretsu* member firms is now breaking down. With respect to investment and employment the new regime has seen the radical technological downgrading and industrial downscaling of the large labour-intensive *cum* capital-intensive 'heavy industries' that previously dominated the production system. It remains capital-intensive, but makes drastically reduced calls not just on labour, but also on energy and material resources, e.g. 'indirect labour' and 'hyper-indirect labour' in the Pasinetti (1981) growth theory.

The weakening of the strong investment pull and effective demand-creating effects previously generated by investments in the traditional capital-intensive, resource-intensive and labour-intensive industries, has reduced significantly the relevance both of the classical investment accelerator and the Keynesian multiplier. This leads Scott for instance to postulate a direct relationship between investment, output and growth without calling on these mechanisms, but also *without* providing more than a very vague (e.g. his 'learning externalities') explanation of how this relationship occurs.

This suggests that the strong 'relational' content of the new production regime as expressed by the growing importance of economic networks implies that key issues pertaining to investment may now need to be discussed in close conjunction with the findings we possess regarding the factors which command network externalities and inter-firm-created interaction.

One hypothesis for instance is that the effectiveness and efficiency of capital formation in terms of performance, as well as the capacity of an initial investment to trigger off subsequent related technology spin-off and investment-pull effects, might depend on the specific properties of the technoeconomic networks within which the investment occurs. Typologies of network linkages of the sort devised by Callon and colleagues at the CSI/École des Mines (see Callon, 1991 and the contribution by Larédo and Mustar in this volume – Chapter 8) could be developed with a view to understanding their implications for investment.

THE THEORY OF INTER-FIRM AGREEMENTS AND TECHNOECONOMIC NETWORKS AND THE THEORY OF THE FIRM

I have been arguing, rather like Zuscovitch and Justman (1993), that inter-firm agreements bearing on technology or highly specialized intermediary inputs possess, in particular when they take the form of networks, resource-, value- and surplus-creating potentialities. While this property is enhanced, possibly strongly, by cooperation, it cannot arise solely from the cooperative relationship. It implies necessarily that the firms linked by these agreements or involved in these networks possess these attributes themselves. This means that work undertaken on inter-firm agreements and innovation-related networks must refer back to a theory of the firm which recognizes this centrally.

This is far from being the case at present. On the contrary many, indeed most, of the studies undertaken on inter-firm agreements have referred to the Coase–Williamson transaction costs theory of the firm, either explicitly or implicitly. The initial Mariti–Smiley (1983) statement presenting inter-firm agreements as an 'intermediate form of organising and managing transactions' which might lie 'somewhere in between markets and hierarchies', has been reiterated since by many authors. This is why we must now turn to the theory of the firm.

Modes of Coordination: Resource Allocating or Resource Creating?

There are in fact two problems with the Mariti–Smiley statement. The first is the idea of the 'continuum' (Williamson's own term in his 1985 book) with agreements being somehow placed somewhere 'in between' the two opposing poles. This highly unsatisfactory way of viewing agreements was disposed of by Richardson quite some time ago when he showed conclusively in 1972 (well before Williamson's first book!) the pervasive character of cooperation, stressing the fact that firms are not islands of planned coordination in a sea of market relations but are linked together in patterns of cooperation and affiliation. Planned coordination does not stop at the frontiers of the individual firm but can be effected through cooperation between firms. The dichotomy between firm and market, between directed and spontaneous coordination is misleading; it ignores the institutional fact of interfirm cooperation and assumes away the *distinct method of coordination* that this can provide. (Richardson, 1972; my emphasis)

This is of course an extremely important statement; if it had been recognized and assimilated we might have avoided being trapped into the sterile Williamson dichotomy between market and hierarchies. It does not however resolve explicitly the question of knowing what 'coordination' is about and what its implications are. Is it simply to do with the allocation of resources or does it also concern their creation? In the latter case does cooperation found resource and surplus creation or does it simply enlarge and enhance it? (Brousseau, 1993)

These questions are really the most important ones. They relate to the second rather more fundamental issue than that of the 'continuum', that is the theoretical foundations for characterizing cooperation and inter-firm agreements as resource- and surplus-creating or enhancing arrangements or 'institutions' and conditions under which this property holds. Above we have for instance already suggested that the extent to which a given network will effectively exhibit this property will depend on the corporate and institutional strategies of the organizations which have established agreements, as well as on the characteristics of the organizational form which has been adopted. This whole approach is in fact incompatible with the Coase–Williamson theory and is not to be found in Richardson either. It refers to a totally different theory of the firm which has now to be formulated explicitly.

In Chapter 3 of *Technology and the Economy: The Key Relationships* (OECD, 1992), the two issues I have just attempted to separate clearly are merged somewhat confusingly. The report begins by arguing that 'the notion of the continuum [between 'markets and hierarchies'] fails to capture the complex realities of know-how trading and knowledge exchange in innovation and stated 'that a "market" and "hierarchies" framework may hinder economists and technology policy makers from properly identifying the theoretical implications of the present diversity of organisational designs' (p. 78). The analysis then goes on to define networks as 'a distinctive form of economic organisation now extensively used for exchanging production [it would be better to say resource] and value-creating assets (…)'. This is in fact a statement made which can only be understood if and when the critique of the Coase–Williamson theory of the firm has been carried out and an alternative view put forward, which also differs from the one which underlies Richardson's defence of cooperation.

Resource, Value and Profit Creation as the Key Attributes of the Firm

Because neoclassical analysis only recognizes individual agents and has no theory of the firm, the Coase–Williamson theory has seemed to be a step forward. Despite its fashionableness it represents a blind alley. Its basic deficiency is that, like neoclassical analysis, it is a theory which encompasses only questions relating to resource allocation (Cantwell, 1989; Lazonick, 1991). The firm is no more than an alternative and indeed a 'second best' instrument of resource allocation, the best one being markets. In the account the Coase–Williamson theory gives of the nature of the firm, transaction cost-related market failures are the principal *raison d'être* of firms whose function is then to identify and save expensive transaction costs, the most basic of which are apparently rooted in traits of human nature such as opportunism, discretionary behaviour by traders or limited rationality in the writing of contracts. In Williamson' s own terms: 'markets and firms are alternative instruments for a related set of transactions' or again, 'only as market-mediated contracts break down are the transactions in question removed from markets and organized internally' (1985, p. 87).

This is a very narrow view of the firm. It omits several key dimensions of corporate activity which really represent the essence of what firms are about, notably their resource-, value- and surplus- (e.g. profit-)creating attributes and their capacity for strategic conduct.

The operations of firms are bounded by their capacity to commercialize their output, e.g. to undergo successfully 'the test of the market'. But they are everything save an 'alternative' to markets. They differ from these in essence: they are the *locus* in market economies (of which capitalism has been the most advanced form) for the creation of resources via their transformation. The production of resources precedes their allocation through exchange and distribution and calls for a particular kind of institution which is both counterpoised to the market and in the closest possible contact with it. In the course of their activity firms acquire the use of resources (raw materials, semi-processed products, technology, etc.), but this acquisition is subordinated to their subsequent transformation and also requires the planned coordination or administrative integration with corporate managerial organization (Penrose, 1959).

Many of the aspects which distinguish firms from one another, and decide the outcome of the competitive process between them, are based on superiority with respect to resource transformation and creation (e.g. the capacity to offer new products, or again more reliable and/or cheaper existing products), involving the analysis of inputs not just as factors of production but as services to the firm (Penrose, 1959). Contemporary studies on corporate competitiveness and performance (e.g. Porter, 1986; Womack et al., 1990) offer a more realistic presentation of the nature of firms than do transaction costs economics. They show that factors such as the capacity of firms to maximize labour productivity by a wide array of decisions regarding the organization of production at the shop-floor level, their capacity to innovate and their ability to manage internal organizational change, are of central importance in their profitability and growth.

Once the nature of the firm as *the* institution in capitalist society where resource and value creation takes place is established, the capacity of firms to minimize the burden of certain transaction costs on markets for intermediary products can at best only represent one of the sources of corporate viability. Similarly the process of internal allocation and coordination of resources carried out by large integrated firms is invariably and quite necessarily part-and-parcel of more fundamental decisions regarding resource and value creation, which require the particular managerial resources discussed by Penrose. This does not mean that there are no specific ownership advantages attached to large size: the capacity to organize the sourcing of key resources in ways which save transaction costs (including through the use of monopsonic power and the capacity to understand the properties of given resources better than the firms which own them) and the capacity to exploit firm-specific advantages through internalization (the 'I advantages' of Dunning's eclectic theory of the multinational enterprise). But as a careful reading of Dunning (1988a and 1988b) shows, the advantages associated with 'internalization' are in fact the combined result of large size, market power (notably monopsony and privileged access to given markets) and the successful internalization *stricto sensu* of certain market transactions, the most important ones today being almost certainly those pertaining to finance. All these factors are invariably part of the overall corporate strategies directed towards resource and value creation and so linked almost indissolubly with firms' core competitive advantages.

Putting aside the apologetics in favour of takeovers and integration contained in Williamson's work, the account it offers leaves no place for a dynamic approach to innovation and production (Cantwell, 1993). It excludes any active role for managerial strategy and leaves the firm as a passive reactor to transactional circumstances (Casson, 1986). However in the context of globalization and contemporary macroeconomic conditions, only a small part of the wide-scale integration activity can be explained by the compulsion to save transaction costs. Independently of the financial and purely speculative dimensions they may often possess, today's mergers and acquisitions are essentially the main and sometimes the only available route open to firms that are already large, for gaining market shares. This is done preferably by buying out firms on the 'home turf' of major competitors (Graham, 1988), within a twofold context of very slow growth and of patterns of international oligopolistic rivalry requiring as far as possible a fairly balanced 'mutual invasion through FDI' at all three poles of the triad.

The Resource-Creating Potential of Networks

Today the resource- and surplus-creating dimensions of corporate activity rely heavily on the mastery of technology. Firms do not build in-house R&D capacities simply because of the problems involved in the writing of contracts bearing on science and technology (Weinstein, 1992) or even for the reasons related more broadly to the appropriation of technology. They do so on account of anticipated and possibly (as in the Japanese case) planned synergies between their technology-creating and their production-related activities, and because they have at least a partial insight that 'technological cumulativeness and accumulation' are firm-specific processes dependent on the *collective* internal corporate capacity of managers, scientists, engineers and production workers to organize the appropriation of results through an efficient linking to production and other areas of corporate activity where 'tacit knowledge' (Dosi, 1988) dominates.

Once the resource- and surplus-creating capacity of firms has been established, one can start looking at the similar potential that networks might possess: organizations which possess the capacity to create resources can take steps to ally their strengths and increase this capacity through cooperation. On the basis of the linkages they can establish among themselves (as well as with innovation-related public institutions) through a wide variety of contractual and informal arrangements, firms can combine and pool innovative and productive capabilities which if properly coordinated can be greater than the sum of the technological knowledge and capabilities of the individual participant firms and institutions.

Zuscovitch and Justman (1993) argue that these properties are of particular importance in the context of the 'information-intensive production system':

> when intensive information is embodied in products both through the explicitation of user needs and through the large scale incorporation of science and technology, the firm tends to rely increasingly on intangible assets to assert their competitive advantage; the real side or the 'book value' decreases in importance. This intangible capital of the firm is much less transferable than physical assets, due partly to the tacit dimension of technological practice and partly to the collective nature of these assets. The cumulative nature of learning makes these assets even more 'local', more specific. If information cannot be efficiently transferred through markets even with the 'right' incentive, then the only way to transmit such experience is by *sharing its production*. In this light networks represent a mechanism for innovation diffusion through collaboration and the interactive relationship becomes not only a coordination device to create resources, but an essential enabling factor of technical progress.

The Reality of Inter-Corporate Relationships

The extent to which a given network will effectively exhibit this type of collective resource-creating characteristic is not given *a priori*. It depends on the corporate and institutional strategies of the organizations which have established agreements as well as on the characteristics of the organizational form displayed by the network. These factors will determine how far mutual advantages are truly conferred by membership in an agreement, thus shaping the level of trust and reciprocity which should ideally characterize inter-firm and inter-institutional technology-creating and -sharing arrangements.

A number of authors have of course presented technology-related inter-firm relationships, in particular those initiated by large firms (notably MNEs) in a rather different way. They have depicted them as an instrument of external technological sourcing where large firms build on the strength of their in-house corporate R&D and choose alternative routes for sourcing complementary technology in the course of which they establish what are basically alternative forms of hierarchical relationships with smaller and weaker firms or organizations (see for instance Chesnais, 1988a, 1988b, 1990; Hamel et al., 1989). Such relationships may include the capacity of larger firms to impose 'leonine' contractual clauses in agreements or lead to situations tantamount to quasi-integration as distinct from integration *stricto sensu*. Studies of this kind highlight some important dimensions of a large number of inter-firm agreements; they can only be understood of course within a non-Williamsonian theory of the firm.

Similarly, some of the less benign, more realistic and so often more clearly critical assessments of inter-firm agreements among the world's largest firms have set these in the context of global oligopolistic competition and concentrated supply structures. They have shown agreements and 'alliances' to be instruments of corporate strategy in the complex interplay of cooperation and competition which characterizes rivalry among oligopolists (Porter and Fuller, 1986; Hamel et al., 1989) and also as involving quite possibly some degree of overt or tacit collusion among partners (Contractor and Lorange, 1985) as well as the building of collective barriers to entry (Chesnais, same references as above). Here again the analysis lies clearly outside the pale of transaction cost economics. It refers to a non-Williamsonian theory of the firm, where the configuration of a firm's value chain, the breadth of activities it performs in-house, the experience it has developed in organizing subcontracting and technology-sourcing agreements to its own advantage and so in appropriating for itself a part of the value produced by other 'allied' firms, are key issues of corporate strategy.

A question to conclude: is network-based economic growth compatible with globalization?

The view of growth which emerges from the arguments I have tried to set out is based on the combined effects of investment, knowledge creation, effective economy-wide externalities supported by adequate public expenditure in infrastructures and education and the particular form of resource- and surplus-creating potential arising from successful network relationships between firms and other innovation-related organizations. This raises the important issue of the geopolitical and spatial framework best (or more exactly least badly) suited to enhancing the interactions between investment (both tangible and intangible) externalities and interactive, network-based processes on which sustainable economic growth could be founded.

The use of the adjective 'national' in relation to innovation systems warrants attention on several counts. It is interesting and somewhat paradoxical that the emergence of interest in 'national systems of innovation' should coincide with the onset of 'globalization' and with a context generally considered as involving a weakening of the structures of national economies as well of the capacity of government to control or monitor key variables, both for political reasons and because of basic worldwide economic processes now totally dominated by financial forces which have been given a free rein.

Considering that mainstream economics, not simply neoclassical but also Keynesian, far from developing a fully fledged theory of the national economy, has ignored it, this sudden, if somewhat belated, emergence is all the more interesting and significant. The credit belongs solely to the various strands of 'heterodox' and 'heretic' economic traditions (those of Marx, List, Schumpeter, Perroux, but also of A. Marshall's little-read *Economics of Industry*) which have, thanks to C. Freeman in particular, combined their efforts in building what is now often loosely called the evolutionary theory of technological change and in imposing the current recognition of the role played in economic growth by externalities and interactive mechanisms associated with cooperation.

The central issue today is whether such mechanisms are compatible with the process of globalization in the way it developed during the 1980s under Thatcherism and Reaganism. A large part of investment is now foreign direct investment both outwards and inwards. The determinants of this investment have to do mainly with the particular requirements of international oligopolistic rivalry among large firms from the triad and are overshadowed by all-powerful, totally unmastered financial markets (see Chesnais in Humbert, 1993, for an interpretation). All large firms are engaged in transoceanic technological alliances designed by considerations of cooperation and rivalry within world oligopolies and have often little interest in committing themselves to the building of domestically or regionally based technoeconomic networks. This weakens the resource-creating potential associated with interactive learning mechanisms (Lundvall, 1992) at the local and regional level, and may even have destructive effects on networks developed before globalization (see Dalum, 1993, for an assessment of the dangers facing the Jutland radiocommunications 'technology district').

The extremely important parallel debate about the relationship between trade and development has also been dominated by the purely ideological approach fostered by the neo-liberals who are at the helm in the GATT, the IMF and hold key positions in the EC and the OECD. Despite some brave sporadic endeavours like the one which led to the OECD Technology/Economy Project, this debate still takes only marginal account of the factors discussed in this paper. The characteristics, size and power to implement technological policy of the type of geopolitical framework which is likely to enhance growth along the lines suggested above are issues which bear directly on this debate.

The Japanese example suggests that the nation state still remains the most effective framework within which organizational and institutional arrangements and linkages conducive to growth can thrive. In Europe this framework could be a 'European Community', but it can certainly not be that of the Single Act and the Maastricht Treaty and the further dilution of the EC by the continuous extension of its membership. But this is another topic which would have to be the subject of a conference on its own.

REFERENCES

Antonelli, C. (ed.) (1988), *New Information Technology and Industrial Change: The Italian Case*, Dordrecht: Kluwer.

Arrow, K. (1962), 'The economic implications of learning by doing', *Review of Economic Studies*, June.

Brousseau, E. (1993), *L'Économie des Contrats: Technologies de l'information et coordination interentreprises*, Paris: Presses Universitaires de France.

Callon, M. (1991), 'Réseaux technico-économiques et irreversibilités', in R. Boyer, B. Chavance and O. Godard (eds), *Les figures de l'irreversibilité en économie*, Paris: Editions de l'EHESS.

Cantwell, J. (1989), *Technological Innovation and Multinational Corporations*, Oxford: Basil Blackwell.

Cantwell, J. (1993), 'Multinational Corporations and Innovatory Activities: Towards a New Evolutionary Approach', Reading University Discussion Papers in International Investment and Business Studies, no. 172.

Casson, M.C. (1986), 'Introduction and summary', in M.C. Casson et al., *Multinationals and World Trade: Vertical Integration and the Division of Labour in World Industries*, London: Allen and Unwin.

Chesnais F. (1986), 'Science, Technology and Competitiveness', *STI Review*, 1, Paris: OECD.

Chesnais, F. (1988a), 'Multinational Enterprises and the International Diffusion of Technology', in Dosi et al. (1988).

Chesnais, F. (1988b), 'Technical Cooperation Agreements between Independent Firms', *STI Review*, 4, Paris: OECD.

Chesnais, F. (1990), 'Accords de coopération interfirmes, dynamiques de l'économie mondiale et théorie de l'entreprise', in Humbert (1990).

Chesnais, F. (1993), 'Globalisation, world oligopoly and some of their implications' in Humbert (1993).

Contractor, F.R. and Lorange, P. (1985), 'Why Should Firms Cooperate? The Strategy and Economics Basis for Cooperative Ventures', in F.R. Contractor and P. Lorange (eds), *Cooperative Strategies in International Business*, Lexington Mass.: Lexington Books.

Dalum, B. (1993), 'North Jutland, A "Technology District" in Radiocommunications Technology?', FAST/MONITOR, Dossier FOP 352, Brussels: EC.

DeBresson, C. and Amesse, F. (1991), 'Networks of Innovators: A Review and Intro-
duction to the Issue', *Research Policy*, **20**, 113–31.
Dosi, G. (1988), 'Sources, Procedures and Microeconomic Effects of Innovation',
Journal of Economic Literature, **26**, September.
Dosi, G., Freeman, C., Nelson, R., Silverberg G. and Soete, L. (1988), *Technical Change
and Economic Theory*, London: Pinter.
Dunning, J.H. (1988a), *Multinationals, Technology and Competitiveness*, London:
Unwin Hyman.
Dunning, J.H. (ed.) (1988b), *Explaining International Production*, London: Unwin
Hyman.
Ferguson, C.H. (1991), 'Macroeconomic Variables, Sectoral Evidence and New Models
of Industrial Performance' in OECD (1991a).
Freeman, C. (1987), *Technology Policy and Economic Performance: Lessons from
Japan*, London: Pinter.
Freeman, C. and Foray, D. (1993), *Technology and the Wealth of Nations*, London: Pinter.
Fusefeld, H. (1986), *The Technical Enterprise: Present and Future Patterns*, Cambridge,
Mass.: Ballinger.
Graham, E.M. (1988), 'Transatlantic Investment by Multinational Firms: A Rivalistic
Phenomenom?', *Journal of Post-Keynesian Economics*, 1.
Hamel, G., Doz, Y. and Prahalad, C.K. (1989), 'Collaborate with your Competitors –
and Win', *Harvard Business Review*, Jan/Feb, **67**.
Hollingsworth, R. (1993), 'Variations in National Production Systems and International
Competitiveness', in Freeman and Foray, (1993).
Humbert, M. (ed.) (1990), *Investissement international et dynamique de l'économie
mondiale*, Paris: Economica.
Humbert, M. (ed.) (1993), *The Impact of Globalisation on Europe's Firms and Industries*,
London: Pinter.
Imai, K.J. and Itami, B. (1984), 'Mutual Infiltration of Organisation and Market –
Japan's Firm and Market in Comparison with the US', *International Journal of
Industrial Organization*, **1** (2).
Kline, S.J. and Rosenberg, N. (1986), 'An Overview of Innovation' in National Academy
of Engineering, *The Positive Sum Strategy: Harnessing Technology for Economic
Growth*,Washington DC.: National Academy Press.
Kodama, F. (1992), 'Technology Fusion and the new R&D', *Harvard Business Review*,
July–August, 70–78.
Lazonick, W. (1991), *Business Organisation and the Myth of the Market
Economy*,Cambridge: Cambridge University Press.
Lucas, R. (1988), 'On the mechanics of economic development', *Journal of Monetary
Economics*, 22, 3–42.
Lundvall, B. A. (1992), *National Systems of Innovation – Toward a Theory of Innovation
and Interactive Learning*, London: Pinter.
Mariti, P. and Smiley, R.H. (1983), 'Cooperative Agreements and the Organisation of
Industry', *The Journal of Industrial Economics*, **XXXI** (4), June.
Mistral, J. (1983), 'Competitiveness of the Productive System and International Spe-
cialisation', mimeo, Paris: OECD.
Nelson, R.R. (ed.) (1993), *National Systems of Innovation: A Comparative Analysis*,
Oxford: Oxford University Press.
OECD (1991a), *Technology and Productivity: The Challenges for Economic Policy*, Paris:
OECD.

OECD (1991b), *Strategic Industries in a Global Economy: Policy Issues for the 1990s*, Paris: OECD.

OECD (1991c), *Technology in a Changing World*, (analytical report by L. Soete), Paris: OECD.

OECD (1992), *Technology and the Economy: The Key Relationships*, Paris: OECD.

Ostry, S. (1991), 'Beyond the Border: The New International Policy Agenda', in OECD (1991b).

Pasinetti, L.L. (1981), *Structural Change and Economic Growth*, Cambridge: Cambridge University Press.

Penrose, E. (1959), *The Theory of the Growth of the Firm* (1980 edn) Oxford: Blackwell.

Porter, M.E. (1986), *Competition in Global Industries* (introductory chapter), Boston: Harvard Business School Press.

Porter, M.E. and Fuller, M.B. (1986), 'Coalitions and Global Strategy', in Porter (1986).

Richardson, G.B. (1972), ' The Organisation of Industry', *Economic Journal*, **82**, (327).

Romer, P. (1986), 'Increasing Returns and Long-run Growth', *Journal of Political Economy*, 94, 1002–1037.

Romer, P. (1989a), 'What Determines the Rate of Growth and Technological Change', *World Bank Working Papers* (WPS 279), World Bank, September.

Romer, P. (1989b), 'Endogenous Technical Change', *Journal of Political Economy,* 98, 71–102.

Scott, M. (1989), *A New View of Economic Growth*, Oxford: Clarendon Press.

Stern, N.H. (1991), 'The Determinants of Growth', *Economic Journal*, **101**, 122–33.

Stiglitz, J.E. (1991), 'Social Absorption Capacity and Innovation', Center for Economic Policy Research Policy Paper 292, Stanford University, Stanford, Ca.

Teece, D. (1986), 'Profiting from Technological Innovation', *Research Policy*, **15**, (6).

Uzawa, H. (1965), 'Optimum Technical Change in an Aggregative Model of Economic Growth', *International Economic Review*, **6**, 18–31.

Weder, R. and Grubel, H.G. (1993), 'The New Growth Theory and Coasean Economics: Institutions to Capture Externalities', *Weltwirtschaftliche Archiv*, **129**, (3).

Weinstein, O. (1992), 'R&D et théorie de la firme', *Économie Appliquée*, **XLV**, (1), 79–104.

Williamson, O.E. (1975), *Markets and Hierarchies: Analysis and Antitrust Implications: A Study in the Economies of International Organisation*, New York: The Free Press.

Williamson, O.E. (1985), *The Economic Institutions of Capitalism*, New York: The Free Press.

Womack, J.P., Jones, D.T. and Roos, D. (1990), *The Machine that Changed the World*, New York: Rawson Associates.

Zuscovitch, E. and Justman, M. (1993), 'Networks, Sustainable Differentiation and Economic Development', in BETA Discussion Paper 9305, Strasbourg: University Louis Pasteur (mimeo).

3. Managerial objectives and technological collaboration: the role of national variations in cultures and structures[1]

Andrew Tylecote

INTRODUCTION

The analysis of technological change must be concerned, explicitly or implicitly, with strategic decision taking by managers; and those decisions must be influenced by managers' objectives, that is the criteria by which they rank options. There is certainly no academic consensus as to what managerial objectives are. Against the traditional assumption that they are to maximize the profit of the firm, or to be more precise maximize the wealth of its shareholders, stand the theories of Marris (1964), Baumol (1959), Leibenstein (1975) and Cyert and March (1963), which assert that managers maximize (subject to some constraint) growth (Marris), sales (Baumol), or nothing at all (the others). As with the other tenets of neoclassical economics the assumption of shareholder wealth maximization (SWM) becomes the more common in economic analysis the further one is from detailed discussion of what is really the case. (It is for example implicit in macroeconomic general equilibrium theory.) This can be justified by the need to abstract from reality in order to construct any theoretical model; and SWM has an elegant simplicity which makes it well suited to all kinds of model building. Moreover there is no doubt that managers of private-sector firms are, everywhere, interested in profits in some sense, whether as an end or as a means to some other end. It will be argued here, however, that SWM will not do as an invariable assumption in theories of technological change, since plausible variations in it have been found to have great explanatory power. (See for example Tylecote and Demirag, 1992; Demirag and Tylecote, 1992; and Demirag, Morris and Tylecote, 1994.) This power, as we propose to show here, turns out to extend fully to theorizing technological collaboration. In particular, it helps to predict and explain important variations in *national* inclinations for technological collaboration.

The chapter proceeds as follows. First we set out three dimensions, of *scope*, *term* and *coherence* on which the objectives of individual managers or groups of managers can be defined. The dimension of scope can itself be broken down into three sub-dimensions, where appropriate – as it is here, since questions of scope are of central importance to technological collaboration. We show in general terms how position on these continua can be expected to affect willingness to undertake and continue technological collaboration, and capacity to benefit from it. Next we consider what determines, and has determined, position on these continua, setting out a number of cultural and structural determinants, considering their interrelationships and their incidence by country. We then discuss, country by country, the implications of the argument for technological collaboration; and conclude by examining the implications for variations among countries in methods of innovation and patterns of technological advantage.

THREE DIMENSIONS OF MANAGERIAL OBJECTIVES

Scope and Technological Collaboration

The economic analysis of innovation lays great stress on the problems of externalities to and appropriability by private agents, and the consequent excess of social over private benefit. But externalities to what? Appropriability by whom? The private agent, presumably – assumed normally to be a firm. The traditional neoclassical firm, the 'black box' of microeconomic theory, is a strange creature: in one plane it is an extensive, seamless whole, without any rift along departmental or divisional lines; in another plane it is rather thin, since only its value to its shareholders is of interest. But those external to *this* agent are not 'the rest of society' as a sort of undifferentiated mass. Most of the appropriation of the fruits of its innovations is likely to be carried out by agents very close to the original – by the firm's employees; by its customers and suppliers; by its competitors. It will be argued below that there are firms, industries and economies for which some of these 'external' agents – let us call them *stakeholders* – are not in any strong sense external, since the objectives of the firm's managers give at least some weight benefits to them; and they reciprocate.

To the extent that managerial objectives are thus broader in scope than mere SWM, this must clearly improve the balance of benefit and cost for innovative activity in general. It will also be argued that it will improve this balance for technological collaboration (TC) in particular. How far this is improved will depend on the relationship between the collaborators. If for some reason firms A and B each perceive the other as not fully 'external', so that benefit to A has value to B, and vice versa, then the benefit/cost relationship of mutual collaboration (formal or informal) improves, for the following reasons:

1. A to some extent values the benefit to B, and conversely;
2. A's own benefit increases as B carries out its commitments more generously, and conversely;
3. A and B's monitoring costs diminish.

There is a more general and weak effect of the inclusion of stakeholders in managerial objectives: to the extent that TC leads to increased innovation, inclusion will encourage TC even between partners who are entirely external to each other. Figure 3.1 illustrates the scope of return to innovation.

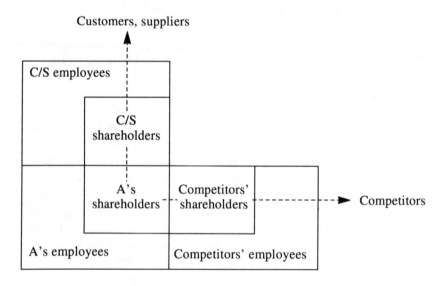

Figure 3.1   Scope of return to innovation

The three sub-dimensions of scope: broadening from SWM
We can think of this broader scope of managerial objectives along three dimensions: *vertical*, *horizontal* and *employee*.

Vertical scope extends outwards to customers and suppliers – among whom it is convenient to include lenders, as suppliers of fixed interest capital. As shareholders' wealth maximization implies a utility function which entirely excludes these stakeholders, one could, as another extreme, define one which fully included them as *filière* wealth maximization. (*Filière* is the French for a 'stream' of production from capital goods etc. as far as the final consumer.) In general, concern with the interests of customers and suppliers can be defined as *filière orientation*.

Horizontal scope extends outwards to other firms in the same sector which are not customers or suppliers – which may indeed be actual or potential competitors. A utility function which, more improbably, fully included them could be defined as *sector* wealth maximization; something less, is *sector orientation*.

Employee scope of course extends downwards from the shareholders to those whose work actually creates their wealth. Since the managers whose objectives we are discussing are employees, not all employees can be excluded! If at the other extreme, they are all fully included, we may, not inappropriately, use the sociologist's German term for 'community', and speak of *Gemeinschaft* wealth maximization: between GWM and SWM we have *Gemeinschaft orientation*.

Narrowing from SWM

So far we have treated shareholder wealth maximization as a narrow starting point from which scope may be broadened. Unfortunately it is possible in theory and in practice to go the other way. To take vertical scope first, Oliver Williamson (1981) has shown that any firm can be seen as a set of small vertically integrated teams. Large firms are highly complex sets of vertical integration, and the vertical integration frequently brings together clearly distinct activities which form separate units for accounting purposes – for cost accounting at least, and nowadays commonly for profit accounting as well. A manager in charge of a profit centre, subjected to the conventional financial control apparatus for monitoring and rewarding that profit centre's performance, might reasonably be expected to care little for the performance of 'customers' and 'suppliers' in the firm. Feelings may go beyond indifference to bitterness, after repeated conflict over the level of shadow prices. By the same token, large firms are normally diversified enough to be divided up 'horizontally' – into product or geographical divisions not (much) linked by vertical integration. Again, the manager of profit centre A is unlikely to care much for the performance of profit centre B. Again, there may be rivalry to the point of antagonism: the easiest way to judge A's performance is relative to B's, and so the more that improves the more explaining A has to do. 'Corporate parenting', as a phrase to describe the relationship of a firm's top management to the profit centres below, is cruelly apt – the jealousy and strife among the 'children' and those who feel themselves to be 'stepchildren', in some of the firms we have been investigating,[2] are awesome to behold. Z's technical director:

> There can appear in the marketplace lots of wonderful opportunities which are very close to your SBU... if it falls between two SBUs what happens when one of them takes it to the parent company? They might say 'it's a super idea, give it to them'.

So half the people with ideas don't bother. Or they'll say, 'you must promise not to tell anyone else, particularly not that bit of Z because the buggers will pinch it from us.' That's a polite version of what they actually said to me in a number of instances. (Demirag, Morris and Tylecote, 1993, p. 10)

So much for loyal devotion to shareholder wealth maximization! Where the managers of a profit centre within a firm – whether vertically or horizontally disaggregated – are inclined to a fairly close approximation to profit maximization for themselves, and are not inclined to put themselves out to improve other profit centres' performance, we can describe their objectives as 'sub-unit profit maximization'; a tendency in that direction is *sub-unit orientation*. The dimensions of objectives by scope are shown in Figures 3.2a and 3.2b.

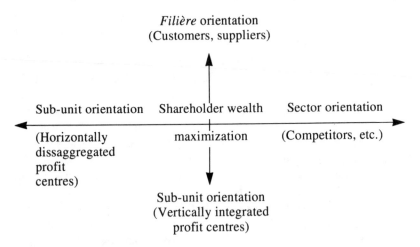

Figure 3.2a   Dimensions of objectives by vertical and horizontal scope

How does sub-unit orientation affect the incentives for innovation generally and TC in particular? Clearly, to the extent that there are technological synergies among profit centres it discourages and hampers innovation. The effect on TC will not be so clear-cut. Since collaborative effort within the firm will be inhibited, there will be some diversion to collaboration with outsiders – TC as usually understood. Moreover there will be a more reckless attitude towards that most dangerous kind of TC – that with actual or potential competitors. Any damage done to one's own firm will almost certainly extend outside the profit centre directly involved; ergo, it will be undervalued by the sub-unit manager. Consequently, TC which should not (for SWM) be undertaken, will be, if the sub-unit management has its way; likewise, what is undertaken will be carried on with less care to avoid disclosure, than it should have been (Hamel, Doz and Prahalad, 1989; 1990).

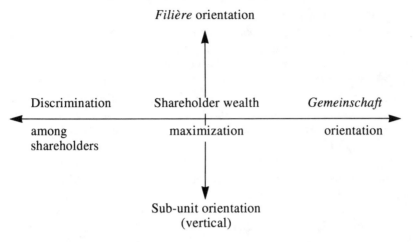

Figure 3.2b   Dimensions of objectives by vertical and employee scope

Termism

If the aim is to maximize the firm's wealth to shareholders, the rational manager will take into account all future costs and benefits, and discount them to the present at its opportunity cost of capital. That will normally be higher than the rate of interest the firm will have to pay on any borrowed funds, since it is appropriate to allow for risk, for any credit rationing, and/or for any effect of extra borrowing on the average rate of interest paid. On the other hand a highly liquid firm may be a lender rather than a borrower, and should then take the (lower) lender's rate of interest as its opportunity cost of capital. Thus the SWM 'optimal' discount rate may vary greatly among firms, industries, and countries and periods.

Short-termism is quite different from such variations. It exists where for some reason managers choose to apply a higher than 'optimal' discount rate and/or to ignore net revenues beyond a certain time horizon. (See Tylecote and Demirag, 1992.) This may arise where the flow of information from firm to shareholders is poor, so that shareholders do not receive good information relating to future prospects, or where they are unable to evaluate it properly: this then creates *external* short-term pressures. Imperfections of information flows between lower and top management, or the latter's incapacity to evaluate them, will compound this problem, in a firm decentralized into a number of tiers of profit responsibility; thus short-termism is likely to be associated with sub-unit orientation. Long-termism, the application of a lower than 'optimal' discount rate, is also possible: particularly when profits are high, the weakness, ignorance or tolerance of shareholders may allow managers to raise extra capital or (most likely) to retain funds where the marginal return is not expected to cover the opportunity cost of capital (Watanabe and Yamamoto, 1992).

Since the average term of costs in innovation is shorter than that of benefits, it is clear that (up to a point) the longer the time horizon, and the lower the discount rate, the better. ('Optimal' for shareholders is not optimal for innovation.) Thus to the extent that TC represents an increment of expenditure on innovation, the length of 'term' is an argument in the inclination to it. Moreover, in so far as successful TC involves trust which it is in the *immediate* selfish interest of each party to betray, long-termism may be a useful alternative or supplement to stakeholder orientation: as Siegel and Fouraker (1960) showed experimentally in the 1950s, a prisoner's dilemma type of game tends more towards a cooperative relationship, the longer the sequence of bids.

However, as we have already seen, TC may well be to a large extent an *alternative* to other routes to innovation, and to that extent the argument may well be the other way about. It is certainly likely to offer a cheaper route, and in so far as the other firm already has knowledge that can be transferred rather than independently learnt, a quicker one. The common disadvantages of TC – that it will tend to leave the firm more dependent than if it reached the same goal by its own efforts, and that it will strengthen an actual or potential rival – weigh relatively heavily in the longer term. (See for example Malerba, 1985, on the consequences in the 1960s electronics industry of licensing in rather than developing in-house R&D capabilities in integrated circuit technologies.) It may thus be a Faustian compact. Term and scope in managerial objectives is illustrated in Figure 3.3.

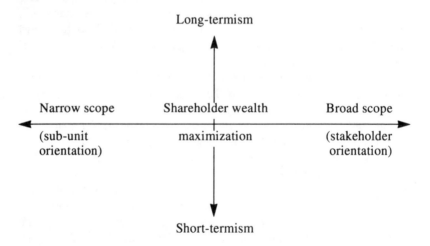

Figure 3.3   Term and scope in managerial objectives

Attitude to Risk

For completeness we should consider a further dimension of objectives: attitude to risk. However it is far from clear how TC compares for general riskiness with other routes to innovation. Innovation in general seems to involve increased risk in the short and medium term and reduced risk in the long term – innovate or die! Thus attitude to risk would have to be considered in conjunction with position on other dimensions: aversion to risk combined with long-termism would increase the incentive to innovate, whereas in combination with short-termism it would decrease it further. Moreover it will largely be a function of position on other dimensions: if risk attaches to individual bids and they are made in sequence, then the longer the sequence to be considered the lower the overall risk. This is true *a fortiori* if there is learning from mistakes. Likewise if individual bids are made by individual profit centres then the more bidding in parallel the lower the overall risk; true *a fortiori* where part of the uncertainty relates to which profit centre will reap the benefit of the bid. Thus risk aversion (in the short and medium term) is likely to be associated with sub-unit orientation and short-termism.

Coherence: Rationality Versus Organizational Slack

So far it has been assumed that we were dealing with a manager or group of managers who could be taken to be maximizing something, probably the net present value of a stream of costs and benefits. The horizon might or might not be foreshortened, the discount rate higher or lower than the cost of capital would imply, and the entity facing the costs and benefits wider or narrower on some dimension than the neoclassical firm, but nonetheless there was some sort of attempt at maximization going on – within the limits of bounded rationality, uncertainty, etc. The objectives of the firm might in some cases be incoherent, but only in the sense that different groups of managers at different levels were pursuing different objectives – top management, say, pursuing SWM while lower down there was sub-unit orientation. However we have to admit of the possibility that there is not even this degree of coherence, and that there is truth in the behavioural theories of the firm, with their conflicts and coalition building, their log rolling, and consequently their clear failure even to seek to maximize anything. These theories we shall treat as contingent: as approximating much more nearly to the truth in one set of circumstances than in another, which we shall specify.

We can interpret the development of the M-form firm in the US in the 1920s, and its subsequent spread (as depicted in, e.g. Chandler, 1977) as a largely successful attempt, as it were, to make behavioural theories untrue. The clear allocation of profit responsibility to general managers at various levels has that tendency, as does the separation of the topmost tier of management from responsibility for operational control of any function or division: it is easy for them to be bound, or to bind themselves, to the interests of the shareholders, with the help of stock options etc., and to hold themselves coldly aloof from the sectional biases of their subordinates. The U-form firm, and the various hybrids between U and M, are more prone to 'irrationality' through the failure to create an entirely separate layer of top management, and the existence of functions or departments which are cost, not profit, centres. By the same token, the M-form firm runs the risk of inducing sub-unit orientation instead. To some extent there is likely to be a choice of evils – but evils of different character. The difference is most clearly brought out where TC is concerned. TC with another firm is usually a route to a goal most easily formulated by and attractive to a *general* manager: to enable a new product to be brought out or processes to be improved. Since technological change is involved, the other functions besides

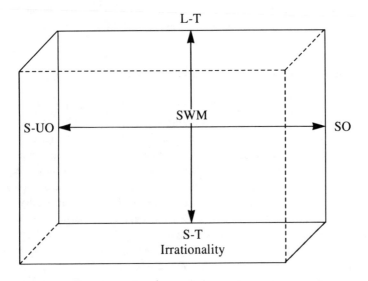

Figure 3.4   Term, scope and rationality in managerial objectives

R&D will have a limited understanding of what is at stake. R&D on the other hand will tend to be biased against TC since external sourcing of technology is an alternative to internal sourcing, i.e. building up their 'empire'. If TC indeed offers a cost-effective path to the goal, general management may value that and go for it; functional management is less likely to do so. Figure 3.4 depicts term, scope and rationality in managerial objectives.

International Patterns of Difference in Managerial Objectives

We have set out the dimensions on which the objectives of managers can be defined, and shown how variations within them can be expected to affect the willingness to undertake TC and the capacity to benefit from it. We shall now sketch how a number of countries (focusing on Germany, Japan and Britain) may be located on the various dimensions of objectives.

There are three main ways of categorizing countries which are relevant to managerial objectives, in terms of:

- sources of capital;
- the density and intimacy of inter-firm relationships; and
- the attachment of the workforce to the firm.

Sources of capital
There are stock exchange-based systems (mainly in the Anglo-Saxon countries), private-sector bank-based systems (Europe north-east of the Rhine, plus Switzerland, North-East Asia) and public-sector bank-based systems (rest of Europe, including Austria). (Public-sector capital plays an important role in some of the 'private bank-based' countries, like Germany and Japan.) The stock exchange/bank distinction largely corresponds to one between dispersed equity ownership and concentrated, mainly family-based ownership. The distinction within the bank-based systems reflects the success of private banking systems in providing risk capital, in the first category, and its failure in the second, the task being taken over by the state. The stock exchange-based systems generate short-term pressures on management to the extent that innovative activities are *invisible* – as they are particularly in the engineering industries, and where firms are diversified and decentralized – a tendency which is encouraged by the ease of acquisition in these systems. The bank-based systems tend to avoid short-term pressures, but they (particularly the public-sector type) may in the absence of strong shareholder control apply little performance pressure of any kind, thus encouraging 'irrationality'. (Tylecote, 1994).

Density and intimacy of inter-firm relationships
In some countries – roughly, the private-sector bank-based ones plus Northern Italy – the density and intimacy of inter-firm relationships is generally high. (On Japan, contrasted with Britain, see Sako, 1992; on Germany, contrasted with Britain and France, Lane, 1989 and 1991; on Italy, Malerba, 1985). Broadly speaking this corresponds to a pattern of historical development without a central state strong enough to suppress local particularism and intermediate organizational forms like guilds. The strength of inter-firm networks clearly implies *filière* and/or sector orientation. (Private-sector banks are part of these

Table 3.1 The departmental hierarchy of pay in ten European countries

	United Kingdom		Switzerland		Germany		Italy		France		Netherlands		Belgium		Sweden		Spain		Ireland	
Typical gross pay of chief executives	£84,670	%	£109,504	%	£118,830	%	£104,098	%	£103,603	%	£83,224	%	£87,413	%	£84,946	%	£94,000	%	£64,766	%
Departmental directors ranked by their typical pay as a percentage of chief executives' typical pay																				
Finance	Pdcn	72	Pdcn	88	Rsch	74	Fin	72	Pdcn	62	Pdcn	76	Mats	72	DP	72	DP	75	Fin	75
Research	Eng	69	Rsch	83	Fin	71	Sales	71	Fin	61	Fin	71	Pdcn	71	Fin	72	Fin	74	Sales	74
Sales	Fin	68	Sales	82	Pdcn	70	Eng	71	Sales	58	Pers	65	Fin	69	Pdcn	71	Pdcn	72	Pdcn	72
Production	Mats	67	Eng	74	Eng	66	Rsch	67	Rsch	58	DP	64	Pers	67	Pers	65	Pers	71	Mktg	71
Marketing	Sales	65	Fin	74	Sales	61	Pdcn	67	Eng	57	Eng	62	Rsch	67	Rsch	65	Mktg	65	Mats	70
DP	Rsch	63	Mats	73	Pers	60	Pers	65	Mktg	56	Mats	60	Sales	66	Sales	65	Sales	69	Pers	70
Engineering	DP	62	DP	70	Mktg	59	Mktg	60	DP	55	Mktg	58	Mktg	65	Mats	63	Mats	65	Eng	67
Materials	Mktg	62	Pers	65	Mats	59	Mats	57	Mats	50	Sales	57	Eng	64	Eng	61	Eng	63	–	–
Personnel	Pers	57	Mktg	64	DP	58	DP	55	Pers	49	Rsch	55	DP	63	DP	53	Rsch	53	–	–

Source: Michael Dixon, 'How Departmental Directors' Pecking-Orders Differ Between Countries', *Financial Times*, 24 June 1992, p. 12.

networks, and have an interest in encouraging them.) The density and intimacy of inter-firm relationships is low in countries where the central state was strong enough to create a large and rather homogeneous economic space and suppressed intermediate organizations within it: that includes Britain and the countries drawing their culture principally from it, and France (Lane, 1989). To this distinction we can assimilate another one with nearly the same origins: aristocratic versus urban culture. The strong British and French states were dominated by aristocrats and their culture showed remarkable resilience and pervasiveness: it embodied a contempt for the activities of production, and it encouraged those with specific skills – accountants, say, or engineers of one sort or another – to constitute themselves as a group apart with aspirations to the high status of the privileged aristocratic orders (lawyers, clerics, etc.). (On France see D'Iribarne, 1989; on Britain, Tylecote, 1982.) In the weaker states the aristocratic culture never triumphed: the dominant culture of industry grew from that of the merchants and craftsmen of the medieval town. Production was respected, and round it the other skills and functions showed more tendency to cohere. Other things being equal, the 'incoherence' of functions should make for 'irrationality'. Where, as in Britain and to a lesser extent the US, management has responded by decentralization so as to force functions together, the result is sub-unit rationality. (On the historical background to these arguments, see Lane, 1991; D'Iribarne, 1989 and Tylecote, 1982. For evidence on the relative status of functions among European countries see Table 3.1.)

Attachment of the workforce to the firm
There is one more distinction, not unrelated to the others. In some countries the workforce, or most of it, is regarded as 'belonging' to the firm, and the firm, to some degree, as belonging to them; in others the relationship of firm and employees is essentially market-based and contractual, and the firm belongs exclusively to the shareholders. The first situation – which clearly corresponds to *Gemeinschaft* orientation – has arisen in different countries in different ways. In the Nordic countries it has evolved within and out of an essentially egalitarian as well as urban culture. In Germany, on the other hand, and even more so in Japan, the cultural traditions were authoritarian, but market-based attitudes to labour were not acceptable (see previous section), so the tendency was to paternalism. Social crisis after defeat in war made that unworkable, and thus the idea of the firm-as-community was reluctantly embraced. (The cultural inclination to strong social bonds within the firm is particularly marked in Japan, due to its late development, 'feudalized Confucianism', and tradition of village cooperation in rice growing.) In the rest, *Gemeinschaft* orientation is weak or (as in the Anglo-Saxon countries) virtually non-existent (Fox, 1974; Fukutake, 1982; Clark, 1979; Berghahn, 1982; Lane, 1989).

MANAGERIAL OBJECTIVES, TECHNOLOGY COLLABORATION AND NATIONAL SYSTEMS OF INNOVATION

We are now in a position to predict and explain national differences in approach to TC. We focus on three and begin with perhaps the best-known case.

Japan

In our terms the typical Japanese firm has the following characteristics:

1. High *filière* orientation. This arises from local particularism and the *zaibatsu* tradition, restored by the development of crossholdings and the *kigyo shudan* or inter-market groups after the war; also the quasi-feudal tradition of the vertical *keiretsu*, of big firms and their multiple tiers of subcontractors (Shokochukin, 1983).
2. Relatively low inclination to *sector* orientation. The particularism and the rivalries between the great *zaibatsu* and their successors make for this. However, the engineering research associations created after 1961 under MITI sponsorship (Freeman, 1992) brought rival firms together, and new small high-technology firms combined in a more independent – and equal – way than the old vertical *keiretsu* (Van Kooij, 1990). Subcontracting firms in general have moved out of dependence on their 'feudal lords' and through supplying several major firms have tended to bring sectors together (Imai, 1989; Shokochukin, 1989; and Small and Medium Enterprise Agency, 1992).
3. High *Gemeinschaft* orientation. The nature of the large Japanese firm as a quasi-community is well known (see above). The exclusion of 'temporary' workers from the care of this community is also well known (Clark, 1979).
4. Long-termism. Safety from takeover (largely through crossholdings) and commitments to the retention and promotion of permanent workers account for this (Hirata and Tylecote, 1993; and Watanabe and Yamamoto, 1992).
5. Low sub-unit orientation (in M-form firms) and organizational slack (in U-form firms). This is connected to 3: long-term employment and the rotation of managers among functions and divisions helps to prevent identification with departments or sub-units.

These characteristics are not immutable; the tendency to long-termism which was sharply increased during the fat years of the Kuznets upswing of the 1980s is likely to be equally reduced by the lean years of the 1990s (Hirata and Tylecote, 1993).

Results
Clearly TC within the *filière* – particularly the *kigyo shudan* and vertical *keiretsu* – will be much encouraged. A number of factors also encourage international

TC. First, there is a tradition of it because until very recently Japanese firms could take it for granted that the most advanced technology was abroad. Second, intra-sectoral rivalries within Japan make international TC the lesser evil – Honda could much more easily join with Rover than with Toyota or Nissan. Third, the low degree of 'irrationality' reduces internal resistance to TC. Fourth, the low degree of sub-unit rationality and irrationality makes it relatively easy to control the collaboration in the firm's own interests – to maximize its value to the Japanese firm and limit undesired value to the foreign partner.

Germany

In general, German firms appear to be characterized by:

1. High sector orientation. Germany has a long tradition of sectoral organizations like the guilds which were protected by the modern state, evolving via the early twentieth-century cartels into the array of modern trade associations, employers' associations, research associations, etc. (Lane, 1991).
2. Moderately high *Gemeinschaft*. Tradition and the co-determination institutions are favourable but the commitment to and of the firm does not go as far as in the Japanese firm (Lane, 1989).
3. Limited *filière* orientation. Local relationships are strong, but beyond that strong bonds do not tend to extend beyond broad sectors (e.g. mechanical engineering). (Lawrence, 1980; Lane, 1991.)
4. A degree of long-termism. The takeover threat is negligible; on the other hand there are in many cases dominant family shareholdings, unlike in large Japanese firms, whose owners are not immune to the attractions of present profit (Tylecote, 1991).
5. Low sub-unit orientation, largely because fully fledged M-forms are rare; but considerable irrationality (compared to Japan) because, conversely, functional responsibilities tend to be centralized and there is a strong identification with one's function, at least in large firms (Guerrieri and Tylecote, 1992). Moreover large firms have gradually become less subject either to shareholder or to bank control (Schreyoegg and Steinmann, 1991) – which would put them in a similar situation to most large Japanese firms, but for the fact that Japanese managers are quasi-shareholders to a degree that German managers are not. (The current unease over the lack of accountability of senior managers in Germany – industrial and financial – and what amounts to the resulting organizational slack is well expressed by Ogger's, 1993, best-selling diatribe against them.)

Results
German TC is very uneven in pattern. On the one hand established *sectoral* institutions – research associations and Fraunhofer institutes – thrive, and there is

Current sources of technology

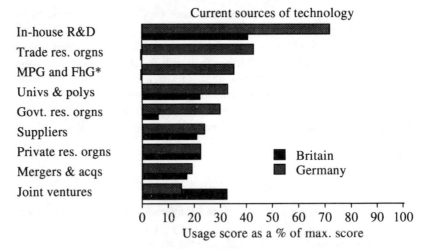

Univs & polys

Joint ventures

0   10 20 30 40 50 60 70 80 90 100
Usage score as a % of max. score

Britain – sources of technology by sector

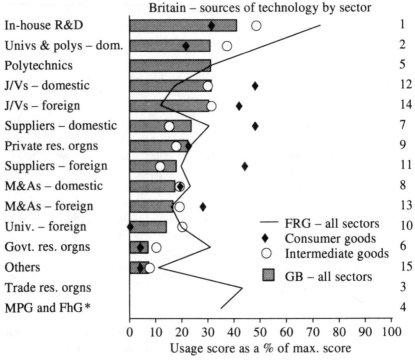

0   10 20 30 40 50 60 70 80 90 100
Usage score as a % of max. score

* Max Planck Gesellschaft and Fraunhoffer Gesellschaft

Source: Cheese (1991), Figures 2.10 and 2.11.

Figure 3.5   Sources of technology in Britain and Germany

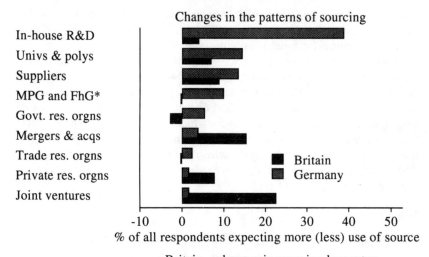

Changes in the patterns of sourcing

In-house R&D
Univs & polys
Suppliers
MPG and FhG*
Govt. res. orgns
Mergers & acqs
Trade res. orgns
Private res. orgns
Joint ventures

Britain
Germany

-10   0   10   20   30   40   50
% of all respondents expecting more (less) use of source

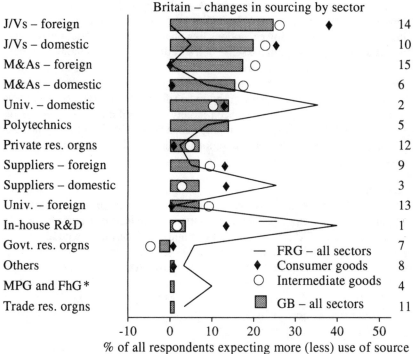

Britain – changes in sourcing by sector

J/Vs – foreign   14
J/Vs – domestic   10
M&As – foreign   15
M&As – domestic   6
Univ. – domestic   2
Polytechnics   5
Private res. orgns   12
Suppliers – foreign   9
Suppliers – domestic   3
Univ. – foreign   13
In-house R&D   1
Govt. res. orgns   7
Others   8
MPG and FhG *   4
Trade res. orgns   11

— FRG – all sectors
♦ Consumer goods
○ Intermediate goods
GB – all sectors

-10   0   10   20   30   40   50
% of all respondents expecting more (less) use of source

* Max Planck Gesellschaft and Fraunhoffer Gesellschaft

Source: Cheese (1991), Figures 2.12 and 2.13.

Figure 3.6   Changes in technology sources in Britain and Germany

strong TC among companies which have become acquainted, so to say, within
the sector and/or locality. Likewise TC with a neighbouring university or
research institute is favoured as a useful complement, rather than substitute, for
in-house research. However, further-flung, particularly international TC is
treated with great reserve, for both good and bad reasons (Cheese, 1991, and
Figures 3.5 and 3.6). The good reasons are that a relationship of trust is hard
to create at a cultural and geographical distance and that there are inevitable
long-term disadvantages or at least risks, which do not attach to in-house R&D
if it is generously funded – which German firms are prepared to do. One bad
reason is irrationality, specifically the selfish interests of in-house R&D; another,
the low level (compared to Japan) of *filière* orientation buttressed by crossholdings
right across sectoral boundaries.

Britain

Very simply and flatly, in Britain *filière* and *Gemeinschaft* orientation are and
always have been virtually non-existent, while sub-unit orientation and short-
termism (for connected reasons) have, since the 1960s, become rampant in most
industries (with interesting exceptions like pharmaceuticals). Sectoral orientation is also weak, except in the sense of a sort of freemasonry among members
of a given occupation ('aristocratic order') who maintain friendly contact – and
frequently move – across the boundaries of firms; but not across the boundaries
of functions. Irrationality, which used to be rife due partly to high attachment
to functional specialization, has been largely squeezed out by fear of hostile
takeovers and the introduction of highly decentralized M-form firms – just the
factors which let loose the sub-unit rationality and the short-termism (Demirag,
Morris and Tylecote, 1994).

Results
There is no preference for national over international TC, because of the lack
of intra-national sectoral or *filière* orientation. There has been a recent upsurge
of enthusiasm for TC for a number of bad and good reasons: the good reasons
include the decline of 'irrationality' and an increased commitment to innovating
somehow; the bad ones include short-termism which encourages neglect of the
long-term dangers of TC and sub-unit orientation, which has a similar effect
and inhibits internal collaboration. Informal exchange of information specific
to a function, as described by Von Hippel (1987, 1988), will have been
encouraged by the occupational 'freemasonry' described above.

CONCLUSIONS

This chapter has argued that the objectives of managers vary along at least three
dimensions: of *term*, from long-termism through shareholder wealth maxi-

mization (SWM) to short-termism; of *scope*, from stakeholder orientation (which can be subdivided) through ER to sub-unit orientation (which can also be subdivided); and of *coherence*, from rationality to increasing organizational slack. It was shown that (on the first two dimensions) long-termism and stakeholder orientation favoured technological innovation in general, but not necessarily TC, since (to the extent that it was an alternative to *in-house* innovation) it was generally more attractive to short-termism and sub-unit orientation. On the third dimension, technological innovation usually and TC almost invariably would be favoured by rationality. There followed sketches of the position and recent movements of the position of three economies on the dimensions described. Japan and Germany – in that order – were much less short-termist than Britain had recently become, and less inclined to sub-unit orientation. They both displayed more stakeholder orientation than Britain, but of different types. Large German firms had acquired some of the slack that their British counterparts had lost. These sketches helped to explain differences in behaviour: notably, that while Japan and Germany were overall quite similar in their commitment to technological innovation, Japan was much more inclined to international TC between firms; and that while British managers' commitment to innovation was much less than Japanese, their enthusiasm for international TC was now similar. They may also help to show that a similar inclination to TC does not imply that rewards from it will be similar.

NOTES

1. I am grateful for the financial support of the Joint Committee on the Successful Management of Technological Change of the Science and Engineering and Economic and Social Research Councils for a recently concluded project on Performance Pressures and Innovation in British Manufacturing (SERC GR/F65149) which involved case studies of a number of British-based firms in pharmaceuticals, mechanical engineering and electrical/electronic engineering. (The project team at Sheffield involved Ben Morris, Research Associate, Istemi Demirag, Accounting and Financial Management, Ian Freeston, Electronic Engineering, Rod Smith, Mechanical Engineering, and Nigel Bax, Pharmacology.) I am also indebted to the British Council and the Sheffield University Research Stimulation Fund. For other help and advice I am grateful to Lars-Erik Gadde, Hakan Hakansson, Tony Moss, Paolo Guerrieri, John Groenewegen and other colleagues in PEPOPPAI (the Pan-European Project on Performance Pressures and Innovation); to Mike Dietrich, Mitsuhiro Hirata and Harukiyo Hasegawa; also to the many managers who gave their time to talk to our team.
2. In the Performance Pressures and Innovation in British Manufacturing project (see note 1 above).

REFERENCES

Baumol, W.J. (1959), *Business Behaviour, Value and Growth*. New York: Macmillan.
Berghahn, V. (1982), *Modern Germany: society economy and politics in the 20th century*, Cambridge: Cambridge University Press.

Chandler, A.D. Jr (1977), *The Visible Hand: The Managerial Revolution in American Business*, Cambridge, Mass.: Belknap Press.

Cheese, J. (1991), *Attitudes to Innovation in Britain and Germany*, London: Centre for the Exploitation of Science and Technology.

Clark, R. (1979), *The Japanese Company*, New Haven and London: Yale University Press.

Cyert, R.N. and March, J.G. (1963), *A Behavioral Theory of the Firm*, (2nd rev. edn, 1992), Oxford: Blackwell.

Demirag, I. and Tylecote, A. (1992), 'The Effect of Cultures, Structures and Market Expectations upon Technological Innovation', *British Journal of Management*, March, 7–20.

Demirag, I., Morris, B. and Tylecote, A. (1993), 'Technological co-operation and performance evaluation in divisionalised companies: A case study of innovation', CRITEC Discussion Paper no.3, Sheffield University Management School.

Demirag, I., Morris, B. and Tylecote, A. (1994), 'Accounting for Financial and Managerial Causes of Short-Term Pressures in British Corporations', *Journal of Business, Finance and Accounting*, **21** (8), December, 1195–1213.

D'Iribarne, P. (1989), *La Logique de l'Honneur*, Paris: Seuil.

Fox, A. (1974), *Beyond Contract: work, power and trust relations*, London: Faber.

Fransman, M. (1990), *The Market and Beyond: Information Technology, Cooperation and Competition in the Japanese System*, Cambridge: Cambridge University Press.

Freeman, C. (1992), *The economics of hope*. London: Pinter.

Fukutake, T. (1982), *The Japanese Social Structure: Its Evolution in the Modern Century*. Tokyo: University of Tokyo Press.

Guerrieri, P. and Tylecote, A.B. (1993), 'National competitive advantages and microeconomic behaviour', CRITEC Discussion Paper no. l.

Hamel, G., Doz, Y. and Prahalad, C.K. (1989), 'Collaborate with your Competitors – and Win', *Harvard Business Review*, Jan/Feb, **67**.

Hirata, M. and Tylecote, A.B. (1993), 'Technological innovation and performance pressures in Europe and Japan', *Hitotsubashi Journal of Commerce and Management*, December.

Imai, K. (1989), 'Evolution of Japan's corporate and industrial networks', ch. 6 in B. Carlsson (ed.), *Industrial Dynamics*, Dordrecht: Kluwer.

Lane, C. (1989), *Management and Labour in Europe: The Industrial Enterprise in Germany, Britain and France*, Aldershot: Edward Elgar.

Lane, C. (1991), 'Industrial Reorganisation in Europe: Patterns of Convergence and Divergence in Germany, France and Britain', *Work, Employment and Society*, **5** (4), 515–39.

Lawrence, P. (1980), *Managers and Management in Germany*, London: Croom Helm.

Leibenstein, H. (1975), 'Aspects of the X-Efficiency Theory of the Firm', *Bell Journal of Economics*, **6**, 580–606.

Malerba, F. (1985), *The Semiconductor Business*, London: Pinter.

Marris, R. (1964), *The Economic Theory of Managerial Capitalism*, London: Macmillan.

Ogger, G. (1993), *Nieten in Nadelstreifen: Deutschlands Manager in Zwielicht*, Munich: Droemer Knaur.

Prahalad, C.K. and Hamel, G. (1990), 'The Core Competencies of the Corporation', *Harvard Business Review*, May–June, 79–91.

Sako, M. (1992), *Prices, Quality and Trust: Inter-firm relations in Britain and Japan*, Cambridge: Cambridge University Press.

Sasaki, N. (1981), *Management and Industrial Structure in Japan*, Oxford: Pergamon.

Schreyoegg, G. and H. Steinmann (1991), 'Zur Trennung von Eigentum und Verfue-gungsgewalt: Eine Empirische Analyse der Beteiligungsverhaeltnisse in Deutschen Grossunternehmen', *Zeitschrift fuer Betriebswirtschaft*, **51** (6), June, 533–57.

Shokochukin, C. (1983), *Shitauke Chushokigyo no Shin Kyokumen: Sono Jiritsuka Shiko to Shitauke Saihensei* (New Phases of Small and Medium-sized Subcontractors in Japan: Their Independence and Reorganisation), Tokyo: Small and Medium Enterprise Agency.

Shokochukin, C. (1989), *Atarashii Bungyo Kozo no Kochiku wo Mezashite: Endakaka no Shitauke Kikaikoguo no Shin Tenkai* (Towards building new system of division of labour in Japan: new development of subcontractors in the mechanical industry under the strong yen), Tokyo: Small and Medium Enterprise Agency.

Siegel, S. and Fouraker, L. (1960), *Bargaining and Group Decision-making: Experiments in bilateral monopoly*, New York and London: McGraw-Hill.

Small and Medium Enterprise Agency (1992), *Chusho Kigyo Hakusho 1992* (White Paper on Small and Medium-Sized Firms), Tokyo: Small and Medium Enterprise Agency.

Tylecote, A.B. (1982), 'German Ascent and British Decline, 1870–1980', pp. 41–68 in E. Friedman (ed.), *Ascent and Decline in the World Economy*, Beverly Hills and London: Sage.

Tylecote, A.B. (1991), 'Performance Pressures and Innovation in Britain and Germany', pp. 65–74 in Cheese, (1991).

Tylecote, A.B. (1994), 'Financial Systems and Innovation', in M. Dodgson and R. Rothwell (eds), *The Handbook of Industrial Innovation*, Aldershot: Edward Elgar.

Tylecote, A.B. and Demirag, S.I. (1992), 'Short-Termism: Culture and Structures as Factors in Technological Innovation', in R. Coombs, P. Saviotti and V. Walsh (eds), *Technological Change and Company Strategies*, London: Academic Press.

Van Kooij, E.H. (1990), *Technology Transfer in the Japanese electronic industry*, Zootemeer, Netherlands: Economic Research Institute for Small and Medium-sized Business.

Von Hippel, E. (1987), 'Cooperation between rivals: informal know-how trading', *Research Policy*, **16** (5), 291–302.

Von Hippel, E. (1988) *The Sources of Innovation*, Oxford: Oxford University Press.

Watanabe, S. and Yamamoto, I. (1992), 'Corporate governance in Japan', *NRI Quarterly*, Winter, 28–45.

Williamson, O.E. (1981), 'The modern corporation: origins, evolution and attributes', *Journal of Economic Literature*, **19**, 1537–68.

4. Learning, trust and inter-firm technological linkages: some theoretical associations[1]

Mark Dodgson

INTRODUCTION

A growing body of theoretical and empirical research addresses the centrality of learning in the organizational and technological renewal of firms, and hence in their continuing competitiveness. Learning in firms is a complex, multi-level concept encompassing a variety of motives, sources, processes and outcomes. It occurs across a broad range of activities, including inter-firm technological linkages. Learning has to be seen in the context of the uncertainties facing firms, and the competitive imperatives and power relationships under which they operate. Firms cooperate as well as compete; business transactions are not always zero sum games. Such cooperation often has a strongly 'social' basis, involving affinity and loyalty. An important aspect of these qualitative links between firms is the existence of trust. By means of a review of a range of theoretical literature this paper's aims are threefold. First, to discuss some of the features of learning and to identify the significance of inter-firm links for its encouragement. Second, to examine the relevance of a 'learning approach' to inter-firm links within a broad range of theoretical explanations for such linkages. Third, to begin to explore the relationship of 'trust' to shared learning between firms. The paper then raises a number of germane research questions in the area yet to be addressed.

LEARNING AND TECHNOLOGICAL CHANGE

Recent interest in the ways in which firms learn, and thereby deal with change, has manifested itself in a range of literatures. The concept of 'learning organizations' has excited great attention in the management literature (Senge, 1990; Howard, 1993), with 'technological learning' as a subset of this (Hayes and Wheelwright, 1984; Dodgson, 1991a). A special edition of *Organization Science* has been dedicated to the subject. Interesting historical accounts have examined the role of learning in technological change (Thomson, 1993). Learning has received the attention of mainstream economics (Malerba, 1992), which, rather belatedly, has identified its significance, and extended the discipline's previously restricted parameters of its constitution. Valuable attempts are beginning to be made to confront the complexity of learning, and empirically examine difficult issues such as the relationship between individual and group learning (see, for example, Pentland, 1992).

All these literatures describe the centrality of learning for corporate survival. However, they are often based on fundamentally different assumptions, and examine very diverse issues under the auspices of 'learning'. The management literature, for example, sees learning variously as a response to environmental contingency, systems logic, or the action of individuals. The economics literature is still chary of looking in the 'black box' and seems primarily concerned with analysis of the sources and outcomes of learning, while organization theory's focal concern is with processes within firms. There is little evidence of inter-disciplinary attempts to merge the theoretical insights of these literatures, although it can be argued that this is a valuable thing to do (Dodgson, 1993a).

Learning can be described as the ways firms build, supplement and organize knowledge and routines around their competences and within their cultures, and adapt and develop organizational efficiency through improving the use of these competences. Competences are the focused combination of resources within a firm which define its business activities and comparative advantage. Common explanations of the need to learn is the requirement for *adaptation* and improved *efficiency* in times of change. In turbulent environments learning can be seen as a purposive quest by firms to retain and improve competitiveness, productivity and innovativeness. The greater the uncertainties facing firms, the greater the need for learning. Learning can be seen to have occurred when organizations perform in changed and better ways, when competences are better defined, more appropriate, and effectively implemented. The goals of learning are useful outcomes, which in the present industrial context include, at best, improved comparative performance; at worst, survival.

Among other factors stimulating environmental uncertainty and learning, two are particularly important at present: responses to technological change, and Western companies' reactions to the competitiveness of alternative forms of industrial organization (particularly Japanese). But the need to learn is more than just a response to external stimuli. There is a continuous and iterative interaction between these stimuli and factors within the firm such as their strategies and organizational forms. Firms need to learn in order to overcome strategic and organizational tendencies towards introspection and parochialism (Morgan,

1986), which can be particularly disadvantageous in turbulent and rapidly changing circumstances.

Learning is a multi-faceted and complex concept. It can be *contradictory*, seen in Clark et al.'s (1985) 'productivity dilemma' of discord between innovation and productivity, change and experience (what economists sometimes refer to as the tensions between 'dynamic' and 'allocative' efficiencies, and organization theorists, the tensions between 'exploration' and 'exploitation'). It can be *conservative* (Morgan, 1986), *unreliable* (March et al., 1991), and *non-uniform* (Marengo, 1992a). Learning *from failure* is important, as is *unlearning* (Hedberg, 1981). The sources of learning *change* over time (Mody, 1990), and the lack of preparedness of firms to fund it (Pucik, 1988a) and problems in establishing incentives to encourage it (Aoki, 1988) provide some of the many reasons why organizations encounter such difficulty in learning (Argyris and Schon, 1978).

Nevertheless, firms do learn, survive and improve comparative performance. This learning progresses beyond the 'everyday' adaptation and improvement organizations can achieve in their existing competences through learning by 'doing' (Arrow, 1962) and 'using' (Rosenberg, 1982), and encompasses 'higher'-level learning (Fiol and Lyles, 1988) which questions the validity of current competences and facilitates the construction of new ones (described in the management literature as 'generative' as opposed to 'adaptive' learning – Senge, 1990 – and by Argyris and Schon, 1978 as 'double-loop' and 'deutero' learning as compared with 'single-loop' learning).

In conditions of rapid and disruptive market and technological change firms, it can be argued, need to learn at a 'higher level' as existing 'lower-level' learning focuses on current systems, products and technologies and not on new competences and opportunities. However, such learning is constrained. Much of the management, innovation and business economics literature points to the conservatism of strategies firms adopt, reflecting what companies are currently best at, rather than what changing markets require. The emphasis of much of this literature is that 'history matters', and that what a firm can do in the future is strongly influenced by its past and its collective learning. Firms' learning is 'path-dependent' (Dosi, 1988), and its technological choices are constrained by their 'technological trajectories' (Dosi, 1982) and 'firm-specific accumulated competences' (Pavitt, 1991). Yet as shown in the longevity of large industrial firms, resiliently operating under very different technological conditions (Pavitt, 1994), firms do learn to learn at a 'higher level', i.e. in ways that question their assumptions about what they do, and transform their competences and routines.

Firms learn through purposefully adopting strategies and structures that encourage learning (Senge, 1990; Malerba, 1992; Dodgson, 1992a). They learn through the activities of key individuals: 'boundary spanners' (Michael, 1973), by executive succession (Tushman et al., 1986), and through recruitment and training programmes. Important in this process is the way they develop shared cultures that facilitate learning (Schein, 1985). Furthermore, the management strategy literature has long pointed to the ways firms not only react to external change, but can seek proactively to shape the environment in which they operate and learn (Ansoff, 1968; Chandler, 1962).

A major mechanism by which firms learn about technology is through their internal R&D efforts. Learning is thus, to a significant extent, a function of the size and focus of R&D budgets, and the strategies for their direction and management. Firms do, of course, learn from a wide range of other functions, particularly from marketing and manufacturing and from the iterative interactions between functions. The learning that takes place in manufacturing, in both development and implementation, is particularly important and leads Baba (1985) and Leonard Barton (1991) to talk of the 'factory as a laboratory'. Furthermore, learning has both an 'internal' and an 'external' component. Given the complexity and multi-faceted nature of learning, it requires a multiplicity of stimuli, processes and outcomes. External learning is valuable in this respect. Malerba (1992) develops a typology of forms of learning: learning from doing, using, searching, interacting, inter-industry spillovers, and advances in science and technology. The first three in this list he describes as primarily internal activities, and the latter three, external. He points to the important role of external sources of knowledge in the generation of incremental technical change, something which, of course, has long been emphasized in the 'innovation studies' literature (Carter and Williams, 1957; Gibbons and Johnston, 1974; Rothwell et al., 1974). External links, with customers, suppliers, and other sources of information, are critical to innovative success. Indeed, it is argued that these links are becoming more central in the innovation process (Rothwell, 1992).

Inter-firm links also assist firms' learning processes (Lyles, 1988). An external orientation assists firms overcome the organizational introspection described in the management and organization theory literature, and applicable to firms' R&D groups. Psychologists refer to the way people learn *vicariously*, by watching before they perform and profiting from the successes and failure of others (Bandura, 1977). Firms similarly can use external links to learn in this way. They can bring new knowledge into the firm of a specific, project-based nature. They also can enable firms to reconsider their existing ways of doing things: be it in R&D organization (Clark et al., 1985), the implementation of new technology (Chew et al., 1991), or indeed if successful they can perhaps lead to a realignment of business strategy through diversification (Ciborra, 1991). Inter-firm links provide an opportunity to observe novelty through the approaches of partners, and can stimulate reconsideration of current practices. They can be an antidote to the 'not-invented-here-syndrome', and learning vicariously can help prevent the repetition of mistakes. Inter-firm links can provide opportunities for 'higher-level' learning (Dodgson, 1991b).

SOME THEORETICAL EXPLANATIONS FOR INTER-FIRM TECHNOLOGICAL LINKAGES

Having established the significance in the literature of learning for technolog-ical and organizational change, and of inter-firm links for that learning, what follows is an examination of four bodies of theory of inter-firm links and con-sideration of their insights for, and relevance to, learning.

There is a broad range of theoretical explanations of inter-firm technologi-cal linkages, and an extensive lexicon of analytical terms used to describe them. Somewhat crudely, this paper distinguishes four broad categories of theory applied to explain linkages between firms. These will briefly be described (for a fuller exposition see Dodgson, 1993b). The categories are: *changing systems of production*; the impact of *technological change*; those that focus on firms and their *economic and competitive relations*; and a final group which specif-ically address *organizational learning*. The categories are not mutually exclusive; there is occasional overlap. Although they address inter-firm technological links, some of the analyses were not specifically designed to focus primarily on them. Allocation of the various theories to each category was done on the basis of the theory's core assumptions. Given the large and expanding literature in the area, this brief review of theory does not claim to be exhaustive, but is instead a reflection of the author's inevitably selective reading into inter-firm links and has a bias towards innovation and management studies, business and industrial economics, and aspects of organization theory.

Changing Systems of Production

This group of explanations for inter-firm technological links sees them as a response to the reorganization and restructuring of industry. For example, Lawton-Smith et al. (1990) refer to the *disorganized capitalism* explanation of collaboration between firms based on the Lash and Urry (1987) thesis of the collapse of 'organized capitalism'. In this view firms face increased uncertainty due to the historical loss of control over markets and extensive industrial restructuring. The adhesion to competitive 'free-market' principles or absence of industrial policy compounds these uncertainties. Extensive inter-firm links are a response to this uncertainty.

Marceau (1992) provides a useful distinction in her analysis of the forces 'reworking the world', of *chains, clusters and complexes*. 'Chains' of production refer to the relationships established between 'core' firms and their suppliers and distributors. These vertical production chains draw together all those activities from raw material extraction to final product marketing and servicing. Inter-firm links integrate and coordinate their activities through, for example, closer subcontracting relationships. 'Clusters' refer to the Marshallian analysis of groups of firms, geographically proximate, which through internal collaboration and competition continually stimulate product and process innovation and assist competitiveness. 'Complexes' integrate not only firms, but also public-sector bodies, industry-funded research organizations, regulatory regimes and public procurement policies (similar therefore, to Callon's, 1991, conception of technoeconomic networks).

The way in which 'industrial districts' can form cohesive social and economic groupings of innovative and self-supporting (small) firms has been the source of much attention, and is an important element of the *flexible specialization thesis* of Piore and Sabel (1984) and its variants. Although highly empirically contestable, this thesis has attracted considerable attention and has valuably highlighted the significance of the social and cultural context of inter-firm links. Recent approaches to industrial districts take greater account of the changing strategies of large companies and the importance of 'bridging institutions' linking the public and private sector in local and regional systems of production.

The approaches in this category of theory emphasize the *systemic* nature of industrial change, with extensive interconnectedness of industrial actors. Marceau (1992), for example, argues that in order to decipher changes in the organization of production it is necessary to examine the relationships of public and private sector, science and technology, large and small firms, and the... '...creative tension or stress...which shapes the outcome at any given time and contains the potential for radical change. If the position of any of the key players changes then changes to the whole system are likely' (p. 469).

Technology and Innovation

This group of theories highlights the role of technology within industrial reorganization and restructuring, and is typified by Freeman and Perez's (1988) work on changing *technoeconomic paradigms*. Technological change and uncertainty are key elements of Marceau's creative tension and stresses within industrial systems. Emphasis lies with the scale, scope and cost of contemporary technologies, and the uncertainties facing the development and market diffusion of pervasive technologies (particularly information and communications technology). Since Schumpeter many analyses of technological change have emphasized the discontinuous nature of innovation, and the problems this poses for firms (Tushman and Anderson, 1987). This uncertainty extends beyond consideration of technological feasibility, i.e. whether a new product can emerge, to how it will subsequently evolve. Market preferences in new technologies are rarely predictable, and the post-innovation improvements necessary for market success provide additional uncertainty.

Characteristic of periods of change in technoeconomic paradigm is the rise of new firms associated with competence in the new technologies and the strategic repositioning of many established firms as they try to cope with the rapid structural and technical change affecting their markets and their very existence. If we take into account also the international aspects of production, marketing and technology development, then clearly a period of great turmoil could have been expected in the 1980s, with many new strategic alliances and networks. (Freeman, 1991, p. 509)

Among the responses to these changes are *innovation networks* described as 'the' organizational form for the new technoeconomic paradigm (DeBresson and Amesse, 1991). Innovation networks are assumed to produce positive sum gains for participants on the level of innovation and profits, deal with technological uncertainty, and help in reducing opportunism and in setting technical standards.

Similarly, Imai (1990) argues that Japanese business organization is evolving from its traditional, formal *zaibatsu* and *keiretsu* business groups to a more adaptable and flexible network organization. He describes network organization as:

a basic institutional arrangement for coping with systemic innovation in the recent technology regime. Networks can be viewed theoretically as interpenetrated forms of market and organization. Empirically they are loosely coupled organizations having a core of both weak and strong ties among constituent members.... Cooperative relationships among firms are a key linkage mechanism in network organization. (p. 185)

Empirical research, such as Saxenian's (1991) in Silicon Valley, argues the innovative advantages of such network organization. However, Hobday (1991) is critical of this view and suggests that the innovative network may only have advantages at the early stages of a new technology's development. A number of analyses of inter-firm links refer to the way the intent, focus and nature of partnership vary with product and technology *life cycles* (Cainarca et al., 1992; Kogut, 1988; Mody, 1989, 1990). Uncertainties at the early stage of product or technology life cycles are argued to lead to inter-firm links between firms in R&D. As products and technologies mature, competition is driven by cost considerations: assemblers and suppliers link in novel ways to reduce cost. When products and production technologies are mature, firms link in order to rejuvenate them or to find alternatives. Life cycle analysis is, of course, much more sophisticated than this simple sequential model. Firms begin to collaborate in production in the early stages of life cycles, and link in R&D activities long before products are mature. Furthermore, firms are argued to have the ability to influence the speed of life cycle changes by influencing the behaviour of competitors. An important aspect of life cycle theory is the way in which it naturally considers the termination of inter-firm technological links, a factor omitted from many other approaches.

Within this category are those approaches, typified by analysts of management information systems, that emphasize the role of technology itself in networking. Whilst not accepting the determinism of some of these approaches, it is important to note the ways linked computer-aided design (CAD) systems in product design, electronic data network (EDN) in supplier relationships, and various other information technologies, facilitate and increase the opportunities for inter-firm linkages.

Other approaches are concerned with the *nature of technological knowledge*. Ouchi and Bolton's (1988) analysis of inter-firm collaboration centres on the nature of intellectual property; some approaches identify the significance of tacit, non-codifiable knowledge for innovation through inter-firm links (Mowery, 1988). This has implications for inter-firm relationships inasmuch as non-integrated firms cannot effectively communicate and share this type of knowledge (an issue pursued in the paper by Senker and Faulkner for this conference – Chapter 5). The Nelson/Winter/Dosi-type evolutionary economics perspective that sees firms as social institutions combining useful productive knowledge – knowledge which is largely tacit (Winter, 1987) – begins to point to the social and 'shared' nature of knowledge accumulation. As Radosovic (1991), in his conception of 'social intelligence', puts it:

> Network relations and linkages represent a natural response to situations where the sharing of tacit knowledge is a prerequisite for the successful production of new technological knowledge. As technological capacity is a mixture of 'firm-specific' knowledge and knowledge acquired through cooperation ... we could talk of knowledge creation as a social process based on sharing. Its effective use, that we call social intelligence, is based on the proposition that information can be sold but knowledge can only be shared. Since sharing is *prima facie* a social phenomenon, knowledge and particularly tacit knowledge is also embodied in social systems (p. 33).

The social basis of inter-firm links is also seen in analyses that focus on *national systems of innovation* (Lundvall, 1992; Nelson, 1993), and *technology systems* (Carlsson, 1994). In Lundvall's analysis the role of learning is key. His approach is based on two assumptions:

1. The most fundamental resource in the modern economy is knowledge and, accordingly, the most important process is learning.
2. Learning is predominantly an interactive and, therefore, a socially embedded process which cannot be understood without taking into consideration its institutional and cultural context.

In Lundvall's view, '...the national system of innovation is a *social* system. A central activity in the system of innovation is learning, and learning is a social activity which involves interaction between people. It is also a *dynamic* system, characterised both by positive feedback and by reproduction' (Lundvall, 1992, p. 1). 'Technology systems' are in some ways similar to national innovation systems, and are defined as: '...network(s) of agents interacting in each specific technology area under a particular institutional infrastructure for the purpose of generating, diffusing, and utilising technology' (Carlsson and Stankiewicz, 1991: 111).

However, technology systems differ from national innovation systems in a number of ways (Carlsson, 1994). First, they are defined by technology rather than national boundaries, and although they are influenced by national culture and institutions, they can also be *international* in nature. Second, technological systems vary in character and extent *within* nations. Third, this systems approach emphasizes technology diffusion and use rather than creation.

These latter two groups of theory place the turbulence and uncertainty facing firms' operating environments within the 'big picture' of changing industrial and economic structures. They provide the context in which firms' motivation to learn can be placed. Envisaging the changes within chains, clusters and complexes helps understanding of the systemic nature of this change. Those approaches focusing primarily on technological change usefully emphasize the extent and focus of much of the uncertainty and turbulence facing firms, and suggest the way in which the cyclical nature of technology development and diffusion may impact upon the motivation for inter-firm links, and their changing focus over time. It furthermore begins to delineate some of the cooperative elements of relationships between firms necessary for learning and technological development. This is highlighted in the examination of the 'social' aspects of systems at the 'national innovation', 'industrial district' and 'technology' levels. The way in which many of these relationships have a social basis, and the fact that the nature of technological knowledge requires 'quality' links between firms to encourage effective transfer and sharing of knowledge, begins to point to some of the elements of the *process* of inter-firm links.

Economic and Competitive Relations

The extent of inter-firm links is profoundly affected by the *structural* nature of markets and industries. Stigler (1951) showed that the inter-firm division of labour is limited by the extent of the market. It is only profitable to extend the division of labour when demand is increasing. Oligopolistic markets provide fewer potential partner firms than do highly segmented ones. Vertically integrated firms have less need for vertical links.

Several approaches to inter-firm links focus on the way that industrial structures (affected by their level of concentration and competition, existence of scale economies and other entry barriers, and general levels of technological change) influence the behaviour of firms (Porter, 1990). In this approach inter-firm links are seen as a means of shaping competition by improving a firm's comparative competitive position through raising entry costs, increasing price performance differentials, or by reducing uncertainties by encouraging mutual dependencies. Globalization is an important element of Porter and Fuller's (1986) analysis, inasmuch as it stimulates structural change. For Hamel, Doz and Prahalad (1989), collaboration needs to be viewed in a competitive power perspective. Collaboration is a continuation of competition, and should be seen, as Harrigan (1986) sees it, as a transitional stage in firm positioning.

Langlois (1989) argues that almost all modern economic theories of vertical integration are transaction costs explanations. And *transaction costs* economics are certainly commonly used to explain inter-firm technological links: 'Transaction costs are economized by assigning transactions (which differ in their attributes) to governance structures (the adaptive capacities and associated costs of which differ) in a discriminating way' (Williamson, 1985, p. 18).

The governance structures selected may range from classical market contracts to highly centralized, hierarchical organization, with mixed forms of market and firm organization in between. The selection of governance structure, and attempts to minimize transactions costs, are affected by: asset specificity, bounded rationality/opportunism, and uncertainty. Inter-firm links are seen as a form of hierarchy, which when transactions are costly, complex and difficult to specify, are a more efficient form of governance structure than contracts in markets (Williamson, 1985). Inter-firm linkage is a means by which 'leakage' of proprietorial information can be restricted to small numbers of firms, rather than having to display this information for broad consumption (and potential replication) in markets.

Transactions costs economics make a number of assumptions about base human behaviour, which is probably the weakest element of the thesis. Managers are presumed to behave opportunistically. Collaborative efficiency is assumed to be achieved when each partner can limit the other's behaviour by means of a 'double-hostage system'. These assumptions are antithetical to those many approaches which emphasize 'social' considerations such as the importance of continuing commitment for excellent communications and effective learning between firms enabling the development of competences (something difficult to envisage when analysis is transaction-specific). The instrumentality of the approach excludes questions of organizational power and the interpersonal relationships which provide some of the reasons for inter-firm links, and are so central to its process and outcome. Another approach which essentially denies cooperativeness is *game theory*. That part of this theory which has at least some empirical grounding points to the way firms send signals to one another, informative and misleading, which are designed to influence other firms' behaviour. The formation of collaborations may be one such signal.

A variety of approaches in this tradition integrate insights from recent *theory of the firm*. Mowery (1988) and Teece, Pisano and Schuen (1990) see firms as 'bundles of resources', and stress the importance of the development of new capabilities and exploitation of new ones, processes in which learning plays a central role. While referring to comparative cost efficiencies in transaction structures they also strongly emphasize the imperfections of transfer mechanisms of knowledge, technology and other assets. For Teece (1986), full commercial rewards from innovation can only be achieved if firms can access 'complementary assets' such as competitive manufacturing and distribution and marketing. These assets can be linked to R&D by means of: arm's-length transactions; vertical integration; and collaboration. Arm's-length transactions can have high costs, but are useful when technology is codified, discrete (non-systemic) and relatively simple. Vertical integration limits transaction costs, but prevents the access of specialisms in other firms. Collaboration allows these specialist skills to be accessed, and can allow complex and tacit knowledge to be transferred, and technology to be 'unbundled'. Important in this analysis is the question of appropriability: how firms protect and utilize their intellectual property.

Other approaches are based on analyses of numbers of firms operating in *networks*. Miles and Snow (1986) in their conception of 'dynamic networks' contend that future industrial structures will be disaggregated, market transactions will replace previously internalized activities, and future competitiveness will depend on the ways in which firms interact with one another. Jarillo (1988) refers to 'strategic networks' which provide an opportunity for joint value creation. Because of specialization they reduce final total costs, and as networks are typified by high levels of trust, transaction costs are also reduced. Jarillo suggests the mechanism for network creation lies in the catalytic role of a 'hub' firm cognizant of the advantages of network organization.

A *strategic management* approach highlights a number of aspects of inter-firm links relevant to their frequency and conduct. It posits that inter-firm links are not only of relevance to immediate or envisaged products and technologies but also as a means of developing the competence and flexibility to produce at present unforeseen technologies and products (Granstrand et al., 1992; Arnold et al., 1992; Dodgson, 1992b). The pragmatism of this perspective of corporate behaviour identifies both the idiosyncrasies of individual firm responses and the frequent shortcomings of inter-firm links and the difficulties in assuring mutual benefits for partner firms. It emphasizes the instability of horizontal linkages and their high failure rates. It points to exclusionary motives and control objectives. Thus links may be formed to pre-empt competitors doing the same (van Tulder and Junne, 1988) or to raise entry barriers. Firms may use links to increase the 'stress' and hence control over suppliers (Lamming, 1992). Alternatively, firms may sacrifice autonomy in the generation and diffusion of technology, and develop strategies for sharing control over technology in order to retain that control (Dodgson, 1989).

The approaches focusing on economic and competitive relations valuably direct analyses to the key motive of inter-firm links: long-term corporate survival and growth. They introduce the question of power between firms, and how dominant positions may be maintained. However, the transactions cost approach to explaining technological inter-firm links is limited in a number of respects. It discounts many of the important characteristics of links discussed in the literature such as their social basis, and those elucidated later in the paper, of interpersonal and organizational trust. Furthermore, it cannot account for those aspects of collaboration which stimulate and facilitate learning in firms across broad technological and organizational competences. Generally, however, these approaches further help our understanding of the motives and stimuli of technological linkages and learning. They usefully highlight the need to consider the competitive and profitability aims of links, the reasons for, and constraints on resource exchange, and the continuing dilemma between firms' competitive aims and cooperative means.

Organizational Learning

There is a literature which places learning centrally in its analysis of inter-firm links (see, for example, numbers of chapters in Contractor and Lorange, 1988; Doz and Schuen, 1988). For Kogut (1988) joint ventures are 'vehicles by which knowledge is transferred and by which firms learn from one another'. These approaches complement elements of the previous categories of theory in that they suggest focused motives and desired outcomes from inter-firm links. Thus, learning is necessary to comprehend and respond to changing industrial and technological systems. It can assist in developing competences and enhancing the power that provides competitive advantage.

The primary ascribed *motive* for learning through inter-firm links is to deal with technological and market uncertainty (Mody, 1990; Ciborra, 1991). Ciborra argues that alliances are the institutional arrangement that most efficiently allows firms to implement strategies for organizational learning and innovation: 'The alliance brings into the corporation new expertise concerning products, marketing strategies, organizational know-how, and new tacit and explicit knowledge. New management systems, operating procedures and modifications of products are the typical outcomes of this incremental learning' (Ciborra, 1991, p. 59).

Ciborra's analysis argues that the *outcomes* of alliances are reduced uncertainties by means of improving predictability of technological development, and that they are a means of reducing the transition costs of firms transferring strategies. These transition costs can be argued to reflect the learning rigidities in firms. Whether by 'iron laws' or 'iron cages' firms do become defensive, introspective and resistant to change. Inter-firm links provide an opportunity to expand learning horizons and to overcome internal introspection (Dodgson, 1991c).

The learning approach also attempts to examine the *process* of inter-firm links. Such a consideration is important for a number of reasons. First, it is necessary to account for adaptability and change in inter-firm links. As Contractor and Lorange (1988) argue, the strategic rationales prevailing when a cooperative venture was formed may shift over time. They argue that the erosion of the fundamental strategic rationales may come from external or environmental sources (such as technological obsolescence) or internal sources, 'such as when one partner learns from the other, and the other partner has nothing to contribute'. Adaptability is necessary in inter-firm links because: the bargaining power of partners varies over time (Kogut, 1988; Doz, 1988); the original reasons for forming the links may become obsolete over time (Harrigan, 1986); and initial agreements surprisingly often focus attention on the wrong sets of issues (Lyles, 1988).

Second, the differential speeds at which partners learn have marked consequences for the outcomes of inter-firm links. In his study of US/Japanese joint ventures, Pucik argues: 'Benefits are appropriated asymmetrically due to differences in the organizational learning capacity of the partners. The shifts in relative power in a competitive partnership are related to the speed at which the partners can learn from each other' (Pucik, 1988b, p. 80). Dodgson (1991b) argues that it is the differential speed of learning that accounts for the high level of linkages between large and small firms in biotechnology, and that it is the ability of smaller firms to 'fast learn' which makes them attractive partners.

Third, consideration of the process of linkage implies examination of the qualitative nature of relationships within and between firms. It is the process by which externally derived knowledge, both tacit and codified, is diffused throughout the organization, for example, from central to divisional R&D, from R&D to manufacturing, from individuals to groups – and hence provides benefits and returns to that learning. In an area ripe for research it is the latter question – how individual learning through inter-firm links extends into group or organizational learning – which is particularly germane, and why recent research such as Pentland's (1992) is so valuable. Another key research question concerns the need for diversity in learning sources. DiMaggio and Powell (1991) refer to 'organizational fields' of organizations which in aggregate constitute a recognized area of institutional life (suppliers, consumers, regulators, etc. that produce similar services or products), and argue that: 'Once disparate organizations in the same line of business are structured into an actual field... (by competition, the state, or the professions), powerful forces emerge that lead them to become more similar to one another' (p. 148).

This tendency towards isomorphism has profound implications for learning. If firms in a network extensively share knowledge over a long period, then they will increasingly come to resemble one another with detrimental consequences for novelty and innovation. Just as Marengo (1992b) argues the need for diversity of learning within firms, it would appear beneficial if firms were to seek heterogeneous sources of external learning, with perhaps long-term, intimate links to assist incremental improvements, and short-term links with companies outside of the network to assist radical, higher-level learning. This area is ripe for research. → bus. history — how have LT survivors adapted and changed ?

TRUST AND INTER-FIRM LINKS

Given the social basis of inter-firm links – as identified by many of the approaches discussed – the quality of relationships between partner firms has obvious implications for outcomes. An aspect of these relationships which has received some attention is the question of trust.

Trust between firms, according to Sako (1991), is '...a state of mind, an expectation held by one trading partner about another, that the other will behave in a predictable and mutually acceptable manner' (p. 377). She argues that there are different reasons for predictability in behaviour, and this allows three types of trust to be distinguished. 'Contractual trust' exists such that each partner adheres to agreements, and keeps promises. 'Competence trust' concerns the expectation of a trading partner performing his role competently. 'Goodwill trust' refers to mutual expectations of open commitment to each other: '...someone who is worthy of "goodwill" trust is dependable and can be credited with high discretion, as he can be expected to take initiative while refraining from unfair advantage taking...trading partners are committed to take initiatives (or exercise discretion) to exploit new opportunities over and above what was explicitly promised' (Sako, 1991, p. 379).

Such high levels of trust often underpin the success of Japanese customer/supplier interactions. The significant role of trust within inter-firm links is emphasized both theoretically (Buckley and Casson, 1988) and empirically, for example, by Lorenz's (1992) historical study of the shipbuilding industry. A wide number of studies show how effective inter-firm links and learning between partners depend on high levels of trust (Jarillo, 1988). Lundvall (1988), for example, argues that in order to overcome the inevitable uncertainties in jointly developed product innovations, 'Mutual trust and mutually respected codes of behaviour will normally be necessary' (p. 52). Saxenian (1991) contends that

'A network of long-term, trust-based alliances with innovative suppliers represents a source of advantage for a systems producer which is very difficult for a competitor to replicate. Such a network provides both flexibility and a framework for joint learning and technological exchange' (p. 430). The firms in this network are argued to exchange sensitive information concerning business plans, sales forecasts and costs, and have a mutual commitment to long-term relationships. This involves '...relationships with suppliers as involving personal and moral commitments which transcend the expectations of simple business relationships' (p. 428).

Håkansson and Johanson (1988) describe a range of these commitments and bonds:

> Interaction between firms develops over time. It takes time to learn about each other's ways of doing and viewing things and how to interpret each other's acts. Relations are built gradually in a social exchange process through which the parties may come to trust in each other. . .Over time, as a consequence of interaction, bonds of various kinds are formed by the parties. There may be technical bonds which are related to the technologies employed by the firms, knowledge bonds related to the parties' knowledge about their business, social bonds in the form of personal confidence, administrative bonds related to the administrative routines and procedures of the firms, and legal bonds in the form of contracts between the firms. These bonds create lasting relationships between the firms. (p. 373)

The importance of cultural affinities within such combinations of inter-firm linkages is strongly emphasized within the 'industrial districts' literature (Hirst and Zeitlin, 1989). Freeman (1991) argues: 'Personal relationships of trust and confidence (and sometimes of fear and obligation) are important both at the formal and informal level... For this reason cultural factors such as language, educational background, regional loyalties, shared ideologies and experiences and even common leisure interests continue to play an important role in networking' (p. 503).

A number of reasons can be suggested to explain why high trust facilitates effective inter-firm links, both horizontal and vertical. The first relates to the sort of *knowledge* being transferred, which is often tacit, uncodified, firm-specific and commercially sensitive. It is, therefore, not readily transferable, requiring dense, reliable and continuing communication paths. Furthermore, it is often *proprietorial*. What is being exchanged is the kind of knowledge and competence which is not easily replicated or purchased by competitors and thus can provide important elements of a firm's defining competence and competitiveness. Partners are expected to share trust in each other's ability to provide valid and helpful responses to uncertainty. But furthermore they are trusted not to use this information in ways which may prove disadvantageous to partners.

A second reason relates to time scale of successful inter-firm links. Trust facilitates continuing relationships between firms (Arrow, 1975). Continuity is valuable because, as we have seen, the objective of inter-firm links may change over time, in line, for example, with changing or new market and technological opportunities. Furthermore, it is only within a long-term horizon that reciprocity in collaboration can occur. At any one time one partner will be a net gainer. The disincentive to cut and run is based on the view of future gains which can only be achieved through continuity of collaboration. Trust militates against opportunistic behaviour (Buckley and Casson, 1988). Similarly, fear of mistrust on the part of future new partners should a firm behave in such a manner is another consideration.

Many user/supplier links have surprising longevity (Håkansson, 1989). This enables effective communication paths to develop, and facilitates the social and other bonds referred to by Håkansson and Johanson (1988) to be established. Macaulay's classic (1963) article arguing the way contract law is often ignored in business transactions is revealing in this regard. He argues that trading partners' primary motives are to remain in business and that they will avoid doing anything which might interfere with this. This includes avoiding the legal system, but also being sensitive to reactions of business partners and concern for business reputation. A priority for business, he argues, is flexibility over the long term. He points out how detailed negotiated contracts can get in the way of good exchange relationships: 'Some businessmen object that in...carefully worked out relationship(s) one gets performance only to the letter of the contract. Such planning indicates a lack of trust and blunts the demands of friendship, turning a cooperative venture into an antagonistic horse trade' (Macaulay, 1963, p. 64).

The advantages of cooperativeness and fairness in continuing reciprocal relationships is demonstrated by Axelrod (1984). In his analysis of the large variety of approaches to the prisoner's dilemma game, he castigates the unsuccessful contestants ('expert strategists') from political science, sociology, economics, psychology and mathematics for their 'systematic errors of being too competitive for their own good, not being forgiving enough, and being too pessimistic about the responsiveness of the other side' (p. 40). He argues that his approach, based on the assumption of continuing interactions, has implications for the conduct of business relationships.

A third reason for high trust in collaboration reflects the high management costs of such linkages. Selecting a suitable partner and building the dense communications paths through which tacit and uncodified information can be transferred has considerable management costs, both real and opportunity. These costs are increased when consideration of interpersonal trust is extended to inter-organizational trust. As Dodgson (1993c) argues, trust between partner firms is commonly analysed by means of relationships between individuals.

However, to survive the problems of labour turnover and the possibilities of communications breakdowns on the part of particular managers, scientists and engineers, trust between firms has to be general as well as specific to individuals. It has to be engrained in organizational routines, norms and values. Inter-organizational trust is characterized by community of interest, organizational cultures receptive to external inputs, and widespread and continually supplemented knowledge among employees of the status and purpose of the links (Dodgson, 1993c). Such features are not costless, and having made the effort to build such strong relationships, jeopardizing them through a lack of trust is not a sensible option.

CONCLUSIONS

This review of some of the theoretical literature on learning, trust and inter-firm linkages identifies some strong associations. Learning is a complicated concept, and it has a plethora of stimuli, motives, processes and outcomes. External learning is an important method by which firms deal with environmental uncertainty and compensate for organizational myopia. It can be viewed as significant input into firms' need to learn, the process by which they do learn, and learning outcomes. A number of theories of inter-firm links point to the context in which firms learn. The diversity of these theories, which encompass changing systems of production, technological change, economic and competitive relations and organizational learning, reflect the multi-faceted and complex nature of inter-firm links and of learning within them. A feature of many of the analyses of links between firms is their social and cultural basis. There is an association between the quality of these links, often reflecting trust between firms, and successful outcomes.

This review of the centrality of learning and trust within inter-firm links highlights tensions and paradoxes in inter-firm relationships; between, for example, firms' competitive aims and cooperative means, and between integration and isomorphism and the need for diversity. In addition to those research questions already raised, addressing the following questions may help our understanding of these complex and interdisciplinary issues:

1. What are the influences of power differentials between firms and learning and trust? Are shared learning and trust primarily a feature of balanced power, not only in an economic or market sense, but only in respect to knowledge and knowledge acquisition? How do power-disadvantaged firms begin to redress this balance, particularly in times of technological turbulence?

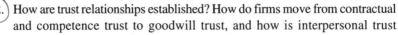

2. How are trust relationships established? How do firms move from contractual and competence trust to goodwill trust, and how is interpersonal trust

extended into inter-organizational trust? What role do 'honest broker' inter-mediary institutions play in this process?
3. Given the advantages of longevity and continuity for learning and trust in inter-firm links, what impact does this have for new, start-up firms whose potential contribution to 'systems' learning may be significant when market and technological change is rapid and uncertain?
4. What cultural factors influence learning and trust, particularly in respect of power and authority in inter-firm links? What cultural influences assist responses of contentment or resentment to positions in hierarchies?

NOTE

1. This paper is an early result of a research project on 'The Technological Linkages Between Large and Small Firms in Britain and Japan', by the author and Mari Sako. Grateful acknowl-edgement is made to the generous support of the Japanese National Institute for Research Advancement and the Daiwa Anglo/Japanese Foundation. Thanks are extended to Mari Sako for her comments on a draft of the paper.

REFERENCES

Ansoff, I. (1968), *Corporate Strategy*, Harmondsworth: Penguin.
Aoki, M. (1988), *Information, Incentives and Bargaining in the Japanese Economy*, Cambridge: Cambridge University Press.
Argyris, C. and Schon, D. (1978), *Organizational Learning*, London: Addison Wesley.
Arnold, E., Guy, K. and Dodgson, M. (1992), *Linking for Success*, London: National Economic Development Office/Institution of Electrical Engineers.
Arrow, K. (1962), 'The Economic Implications of Learning by Doing', *Review of Economic Studies*, **29** (2), 155–73.
Arrow, K. (1975), 'Gifts and Exchanges' in E. Phelps, *Altruism, Morality and Economic Theory*, New York: Russel Sage.
Axelrod, R. (1984), *The Evolution of Cooperation*, London: Penguin.
Baba, Y. (1985), 'Japanese Colour TV Firms' Decision-making from the 1960s to the 1980s', unpublished DPhil dissertation, University of Sussex.
Bandura, A. (1977), *Social Learning Theory*, Englewood Cliffs, NJ: Prentice-Hall.
Buckley, P. and Casson, M. (1988), 'A Theory of Cooperation in International Business' in Contractor and Lorange(1988).
Cainarca, G., Colombo, M. and Mariotti, S. (1992), 'Agreements Between Firms and the Technological Life Cycle Model: Evidence from Information Technologies', *Research Policy*, **21**, 45–62.
Callon, M. (1991), 'The Dynamics of Techno-Economic Networks' in R. Coombs, P. Saviotti and V. Walsh (eds), *Technological Change and Company Strategies*, London: Academic Press.
Carlsson, B. (1994), 'Technological Systems and Economic Performance' in M. Dodgson and R. Rothwell (eds), *The Handbook of Industrial Innovation*, Aldershot: Edward Elgar.

Carlsson, B. and Stankiewicz, R. (1991), 'On the Nature, Function, and Composition of Technological Systems', *Journal of Evolutionary Economics*, **1** (2), 93–118.

Carter, C. and Williams, B. (1957), *Industrial and Technical Progress: Factors Governing the Speed of Application of Science*, London: Oxford University Press.

Chandler, A. (1962), *Strategy and Structure*, New York: McGraw-Hill.

Chew, W. et al. (1991), 'Beating Murphy's Law', *Sloan Management Review*, **32** (3).

Ciborra, C. (1991), 'Alliances as Learning Experiences: Cooperation, Competition and Change in High-Tech Industries', in L. Mytelka, *Strategic Partnerships and the World Economy*, London: Pinter.

Clark, K., Hayes, R. and Lorenz, C. (1985), *The Uneasy Alliance: Managing the Productivity Technology Dilemma*, Cambridge, Mass.: Harvard Business School Press.

Contractor, F. and Lorange, P. (1988) (eds), *Cooperative Strategies in International Business*, Lexington Mass.: Lexington Books.

DeBresson, C. and Amesse, F. (1991), 'Networks of Innovators: A Review and Introduction to the Issues', *Research Policy*, **20**, 363–79.

DiMaggio, P.J. and Powell, W.W. (1991), *The New Institutionalism in Organisational Analysis*, Chicago: University of Chicago Press.

Dodgson, M. (1989), 'Introduction' in M. Dodgson, *Technology Strategy and the Firm: Management and Public Policy*, Harlow: Longman.

Dodgson, M. (1991a), 'Technology Learning, Technology Strategy and Competitive Pressures', *British Journal of Management*, **2**, 133–49.

Dodgson, M. (1991b), *The Management of Technological Learning*, Berlin: De Gruyter.

Dodgson, M. (1991c), 'Technological Collaboration and Organisational Learning: A Preliminary Review of Some Key Issues', DRC Discussion Paper no. 85, Science Policy Research Unit, University of Sussex.

Dodgson, M. (1992a), 'Strategy and Technological Learning: An Interdisciplinary Microstudy', in R. Coombs, P. Saviotti and V. Walsh, *Technological Change and Company Strategies*, London: Academic Press.

Dodgson, M. (1992b), 'The Strategic Management of R&D Collaboration', *Technology Analysis and Strategic Management*, **4** (3), 227–44.

Dodgson, M. (1993a), 'Organizational Learning: A Review of Some Literatures', *Organization Studies* **14** (3).

Dodgson, M. (1993b), *Technological Collaboration in Industry*, London: Routledge.

Dodgson, M. (1993c), 'Learning, Trust and Technological Collaboration', *Human Relations*, **46** (1), 77–96.

Dosi, G. (1982), 'Technological Paradigms and Technological Trajectories. A Suggested Interpretation of the Determinants and Direction of Technological Change', *Research Policy*, **3** (3).

Dosi, G. (1988), 'Sources, Procedures, and Microeconomic Effects of Innovation', *Journal of Economic Literature*, **26**, 1120–71.

Doz, Y. (1988), 'Technology Partnerships Between Larger and Smaller Firms: Some Critical Issues', in Contractor and Lorange, (1988).

Doz, Y. and Shuen, A. (1988), 'From Intent to Outcome: A Process Framework for Partnerships' paper presented at the Prince Bertil Symposium Corporate and Industry Strategies for Europe, Stockholm, 9–11 November.

Fiol, C. and Lyles, M. (1988), 'Organisational Learning', *Academy of Management Review*, **10** (4), 803–813.

Freeman, C. (1991), 'Networks of Innovators: A Synthesis of Research Issues', *Research Policy*, **20**, 499–514.

Freeman, C. and Perez, C. (1988), 'Structural Crises of Adjustment: Business Cycles and Investment Behaviour', in G. Dosi, C. Freeman, R. Nelson, G. Silverberg and L. Soete (eds), *Technical Change and Economic Theory*, London: Pinter.

Gibbons, M. and Johnston, R. (1974), 'The Roles of Science in Technological Innovation', *Research Policy*, **3**, 220–42.

Granstrand, O., Sjolander, S. and Hakanson, L. (1992), *Technology Management and International Business*, Chichester: Wiley.

Håkansson, H. and Johanson, J. (1988), 'Formal and Informal Cooperation Strategies in International Industrial Networks', in Contractor and Lorange, (1988).

Håkansson, H. (1989), *Corporate Technological Behaviour: Cooperation and Networks*, London: Routledge.

Hamel, G., Doz, Y. and Prahalad, C. (1989), 'Collaborate with your Competitors – and Win', *Harvard Business Review*, Jan–Feb 133–9.

Harrigan, K. (1986), *Managing for Joint Venture Success*, Lexington Mass.: Lexington Books.

Hayes, R. and Wheelwright, S. (1984), *Dynamic Manufacturing: Creating the Learning Organisation*, New York: Free Press.

Hedberg, B. (1981), 'How Organizations Learn and Unlearn', in P. Nystrom and W. Starbuck (eds), *Handbook of Organizational Design: Vol 1*, Oxford: Oxford University Press.

Hirst, P. and Zeitlin, J. (1989), *Reversing Industrial Decline? Industrial Structure and Policies in Britain and her Competitors*, New York: St Martin's.

Hobday, M. (1991), 'Dynamic Networks, Technology Diffusion and Complementary Assets: Explaining US Decline in Semiconductors', DRC Discussion Paper no 78, Science Policy Research Unit, University of Sussex.

Howard, R. (1993), *The Learning Imperative*, Cambridge Mass.: Harvard Business School Press.

Imai, K.'I. (1990), 'Japanese Business Groups and the Structural Impediments Initiative', in K. Yamamura (ed.), *Japan's Economic Structure: Should it Change?* University of Washington: Society for Japanese Studies.

Jarillo, J. (1988), 'On Strategic Networks', *Strategic Management Journal*, **19**, 31–41.

Kogut, B. (1988), 'A Study of the Life Cycle of Joint Ventures' in Contractor and Lorange (1988).

Lamming, R. (1992), 'Supplier Strategies in the Automotive Components Industry: Development Towards Lean Production', unpublished D.Phil thesis, University of Sussex.

Langlois, R. (1989), 'Economic Change and the Boundaries of the Firm', in B. Carlsson (ed.), *Industrial Dynamics*, Berlin: Kluwer.

Lash, S. and Urry, J. (1987), *The End of Organised Capitalism*, Cambridge: Polity Press.

Lawton-Smith, H., Dickson, K. and Lloyd Smith, S. (1991), 'There are Two Sides to Every Story: Innovation and Collaboration Within Networks of Large and Small Firms', *Research Policy*, **20**, 457–68.

Leonard Barton, D. (1991), 'The Factory as a Learning Laboratory', Harvard Business School Working Paper, no. 92–023, Harvard, Cambridge, Mass.

Lorenz, E. (1992), *Economic Decline in Britain: The Shipbuilding Industry, 1890–1970*, Oxford: Clarendon Press.

Lundvall, B.-A. (1988), 'Innovation as an Interactive Process: from User–Producer Interaction to the National System of Innovation', in G. Dosi, C. Freeman, R. Nelson, G. Silverberg and L. Soete (eds), *Technical Change and Economic Theory*, London: Pinter.

Lundvall, B.-A. (1992), *National Systems of Innovation*, London: Pinter.

Lyles, M. (1988), 'Learning Among Joint Venture-Sophisticated Firms', in Contractor and Lorange (1988).

Macaulay, S. (1963), 'Non-Contractual Relations in Business: A Preliminary Study', *American Sociological Review*, **28** (1), 55–66.

Malerba, F. (1992), 'Learning by Firms and Incremental Technical Change', Economic Journal, **102**, 845–59.

Marceau, J. (1992), *Reworking the World: Organizations, Technologies and Cultures in Comparative Perspective*, Berlin: De Gruyter.

March, J., Sproull, L. and Tamuz, M. (1991), 'Learning from Samples of One or Fewer', *Organization Science*, **2** (1), 1–13.

Marengo, L. (1992a), 'Knowledge, Coordination and Learning in an Adaptive Model of the Firm', unpublished DPhil dissertation, Science Policy Research Unit, University of Sussex.

Marengo, L. (1992b), 'Coordination and Organizational Learning in the Firm', *Journal of Evolutionary Economics*, **2**, 313–26.

Michael, D. (1973), *On Learning to Plan – and Planning to Learn*, San Francisco: Jossey-Bass.

Miles, R. and Snow, C. (1986), 'Organizations: New Concepts for New Forms', *California Management Review*, **27** (3), 62–73.

Mody, A. (1989), 'Changing Firm Boundaries: Analysis of Technology-Sharing Alliances', Industry Series Paper no. 3, Washington DC: The World Bank.

Mody, A. (1990), 'Learning Through Alliances', Washington DC: The World Bank.

Morgan, G. (1986), *Images of Organization*, Beverly Hills: Sage.

Mowery, D. (1988), *International Collaborative Ventures in US Manufacturing*, Cambridge, Mass.: Ballinger.

Nelson, R.R. (ed.) (1993), *National Innovation Strategies,* New York: Oxford University Press.

Ouchi, W. and Bolton, M. (1988), 'The Logic of Joint Research and Development', *California Management Review*, **30** (3), 9–33.

Pavitt, K. (1991), 'Key Characteristics of the Large Innovating Firm', *British Journal of Management*, **2**, 41–50.

Pavitt, K. (1994), 'Key Characteristics of Large Innovating Firms', in M. Dodgson and R. Rothwell (eds), *The Handbook of Industrial Innovation*, Aldershot: Edward Elgar.

Pentland, B. (1992), 'Organizing Moves in Software Support Hot Lines', *Administrative Science Quarterly*, **37**, 527–48.

Piore, M. and Sabel, C. (1984), *The Second Industrial Divide*, New York: Basic Books.

Porter, M. and Fuller, K. (1986), 'Coalitions and Corporate Strategy' in M. Porter (ed.), *Competition in Global Industries*, Boston: Harvard Business School Press.

Porter, M. (1990), *The Competitive Advantage of Nations*, New York: Free Press.

Pucik, V. (1988a), 'Strategic Alliances, Organizational Learning, and Competitive Advantage: the HRM Agenda', *Human Resource Management*, **27** (1), 77–93.

Pucik, V. (1988b), 'Strategic Alliances with the Japanese: Implications for Human Resource Management', in Contractor and Lorange (1988).

Radosovic, S. (1991), 'Techno-economic Networking and Social Intelligence as Useful Concepts in Technology Policy Making', in B. Cronin and N. Tudor-Silovoc (eds), *From Information Management to Social Intelligence*, London: Aslib.

Rosenberg, N. (1982), *Inside the Black Box: Technology and Economics*, Cambridge: Cambridge University Press.

Rothwell, R., Freeman, C., Horley, A., Jervis, V., Robertson, Z., and Townsend, J. (1974), 'SAPPHO updated – Project SAPPHO, Phase II', *Research Policy*, **3**, 258–91.

Rothwell, R. (1992), 'Successful Industrial Innovation: Critical Factors for the 1990s, *R&D Management*, **22** (3), 221–39.

Sako, M. (1991), 'The Role of "Trust" in Japanese Buyer–Supplier Relationships', *Ricerche Economiche*, **45** (2–3), 375–99.

Sako, M. (1992), *Prices, Quality and Trust: How Japanese and British Companies Manage Buyer Supplier Relations*, Cambridge: Cambridge University Press.

Saxenian, A. (1991), 'The Origins and Dynamics of Production Networks in Silicon Valley', *Research Policy*, **20**, 423–38.

Schein, E. (1985), *Organizational Culture and Leadership*, San Francisco: Jossey-Bass.

Senge, P. (1990), 'The Leader's New Work: Building Learning Organizations', *Sloan Management Review*, **32** (1), 7–23.

Stigler, G.J. (1951), 'The Division of Labour is Limited by the Extent of the Market', *Journal of Political Economy*, **59** (3).

Teece, D. (1986), 'Profiting from Technological Innovation: Implications for Integration, Collaboration, Licensing and Public Policy', *Research Policy*, **15**, 285–305.

Teece, D., Pisano G. and Schuen, A. (1990), 'Firm Capabilities, Resources, and the Concept of Strategy', CCC Working Paper no. 90–8, Berkeley: University of Berkeley.

Thomson, R. (1993), *Learning and Technological Change*, New York: St Martin's Press.

Tushman, M., Virany, B. and Romanelli, E. (1986), 'Executive Succession, Strategic Reorientation, and Organizational Evolution', in M. Horwitch (ed.), *Technology in the Modern Corporation*, New York: Pergamon.

Tushman, M. and Anderson, P. (1987), 'Technological Discontinuities and Organizational Environments', in A. Pettigrew (ed.), *The Management of Strategic Change*, Oxford: Blackwell.

Van Tulder, R. and Junne, G. (1988), *European Multinationals in Core Technologies*, Chichester: Wiley.

Williamson, O. (1985), *The Economic Institutions of Capitalism*, New York: Free Press.

Winter, S. (1987), 'Knowledge and Competence as Strategic Assets' in D. Teece (ed.), *The Competitive Challenge,* Cambridge, Mass.: Ballinger.

5. Networks, tacit knowledge and innovation[1]

Jacqueline Senker and Wendy Faulkner

INTRODUCTION

Studies of innovation, technology transfer and technology diffusion identify tacit knowledge as an important component of the knowledge used in innovation (e.g. Dosi, 1988; Rosenberg, 1976, 1992). However, none of these discussions provides a satisfactory definition of tacit knowledge or gives a detailed, systematic account of its role in technological innovation. Nor do they provide guidance on how its importance may differ according to the industrial sector or technology being studied or how firms may acquire it.

This chapter is an attempt to begin to fill some of these gaps, drawing on literature from a wide variety of disciplines including the economics of innovation, sociology of science, management of technology, psychology and the history of science and technology. It focuses on the contribution of tacit knowledge to innovation and the role of networks in acquiring tacit knowledge. It argues that the generation of tacit knowledge is an inevitable adjunct to advances in science and technology, and that firms acquire such knowledge to support innovation in a purposive manner. Networking is an important means by which companies acquire and exchange tacit knowledge, through personal interaction both with colleagues inside the company and, externally, with researchers in other companies and in the public-sector. Moreover, tacit knowledge is an important element of the knowledge flows associated with internal or external networks. The chapter was prompted by a desire to understand more about the findings of a recent study of industry links with public-sector research in three emerging technologies. It found that the firms' innovation activities involve a great deal of informal interaction with external sources of scientific and technological knowledge, and that much of the knowledge so acquired is tacit in nature (see Senker and Faulkner, 1992).

The chapter has three substantive sections. The first discusses the role of tacit knowledge in innovation. It proposes a working definition of tacit knowledge in science and technology, then examines the routes by which such knowledge becomes codified, and the reasons why, despite the dramatic increase in codification activities in the twentieth century, tacit knowledge continues to be of such importance in innovation. The second discusses the role of networks in innovation and contains our main arguments concerning the importance of tacit knowledge flows in personal networking activities. Empirical evidence on both the role of tacit knowledge in innovation and the use of networks to acquire tacit knowledge is presented in the third section.

TACIT KNOWLEDGE

The Role of Tacit Knowledge in Innovation

Polanyi (1966) encapsulates the essence of tacit knowledge in the phrase, 'We know more than we can tell' and provides further clarification in such commonplace examples as the ability to recognize faces, ride a bicycle or swim without even the slightest idea of how these things are done. By contrast, in science and technology, *conscious efforts* are pursued to elucidate and/or utilize tacit knowledge. In science the aim is constantly to extend theoretical knowledge of the natural world; in technology the aim is to develop physical devices and equipment to solve specific problems. Rosenberg's description of traditional technological knowledge, accumulated in crude empirical ways with no reliance upon science, provides a good working definition for tacit knowledge in both science and technology: 'the knowledge of techniques, methods and designs that work in certain ways and with certain consequences, even when one cannot explain exactly why' (Rosenberg, 1982, p. 143). This heuristic, subjective and internalized knowledge is not easy to communicate and is learned through practical examples, experience and practice.

By contrast, 'articulated knowledge' is transmittable in formal, systematic language. It has many forms, but a main constituent is the general principles and laws acknowledged by the scientific and engineering communities as supplying the foundation for further practice. These principles and laws are written down in great detail in manuals and textbooks and taught to students. They tend to reflect the prevailing Kuhnian paradigms: the accepted examples of actual scientific practice, which include law, theory, application and instrumentation, and which provide models for scientific research (Kuhn, 1970, p. 10). Other forms of articulated knowledge are available in scientific and technical journals, in the technical specifications of materials or components; and in operating manuals for commercial process plant and research equipment.

The distinction between tacit and articulated knowledge must be treated with caution. Polanyi has pointed out that these two are not sharply divided. While tacit knowledge can be possessed by itself, explicit knowledge must rely on being tacitly understood and applied. Hence all knowledge is *either tacit or rooted in tacit knowledge* (Polyani, 1969, p. 114).

This observation raises a question which is central to this chapter. How is tacit knowledge acquired, transmitted and codified? First, it is necessary to stress the essential difference between skills and tacit knowledge, and to establish the general importance of tacit knowledge in both science and technology.

There are some fundamental differences between skill and knowledge. Knowledge implies understanding. The acquisition of knowledge is a purely perceptual, cognitive process. Skill implies knowing how to make something happen; it involves cognition, but also other aspects such as manual dexterity or sensory ability. In some instances skills may be based entirely on tacit knowledge and in others they may rely entirely on a thorough understanding of the scientific principles involved. In most instances skills draw on a combi-nation of tacit and articulated knowledge. The term 'tacit skills' is often used in the literature. We would argue that this usage is confusing and mistaken since it is important to distinguish between tacit knowledge, which is embodied in skills and can therefore be copied, and tacit knowledge which cannot be demon-strated and so is very difficult to transfer (e.g. the recognition of a musical note). To avoid confusion we choose to talk of tacit knowledge and skills rather than tacit skills. This differentiation between tacit knowledge and skills marks a fun-damental disagreement with Nonaka (1992), who suggests that tacit knowledge involves cognitive dimensions (schemata, paradigms, mental models etc.), as well as a technical dimension (concrete know-how, crafts and skills which apply to specific contexts). 'Expertise' is a better definition of skills based on appropriate combinations of tacit and formal knowledge in specific contexts.[2]

The public image of science tends to stress the role of 'solid facts' and plays down the role of tacit knowledge or skills. Yet scientific research demands a large range of skills and tacit knowledge: 'the scientist must be an accomplished craftsman [sic]; he [sic] must have undergone a lengthy apprenticeship, learning how to do things without being able to appreciate why they work' (Ravetz, 1971, pp. 14–15). This apprenticeship teaches scientists methods for manipulating and using tools (e.g. physical apparatus, statistical techniques), including how to assess data and information and how to avoid pitfalls involved in their use. Simple precepts may form the basis for some of this learning, but imitation and experience are the only methods for acquiring the skills to formulate scientific problems and develop strategies aimed at their solution. In short, such tacit knowledge may be vital to the successful replication of experimental results. Collins's (1974) study of the diffusion of knowledge relating to the building of the TEA laser suggests that in new fields little of the corresponding tacit knowledge is learned during scientists' apprenticeships; furthermore, the systematic transfer of new knowledge has sometimes been impossible, because the originating scientist may have been unaware of all the relevant parameters.

With the growth of industrial R&D during the twentieth century and the widespread recruitment by firms of qualified scientists and engineers, firms have been enabled to apply scientific knowledge – both formal and tacit – to solve their technical problems. Kline (1990a), among others, has argued that the role of science in innovation is felt not so much in knowledge *per se* as in the area of methodology: 'Both scientific methodology and the scientific view of the world are absolutely essential to all workers on technical problems everywhere'. In any case, technology develops from a variety of sources which go far beyond the application of prior scientific knowledge (see Faulkner, 1992). As noted by Rosenberg, crude empirical methods have traditionally provided the basis of much technological knowledge acquisition and accumulation, and much productive activity takes place without 'a deep scientific knowledge of why things perform the way they do' (Rosenberg, 1982, p. 143).

Scientific culture tends to play down the role of skills and tacit knowledge. In contrast, the tacit dimension of technology is widely recognized. In technology transfer, for example, the vital importance of know-how, 'a kind of knowledge which cannot be wholly formalised, nor transmitted solely through written documents' (Madeuf, 1984) has been evident from the earliest period of industrialization through to the present day. By definition, know-how transfer requires personal interaction through secondment, training and so forth. Its importance is reflected in the fact that contracts for technology transfer seldom deal exclusively with patents or intellectual property rights; and that technology payments for agreements which do not involve patents outweigh payments for those involving patents (Madeuf, 1984). More generally, the acquisition of tacit knowledge to support innovation is a purposive activity of much industrial development, design and testing of prototypes and pilot plant.

Pavitt (1987) has characterized most technology as 'specific, complex, often tacit and cumulative in its development.' Technological information is often common to firms operating within the same 'technological regime' (Metcalfe and Gibbons, 1989), but individual firms also develop specific knowledge and experience relating to its products and processes. In Hall and Johnson's (1970) terminology, firms build up or acquire system-specific and firm-specific knowledge. The former is related to the tasks or projects involved in manufacturing a specific item; the latter results from a firm's overall activities. System-specific knowledge is likely to be common to firms developing the same item, who tend to obtain the same or similar technology. This applies even when such knowledge is developed by largely tacit means, as demonstrated by Vincenti's (1990) study of flush riveting in airplanes. Here, system-specific knowledge was acquired individually by firms because although books and word-of-mouth could provide some of the necessary knowledge, complete mastery required hands-

on experience: 'All the acquired knowledge in matters of this kind is not sus-
ceptible to codification or communication'. The separate programmes resulted
in widespread simultaneous innovation throughout the industry. Firms may
formalize or codify some of their specific knowledge for in-house use, but its
further dissemination is generally out of the question – either because it is entirely
firm-specific (or contingent on local conditions) or because it is proprietary
knowledge, promising to provide competitive advantage.

Differences in proprietary regimes and in ease of transfer are central concerns
for economists of technology. Sidney Winter (1987) has developed a taxonomy
of knowledge to explain these differences which recognizes that knowledge may,
or may not, be observable, teachable and articulable. Winter's category of
'observability in use', which relates to how easily the underlying knowledge
embodied in a product is revealed in practice, highlights the ease with which
skills based on tacit knowledge may be transferred by example. The non-artic-
ulation of articulable knowledge may pose a greater barrier to the transfer of
knowledge than tacitness itself. This is demonstrated in the widespread problems
caused by failure to document software programmes adequately.

In sum, both scientific and technological inputs to innovation embody a considerable tacit component which can only be required by practical experience.
Firms build up their own practical experience internally, by conducting research,
design and development activities and through interaction with production. Firms
may also access or acquire practical experience from external sources. We
return to this theme in our discussion of firms' networking activities. First we
consider how tacit knowledge becomes codified in science and technology, and
why it continues to be of such importance to innovation.

How is Tacit Knowledge Codified?

The innovation literature suggests that there are two main routes by which tacit
knowledge becomes codified: through conducting *research*, and by the introduction of *automation*. We distinguish two models for the codification of tacit
knowledge by research, which we label crudely 'science push' and 'technology
pull'. In the 'science push' model codification arises from 'blue-sky' research,
which has no strategic objectives, save increasing understanding; from the
investigation of unforeseen but interesting occurrences which crop up during
the course of research; or as the result of strategic research aimed specifically
at filling gaps in knowledge. This research is most likely to take place within
public-sector institutions and relies largely on government funding.

In the 'technology pull' model codification results from the exploration of
the phenomena and problems arising in industrial products and processes and/or
the practical methods developed in industry to solve problems. This research
can receive government and/or industrial support and takes place in industry

or public-sector research establishments. Unlike 'science push' research, its results will tend to be subject to fairly immediate commercial exploitation.

Patenting is excluded from this discussion because although patents embody considerable codification of tacit knowledge, as is well known, such codification represents the minimum required for legal purposes; it cannot easily be reproduced by others without access to associated 'know-how'.

The recent development of biotechnology is a prime example of the science push model. The elucidation of the structure of DNA in 1953 by Crick and Watson laid the groundwork for the growth of molecular biology aimed at understanding the micro-level mechanisms of biological development and inheritance. Research in the field proliferated, especially in the US where there was massive federal support from the National Institute of Health and various medical charities.[3] Increasing knowledge about gene function, coding and expression in turn led to the development of genetic engineering, a range of techniques which allow genes to be moved from one organism to another so that the host acquires traits (e.g. the production of specific proteins) which are unnatural to it. Excitement about the potential of these techniques has subsequently generated worldwide support for biotechnology research – by governments, pharmaceutical companies and venture capitalists – with continued rapid advance in knowledge, techniques and codification.

Within the technology pull model, government and/or company intervention stimulates the codification of knowledge through the funding of research to solve problems which have arisen in existing technology. This is well demonstrated by the history of semiconductor electronics. For instance, industrial engineers investigating the cause of short circuits in electronic equipment in the late 1940s, discovered the cause to be strong but flexible filamentary growths – so-called whisker crystals. The discovery provoked an extensive research programme, which provided a fundamental understanding of crystal growth and proved of great value to the electronics industry. Solid-state physics was barely on the curriculum of most universities before the discovery of the transistor in the Bell Laboratories in 1948. William Stockley, the head of the research group, was persuaded to run in-house courses for laboratory personnel in transistor physics and, two years later, another for 30 university professors (Golding, 1971; Rosenberg, 1982, p. 155). Bell Laboratories, partly to contain danger from an anti-monopoly lobby, 'embarked on a policy of public divulgation of its transistor knowledge.... By publishing, holding seminars and licensing widely' (Braun and MacDonald, 1978). Subsequent innovation and growth in semiconductors were stimulated by substantial government funding though, unlike biotechnology, this was largely military-related and focused on development work in industry.[4]

In moving on to consider automation as a route to codification, we should note that the way in which researchers and companies cope with tacit elements of the knowledge they require is to develop routines. Such routines *replicate* previously successful practice. They help people to deal with complexity and with the unknown, and so guide research, development, production and problem solving. In practice such routines involve a large human element: if things go wrong it is not clear whether this is a result of variation in the procedure or of the human role. Automation is an attempt to capture the human element and so is a more complex and extreme case of replication. Historically, it has been a powerful force driving the codification of tacit knowledge, most notably in the automation of machines tools since the Second World War. The transformation of a general-purpose machine tool into a special-purpose machine, through the use of variable programmes, involves two separate processes: developing the equipment to read instructions and control the machine; and getting the instructions recorded in the first place. Two approaches were adopted for the latter task. 'Record–playback', developed by General Electric, was based on reproducing the accumulated manual skills of the experienced metalworker (Noble, 1979, p. 22). Numerical control (NC), largely developed at MIT, and the approach eventually adopted, depended on codification – breaking down the specifications for a part as contained in an engineering blueprint into a mathematical representation of the part, then into a mathematical description of the desired path of the cutting tool along up to five axes, and finally into hundreds of thousands of discrete instructions, translated for economy into a numerical code which is read and translated into electrical signals for the machine controls (Noble, 1979, p. 23).

Nevertheless, in many cases, the effective use of NC machine tools continues to require the intervention of skilled operators to make tool adjustments, correct for tool wear and rough castings, and to correct programming errors and machine malfunctions (Noble, 1979, p. 41).

It appears, therefore, that there are limits to the codification of tacit knowledge by such means. These limits were also exposed in attempts to produce general solutions to automation by the development of industrial robots. In practice, successful implementation depends on 'detailed and specific knowledge about the particular situation in which it is proposed to introduce a robot, and about the technology itself' (Fleck, 1983 and n.d.). Besides being widely distributed throughout an organization, much of this knowledge is tacit and uncodified. Significantly, however, a body of knowledge in robotics is gradually being built up by the systematization of rules of thumb and other techniques and methods discovered through experience. This same process is also gradually eroding barriers to codification, with knowledge being advanced in the course of academic research designed to discover the underlying cause of problems experienced in the industrial use of robots. Thus, codification can be an iterative process, with the development of artefacts, observation of empirical results and problems feeding back into academic research; in time, the results of research become part of the formal knowledge system, and may be incorporated in the artefacts themselves. Developments in robotics exemplify this process; while early robots were based on the 'record–playback' principle, modern robots incorporate radical developments in software and control (Fleck, 1988, p. 25).

A similar pattern seems to be evident in the development of expert systems. However, the complexity of systems can pose limits to the codification of knowledge. Fleck has suggested that: 'the artefactual crystallisation of the non-technical is easiest where contingencies of the application domain are closely controlled and stabilised, with functions tightly circumscribed. These provisos also extend to areas where purely intellectual or mental skills are concerned' (Fleck, n.d., p. 21).

We shall return to the issue of complexity below, and to the suggestion that codification of knowledge increases as a technology matures.

Why is Tacit Knowledge Still Important?

Putting aside the issue of any limits to codification, how can the persistence of tacit knowledge in innovation be explained alongside the twentieth century's constantly expanding stock of scientific knowledge and the growth of industrial R&D? First, we should reinforce the point made above, that science and technology *in themselves*, *necessarily* involve the use and creation of tacit knowledge. For example, genetic engineering techniques continue to incorporate many empirical and tacit elements; even in the more codified microbial systems, it is not always possible to specify precisely which gene fragment will be spliced or, where this is possible, to explain the effect of specific procedures. Thus, codification by research is a contradictory process in that *new* tacit knowledge is generated as former tacit knowledge becomes codified.

There are other reasons for the continuing importance of tacit knowledge and skills in innovation. Part of the explanation lies in the fact that different industrial sectors and technological regimes are embedded in very different traditions of technological change:

> [Technological] Regimes differ according to the proportion of knowledge which is discovered by scientific or empirical means; they differ in the division of knowledge between codifiable, publicly available, and tacit firm, specific forms; and, they differ according to their dependence on other knowledge bases that are generated outside the industry (Metcalfe and Gibbons, 1989, p. 164).

The direction of technological change within technological regimes is largely defined by the technology already in use. When innovations have been developed successfully (on whatever basis), there is no reason for companies to change their established practices; their aim will be to improve existing technology through minor changes. These will tend to be based on learning by doing and learning by using, rather than on the conduct of research to understand the underlying nature of any problems arising. In other words, companies will tend to adhere to previously successful practice whether or not they have a fundamental understanding of why it works. A change to established practices is likely to occur only when problems arise which demand a more fundamental understanding, or when one firm within a technological regime gains competitive advantage by applying scientific knowledge.

Firms or sectors where there is a lack of relevant scientific knowledge, or qualified scientists and engineers on their staff able to apply such knowledge (Gibbons and Johnston, 1974), perforce are more dependent on tacit knowledge to solve any technical problems which arise. There are still many traditional sectors in the UK, such as construction, where in-house R&D is very rare (Gann et al., 1992). These sectors have been characterized by Pavitt (1984) as *supplier-dominated* firms and they make only a minor contribution to their product or process technology. Most innovations derive from the companies which supply their equipment or materials.

The predominant reason, however, for the application of tacit knowledge and skills to innovation, even in companies which employ large numbers of scientists and engineers, is the complexity of systems that are impossible to model in a laboratory. Kline (1990b) has discussed the difficulty for the physical sciences and engineering of analysing systems with even a moderate degree of complexity. He argues that whilst many powerful tricks have been evolved for reducing complexity in order to make analyses simpler, there are few predictive paradigms of any reliability for complete systems, though they may exist for parts of systems. He suggests that innovation can be created only through 'observing the system, creating perturbations, and then observing what happens. That is, we control and improve such systems by open-loop feedback processes using human intelligence in a learning-by-doing mode.'

To summarize, continuing dependence on skills and tacit knowledge for innovation arises from the tendency for advances in knowledge and techniques to be associated with new tacit knowledge; from adherence to previous successful practices; from the lack of scientific or technological expertise within specific firms or sectors; and, possibly most commonly, from the complexity of systems. Vincenti's (1990) observation that uncertainty diminishes as a technology becomes older suggests a fourth category where tacit knowledge is of importance, namely in the emergence of new technologies.

Networks and Tacit Knowledge

Firms utilize a variety of scientific and technological knowledge inputs in the course of research, development and demonstration (RD&D) leading to innovation. These knowledge inputs come from a range of sources, both internal and external. The external sources comprise chiefly other companies and public-sector research (PSR) institutions. Cross-sector studies have found that external sources contribute around one-third of all knowledge used in innovation, with more being obtained from other companies than from PSR, though the relative contribution of PSR can be significantly greater (Rothwell, 1977). Of the two thirds that are obtained internally, half is knowledge which is *personally held* by company staff, as a result of previous education and work experience, while the other half is collectively *generated*, mostly as a result of RD&D activities (Gibbons and Johnston, 1974). This is an important distinction. Kline (1990b) notes that when a problem arises available sources of *knowledge* (i.e. people and literature) will be consulted in the first instance, and that only if these fail to provide a solution will *research* be conducted. In short, when companies employ scientists and engineers they are acquiring a body of accumulated knowledge and skills (both tacit and codified); the ability to access and utilize knowledge generated elsewhere; plus the ability to generate new knowledge by engaging in relevant RD&D.

Tacit knowledge is obtained from the same *broad sources* as other forms of knowledge used in innovation, i.e. from the personal knowledge of scientists and engineers, by accessing external sources and by conducting RD&D. What distinguishes tacit knowledge is the *channels* through which it is obtained. Since by its very nature tacit knowledge cannot be written down, it must be acquired by example or experience – that is, in 'person-embodied' form. In principal, all knowledge may be transferred by personal interaction. However, personal interaction or movement is (for the most part) the *only* channel by which tacit knowledge can be transferred, whilst many types of codified knowledge can be effectively transferred in written form. On this basis, we hypothesize that *tacit knowledge is a very important element of the knowledge transferred through personal networks*.

To our knowledge, there is no evidence which might enable us to establish the relative importance of tacit and codified knowledge flows in networks. Indeed, it is difficult to imagine how this might be achieved methodologically. Our own findings (presented below) are suggestive. So too is a recent paper by Imai (1991) on the Japanese innovation system, which considers knowledge flows in Kline's 'chain-linked' model of innovation (see Figure 5. 1).

Kline's model recognizes that development, design and production engineering, the production process and customer feedback usually make the largest contribution to innovation (see Pavitt, 1987; von Hippel 1988). It thus incorporates information links and feedback loops between market findings, design, production, distribution and research (Kline, 1990b). In Imai's (1991) discussion of the Japanese innovation system we get hints as to which of these links may incorporate tacit knowledge and skills. He suggests that personal interaction is a necessity for information exchange between design, test, redesign, production and distribution, and that such interactions must be quick and dense. They enable firms to cope with the unexpected situations which frequently crop up during

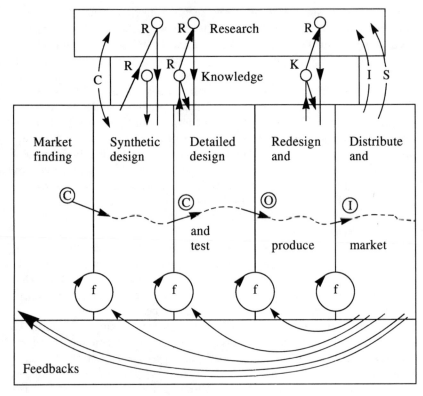

F and f = feedback links
I   = supply of instruments from manufacturing sector
S   = support for fundamental research in industrial research laboratories
C   = two-way flow of ideas between scientific research and synthetic design
K   = the store of accumulated technical knowledge
R   = research

Source: Kline (1990a).

Figure 5.1   Chain-linked model of innovation

the innovation process, and facilitate cooperative learning for designers,
production managers, marketers and machine suppliers. With regard to links
with production, personal information exchange is vital to the upstream stage
of key component and device manufacturing, but has little utility for final
component assembly, the downstream stage, which uses traditional manufacturing techniques.

Building on Kline's distinction between existing *knowledge* and *research* which
generates new knowledge, Imai argues that existing technical knowledge is
embedded in social networks:

Sometimes it is summarised and stored in a data bank as a patent or a [sic] documented know-how. But usually such information, useful for an unsolved problem, exists randomly in the society as tacit knowledge. In this sense it depends on the context of a special problem. To approach such information, 'know-who' is crucial (Imai, 1991, p. 10).

He further argues that whilst personal networks are necessary to access technical knowledge, knowledge generated through research is 'embedded in a theoretical context, not a social context'. Therefore, information exchange can take place through such media as e-mail and fax, and personal interaction is less important. Implicit agreement with this view appears to come from Sørenson and Levold's (1992) discussion of the science–technology distinction: 'While the set-up and carrying out of an experiment may be demanding in terms of locally acquired, tacit skills, the application of the results is affected by tacit skills that are common to a much larger group of scientists'.

However, on the basis of Collins's study, it appears that skills based on tacit knowledge are likely to be held by large groups of scientists only in established areas of knowledge.

The chain-linked model of innovation is valuable in providing a more realistic representation than the linear model. In particular, it captures some of the rich diversity and iteration of interactions between various groups and activities *within* the firm. However, it says little about knowledge and information flows between the firm and any external sources. Imai appears to acknowledge implicitly that accessing technical knowledge might involve external personal networks. He also recognizes that periodic contact with an international community of business professionals, consultants and university and government researchers is vital for *screening* information and ideas which might contribute to concept and analytical design activities. Gambardella suggests that the increasing complexity and interdisciplinarity of knowledge makes external information critical to the development of innovations:

Information exchange ... requires that one be prepared to diffuse research findings in exchange for knowledge produced by others. To be part of a network, and to be able to effectively exploit the information that circulates in the network, has become even more valuable than being able to generate new knowledge autonomously. (Gambardella, 1992)

The importance of networks with other companies is most easily explained in terms of the supply chain. Success in innovation rests crucially on the quality of knowledge flows about user needs, the relationship being especially strong with specialist users of complex technologies. Moreover, innovations of all types demand knowledge from suppliers of materials or components incorporated into the final product. Such considerations should not blind us to the importance of knowledge flows between competitors, however. Nelson (1982) has argued that in addition to companies' individual interests in securing proprietary advantage by keeping knowledge private, companies have a collective interest in keeping much knowledge in the public domain; without this knowledge, no companies on their own would be innovative.

Some formal knowledge is shared through the patent system and other publications. It may be that informal knowledge sharing between competitors has more importance. Barden and Good (1989) found such interaction, though not frequent, to be highly influential in terms of the direction of projects. So, we would suggest that *some types of tacit knowledge are quite extensively shared through informal interaction between competitors.*

The relative importance of informal networking is periodically highlighted (see, e.g. Senker, 1992; Kreiner and Schultz, 1990), but seems to run counter to the current fashion for formal collaboration. In this connection, Stuart Macdonald (1992) suggests that formal collaboration may actually undermine the informal information networks on which firms in competition rely. Similarly, in a paper suggestively entitled 'The strength of weak ties', Granovetter (1973) argues that the most valuable knowledge flows might generally take place as a result of the least visible forms of networking.

TACIT KNOWLEDGE AND NETWORKS IN EMERGING TECHNOLOGIES

Our interest in tacit knowledge and networking was stimulated by the results of a study comparing industrial linkage with public-sector research (PSR) in three areas of advanced technology – biotechnology (in large pharmaceutical companies), advanced engineering ceramics and parallel computing.[5] It highlighted the importance of informal links to facilitate knowledge flows between industrial researchers and external sources of knowledge, and revealed that tacit knowledge is an important component of these knowledge flows. We now present material from this study to illuminate the theoretical ideas presented in the previous section.

The Nature and Role of Tacit Knowledge in Innovation

During an extensive interviewing programme with 36 companies, industrial researchers were asked to spell out, in as much detail as possible, the specific knowledge which they routinely utilized in the course of innovation. They were prompted to supply such information in terms of the detailed categories shown in Table 5.1, and, for each category, asked to identify whether such knowledge was formal and codified, or tacit in nature. They were then asked to identify the source of such knowledge – did it derive from in-house activities, from other companies or from PSR?

Table 5.1   Categories of knowledge inputs to innovation

Knowledge of particular fields
Scientific theory, engineering principles, properties etc.

Technical information
Specifications and operating performance or products, components or materials

Skills
Specific skills e.g. programming, hardware design
Research or production competence

Artefacts
Process plant
Research instrumentation

There was considerable similarity between technologies in regard to knowledge of particular fields and skills, both of which make an important contribution to new product development. Researchers reported that their knowledge of particular fields is largely formal and codified, and that it is acquired during education and through reading the literature. It is interesting to note that, in addition to absorbing formal knowledge during their scientific training, these researchers had also absorbed an attitude which failed to recognize the tacit knowledge and skills acquired at the same time. Companies, however, recognize that formal qualifications are evidence of researchers' tacit ability to acquire and use knowledge in a meaningful way; they regard this attitude of mind – Kline's 'scientific view of the world' – as a most important contribution to new product development.

All the researchers reported that while knowledge of particular fields is necessary for innovation, it is inadequate by itself. They also depend heavily on skills, the learning by doing which takes place largely 'on-the-job'. The researchers perceive that the tacit knowledge and skills which they acquire in-house supplement and build on the formal knowledge derived from their education. Accordingly, they report that they rely particularly heavily on the formal knowledge base at the beginning of their careers, because that is all they have, but that the expertise which they develop over time through carrying out research becomes increasingly important. The general importance of tacit knowledge to skills is emphasized by the reports of many we interviewed that most of the knowledge they use has not yet been published or documented anywhere. It appears that, in addition to overlooking the tacit knowledge they acquire during their formal education, researchers forget the extent to which their skills may rely on formal knowledge. One of those interviewed remarked: 'I didn't realise until I began tutoring for the Open University ... how much of what I learned at university is still relevant as background. I tend to take it for granted while, unknowingly, using that formal knowledge all the time'.

There is a difference between the three technologies in the extent to which knowledge related to technical information and artefacts is used in the course of innovation. Technical information is largely codified and mainly derived from other companies; it makes a significant contribution to new product development in ceramics and parallel computing. Ceramics processors and users rely heavily on materials specifications, but reported that it is impossible for some aspects of such specifications to be documented. This difficulty is overcome by tacit knowledge transfer from their suppliers, with whom they therefore maintain close relationships. Although firms in parallel computing utilize a great deal of technical information from manuals and the scientific literature in relation to components, emerging standards for architecture performance or competitive products, they also rely heavily on tacit information about the performance of, for example, specific compilers of software, which they obtain through informal interaction with users, suppliers and competitors. Researchers involved in biotechnology could think of only one instance where technical information makes a contribution to their work.[6]

The divergence between technologies in relation to knowledge inputs was greatest in artefacts, both in relation to the type of artefacts which were important and the source of the largely tacit information associated with these artefacts. Knowledge relating to process plant has no relevance to biotechnology or parallel computing. Most parallel computing companies contract out product assembly. Production equipment for pharmaceutical production is generally bought 'off the shelf' and once plant has been built, it will rarely be changed (Reuben and Wittcoff, 1989, p. 108). In contrast, ceramics processors stress the important contribution made by tacit in-house knowledge of process plant, much of which they design and build themselves. Their main interest is directed towards improving their processes. Process plant information is also relevant to ceramics end-users, who seek knowledge about how specific processes affect ceramics characteristics. This difference between technologies in relation to process plant appears to validate Imai's suggestion that little utility is gained from interaction between traditional manufacturing and research.

Knowledge inputs relating to research equipment, which is largely tacit, are utilized by companies in all three technologies. Ceramics companies with central research laboratories have some relevant equipment and expertise in-house. In using this equipment, they rely on their tacit knowledge about the capability of specific techniques to measure the characteristics they are attempting to capture. However, few laboratories are big enough to do everything, and many small companies do not have research facilities. This explains the general tendency to contract out testing to the public-sector. In so doing, company researchers not only gain access to specific pieces of instrumentation, but also to the experts with the tacit knowledge to understand the results. Such interpretation provides the bulk of the information they seek and, as one researcher said, 'As far as the use of university instrumentation is concerned, you only get 10 per cent of the information from the equipment: the other 90 per cent is interpretation. We use universities to get the results interpreted by the experts.'

Biotechnology researchers describe research equipment and materials as a necessity, but most tend to have little awareness of the contribution of knowledge from this source. We suspect that they tend to take their companies' well equipped laboratories for granted. External sources make a minor contribution to knowledge acquisition, with PSR being used for training researchers in new research skills and techniques; representatives of research instruments companies also provide a useful source of tacit knowledge about machines and methodologies appropriate for specific applications.

Parallel computing, unlike ceramics and biotechnology, makes no use of PSR instrumentation. This reflects the fact that the parallel computers are the main instruments used in the development of new parallel computers. Companies use their own machines for testing, modelling and simulation work necessary to the development of new products. They also use work stations and some test and measurement equipment from other suppliers.

To summarize, in all three technologies the in-house tacit knowledge used for innovation relates to the personal skills developed through experience, and to research instrumentation. Ceramics is unlike the other two technologies in utilizing in-house tacit knowledge relating to its process plant. There are also similarities between the technologies in their external sources of tacit knowledge. Other companies provide tacit knowledge relating to technical specifications of products and research instrumentation. PSR contributes tacit knowledge associated with knowledge of particular fields and, except for parallel computing, with research instrumentation and techniques.

The Use of Networks to Acquire Tacit Knowledge

The interviews focused specifically on links with PSR and therefore researchers were asked to identify the general channel through which knowledge was obtained from this source. However, we also gained some fragmentary evidence about the channels used for knowledge inputs from other companies.

The three technologies differ in terms of their relative use of publications and personal contacts to access knowledge from PSR. In biotechnology, the literature is more important than personal contacts; in ceramics, contacts are marginally more important than the literature. In parallel computing, all researchers rely far more on contacts than on publications; they find the literature is of little practical value because it is either too abstract or tangential to their interests.

Significantly for our purposes, researchers also revealed that the literature and contacts provide distinctly different types of knowledge input and are frequently used in tandem with each other. In the case of knowledge from PSR, for instance, the literature is scanned to identify new developments and researchers with specific expertise; it provides access to relevant underpinning knowledge and information about specific research or test procedures. The use of publications has limitations because important relevant knowledge about the research is often not included, and the publications cannot be interrogated. As a consequence, reading is often followed by getting in touch with the author informally. Personal contacts are used to provide knowledge of a largely tacit nature – in particular, further information or clarification about the techniques used – but also an interpretation or informed judgement of the relevance or significance of a specific paper.

Our findings confirm that social networks, or Imai's 'know-who', are also used when researchers have a problem which they or their immediate colleagues are unable to solve. Personal contacts will often point them towards relevant published literature or experts who can solve their problem. However, our findings show that Imai and Sørensen and Levold are wrong to assume that the theoretical language used by researchers avoids the need for personal interaction. Theoretical language is only capable of transmitting partial information; the application of that information also requires personal interaction for the transmission of relevant tacit knowledge and skills. Our study suggests that this may be particularly important in dynamic fields where new knowledge and techniques are emerging at a high rate.

In addition to the divergence between technologies in relation to knowledge inputs and channels for seeking knowledge from PSR, the study also revealed differing recruitment strategies for research staff. The companies involved in biotechnology had strategies to recruit career scientists with PhDs and postdoctoral research experience abroad. Ceramics and parallel computing companies recruit graduates and postgraduates, but their preference is for researchers with previous industrial experience.[7]

A partial explanation for these differing recruitment strategies is suggested by the type of tacit knowledge which companies seek to exploit in each technology which, in its turn, is affected by the type of innovation process pursued. Whereas ceramics and parallel computing firms approximate to the chain-linked model of innovation, with research closely linked to and affected by feedback from design, production and customers, pharmaceutical companies are closer to the classic linear model. New product development is strongly knowledge-led, and research is comparatively remote from the user and production. It follows that much relevant tacit knowledge in ceramics and parallel computing is developed in industry, both in-house and in other companies, which explains the attraction of recruits with industrial experience.

Recruitment policy for biotechnology has to be considered in the context of intensified global competition among pharmaceutical companies. The application of biotechnology is a necessity for firms which wish to stay competitive, because it provides the potential to speed up the drug discovery process (see Sapienza, 1989). Substantial worldwide support for public-sector research has led to a rapid expansion of scientific knowledge along a broad front, but specific expertise in many areas, for instance receptorology, is scarce. The recruitment of researchers with foreign postdoctoral experience may be explained by the need to gain relevant, scarce tacit knowledge, skills and techniques associated with rapid advances in underpinning knowledge.

Researchers in all three technologies have a strong network of informal links with other companies. As discussed above, links with suppliers of instrumentation, materials and components provide useful knowledge inputs. But informal links also provide market knowledge and information about product performance, competitor activities and scientific procedures. Customers provide market knowledge to parallel computing and ceramics companies; in the latter technology, knowledge about product performance provided by customers is fed back into development activities. Ceramics companies' customers are also a source of information about competitors' activities.

We also found that workers involved in industrial RD&D in all technologies quite frequently communicate with their opposite numbers in competitor companies, confirming our earlier suggestion. For instance, researchers from various pharmaceuticals companies frequently share ideas on topics such as the containment of genetically engineered organisms, or appropriate animal models for testing various diseases. Opportunities to meet are provided when technical people come together at government, professional or industry meetings, for instance to set standards. They are well used to focusing such discussion on technical areas of common concern – including the largely tacit knowledge related to research and design instrumentalities – thereby avoiding disclosure of proprietary information.

CONCLUSIONS

This chapter demonstrates that tacit knowledge is an important constituent of the scientific and technological inputs to innovation. Firms make deliberate efforts to capture tacit knowledge. They do this by recruiting scientists and engineers who embody the required skills and tacit knowledge; by conducting in-house RD&D; and by promoting networking. By its very nature tacit knowledge is primarily transferred by example and practical experience. The *channels* through which tacit knowledge is obtained are thus primarily person-embodied rather than literature-based. Personal networks include internal links with other members of staff, with technical people in other companies (users, suppliers and competitors) and in public-sector research institutions. Kline and Imai have analysed the internal networks; our material extends to external networks. Unlike Imai, we believe that flows of tacit knowledge are important not only for access to technical information to solve problems, but also for access to new knowledge generated through research. We suspect that much of the knowledge transferred through personal networks is tacit, but our evidence is suggestive in this regard. It may be, however, that the extent of tacit knowledge flows is higher than usual in the examples presented *because* we focused on newly emerging technologies.

NOTES

1. The authors would like to acknowledge the financial support of the ESRC both through the Designated Research Centre on Science, Technology and Energy Policy at the Science Policy Research Unit, which enabled this chapter to be written; and for the project entitled 'Public–private research linkages in advanced technologies' (ESRC award number Y 306 25 3001) conducted under the Science Policy Support Group/ESRC programme *Public Science and Commercial Enterprise* from which the empirical results derive. Our thanks also to colleagues, too numerous to mention individually, who have commented on earlier drafts of this chapter.
2. It should be recognized that the term 'expertise' extends beyond the narrowly cognitive or technical domains to encompass the social context which gives meaning and status to one set of knowledge and skills over another.
3. By the late 1970s, 11 per cent of all federally funded R&D was directed toward basic biomedical research, and the number of basic researchers such as molecular biologists, immunologists and biochemists also increased rapidly. See Teitelman (1989).
4. One estimate suggests defence customers paid for nearly half of all semiconductor R&D in the US from the late 1950s to the early 1970s. See Flamm (1988).
5. See Senker and Faulkner (1992) for details of methodology and partial results. Further information in Senker and Faulkner (1994) and Senker and Faulkner (1995).
6. The only example given was catalogues of companies which market molecular biology materials and give guidance on the availability and suitability of, for instance, different strains of micro-organisms or vectors.
7. Ceramics and parallel computing firms generally cannot offer the rewards or security offered by pharmaceutical companies and therefore cannot be as selective in recruitment.

REFERENCES

Barden, P. and Good, P. (1989), *Information flows into industrial research*, London: CEST.

Braun, E. and Macdonald, S. (1978), *Revolution in Miniature*, Cambridge: Cambridge University Press.

Collins, H. M. (1974), 'The TEA Set: Tacit Knowledge and Scientific Networks', *Science Studies*, **4**, 165–86.

Dosi, G. (1988), 'The nature of the innovative process', in G. Dosi, C. Freeman, R. Nelson, G. Silverberg and L. Soete (eds), *Technical Change and Economic Theory*, London: Pinter.

Faulkner, W. (1992), 'Conceptualising knowledge used in innovation', paper presented to PICT Workshop on 'Exploring Expertise', Edinburgh, November.

Flamm, K. (1988), *Creating the Computer*, Washington, DC: The Brookings Institution.

Fleck, J. (n.d.), 'Configurations: Crystallising Contingency', paper prepared for special issue of the *International Journal of Human Factors in Manufacturing on Systems, Networks and Configurations: Inside the Implementation Process.*

Fleck J. (1983), 'The Effective Utilisation of Robots: The Management of Expertise and Know-how', *Proc. 6th British Robot Association Annual Conference*, Bedford: IFS.

Fleck J. (1988), 'Innofusion or Diffusion? The Nature of Technological Development in Robotics', Edinburgh PICT Working Paper no. 4, University of Edinburgh.

Gambardella, A. (1992), 'Competitive advantages from in-house scientific research: The US pharmaceutical industry in the 1980s', *Research Policy*, **21**, 391–407.

Gann, D., Matthews, M., Patel, P. and Simmonds, P. (1992), *Analysis of Private and Public Sector Funding of Research and Development in the Construction Sector*, Brighton: IPRA.

Gibbons, M. and Johnston, R. (1974), 'The Roles of Science in Technological Innovation', *Research Policy*, **3**, 220–42.

Golding, A. (1971), 'The Semiconductor Industry in Britain and the United States. A Case Study in Innovation, Growth and the Diffusion of Technology', DPhil thesis, University of Sussex.

Granovetter, M.S. (1973), 'The strength of weak ties', *American Journal of Sociology*, **78**, 1360–80.

Hall, G.R. and Johnson, R.E. (1970), 'Transfers of United States Aerospace Technology to Japan', in R. Vernon (ed.), *The Technology Factor in International Trade*, New York: National Bureau of Economic Research.

Imai, K. (1991), 'Globalisation and Cross-border Networks of Japanese Firms', Paper presented to Conference, 'Japan in a Global Economy', Stockholm School of Economics, 5–6 September.

Kline, S.J. (1990a), 'Innovation Styles in Japan and the United States: Cultural Bases; Implications for Competitiveness', The 1981 Thurston Lecture, Report INN-3, Dept. of Mechanical Engineering, Stanford University.

Kline, S.J. (1990b), 'Models of Innovation and Their Policy Consequences', Dept. of Mechanical Engineering, Stanford University. Paper Presented at NISTE International Conference on Science and Technology Policy Research: 'What Should be Done? What Can be Done?' Tokyo.

Kreiner, K. and Schultz, M. (1990), 'Crossing the Institutional Divide. Networking in Biotechnology', Copenhagen School of Economics and Social Science. Paper for 10th International Conference 'Strategic Bridging to Meet the Challenge of the 90s', Strategic Management Society, Stockholm, September.

Kuhn, T.S. (1970), *The Structure of Scientific Revolutions*, 2nd edn, Chicago: University of Chicago Press.

Macdonald, S. (1992), 'Formal collaboration and informal information flow', *International Journal of Technology Management*, Special Issue on Strengthening Corporate and National Competitiveness through Technology, **7** (1–3), 49–60.

Madeuf, B. (1984), 'International technology transfers and international technology payments: Definitions, measurement and firms' behaviour', *Research Policy*, **13**, 125–40.

Metcalfe, J. and Gibbons, M. (1989), 'Technology, Variety and Organisation', in R. Rosenbloom and R. Burgelman (eds), *Research on Technological Innovation, Management and Policy*, Vol. 4, Greenwich, CT: JAI Press, 153–93.

Nelson, R. (1982), 'The role of knowledge in R&D efficiency', *Quarterly Journal of Economics*, **97** (3), 453–70.

Noble, D.F. (1979), 'Social Choice in Machine Design: The Case of Automatically Controlled Machine Tools', in A. Zimbalist (ed.), *Case Studies on the Labour Process*, New York and London: Monthly Review Press.

Nonaka, I. (1992), 'Managing Innovation as an Organisational Knowledge Creation Process', Paper prepared for (*Tricontinental*) *Handbook of Technology Management*, Institute of Business Research, Hitotsubashi University, Tokyo.

Pavitt, K. (1987), 'The objectives of technology policy', *Science and Public Policy*, **14**(4), 182–8.

Polanyi, M. (1966), *The Tacit Dimension*, London: Routledge and Kegan Paul.

Polanyi, M. (1969), 'The Logic of Tacit Inference', *Knowing and Being*, London: Routledge and Kegan Paul.

Ravetz, J.R. (1971), *Scientific Knowledge and its Social Problems*, Oxford: Clarendon Press.

Reuben, B.G. and Wittcoff, H.A. (1989), *Pharmaceutical Chemicals in Perspective*, Chichester: John Wiley.

Rosenberg, N. (1976), *Perspectives on Technology*, Cambridge: Cambridge University Press.

Rosenberg, N. (1982), *Inside the Black Box, Technology and Economics*, Cambridge: Cambridge University Press.

Rothwell, R. (1977), 'The characteristics of successful innovators and technically progressive firms', *R&D Management*, **7**(3), 191–206.

Sapienza, A. (1989), 'R&D Collaboration: a global competitive tactic in the biotechnology and ethical pharmaceutical industry', *R&D Management*, **19**(4), 285–96.

Senker, J. (1992), 'Informal Contacts between academic and industrial researchers: a key to effective technology transfer', Technology Transfer and Implementation Conference *Proceedings*, Day 1, TCS, Faringdon.

Senker, J. and Faulkner, W. (1992), 'Industrial use of public sector research in advanced technologies: a comparison of biotechnology and ceramics', *R&D Management*, **22**(2), 157–75.

Senker, J. and Faulkner, W. (1994), 'Making sense of diversity: public–private sector research linkage in three technologies', *Research Policy*.

Senker, J. and Faulkner, W. (1995), *Knowledge Frontiers: Public Sector Research and Industrial Innovation in Biotechnology, Engineering Ceramics, and Parallel Computing*, Oxford: Oxford University Press.

Sørensen, K.H. and Levold, N. (1992), 'Tacit networks, heterogeneous engineers and embodied technology', *Science, Technology, and Human Values*, **17**(1), 13–35.

Teitelman, R. (1989), *Gene Dreams*, New York: Basic Books.

Vincenti, W. (1990), *What Engineers Know and How They Know It: Analytical Studies from Aeronautical History*, Baltimore and London: The Johns Hopkins University Press.

Von Hippel, E. (1988), *The Sources of Innovation*, Cambridge: Cambridge University Press.

Winter, S. (1987), 'Knowledge and Competence as Strategic Assets', in D. Teece (ed.), *The Competitive Challenge, Strategies for Industrial Innovation and Renewal*, Cambridge, Mass.: Ballinger.

6. Strategic technological collaboration in Canadian industry: towards a theory of flexible or collective innovation

Jorge Niosi

Technological collaboration among firms, and between firms and universities and state laboratories, has been rapidly increasing in the 1980s and early 1990s. Its growth was most often observed in high-technology activities, like the production of advanced materials, biotechnology and electronics, but this organizational form is also spreading to transportation equipment manufacturing, utilities and engineering, and generally across the industrial spectrum, with different intensities and in different forms.

There is no established theory of technical alliances and collaboration. The economics and management literature provides several *ad hoc* explanations, many of them probable and even convincing, but with little theoretical support; they include the companies' search for complementary knowledge, R&D economies of scale and scope, and synergies and standards (Kanter, 1989; Bleeke and Ernst, 1993). Also mentioned is the implementation of Japanese methods of management favouring technical cooperation between assemblers and suppliers. The first part of this paper shows the elements of a theory of cooperative innovation. These elements challenge our conventional knowledge about technical change. The second part displays some characteristics of Canadian strategic technical alliances in high technology, supporting the previous theoretical debate. The third part consists of a few case studies illustrating recent Canadian alliances. The paper concludes that technical cooperation unveils new, hidden dimensions of the process of technological innovation, and that technical change must be rethought in the light of this new trend.

TOWARDS AN EVOLUTIONARY THEORY OF COOPERATIVE INNOVATION

Innovation is supposed to constitute a key component of the strategic behaviour of the firm. Through technological innovation, firms create new products and processes, assuring them a temporary monopoly, and the associated high profits. In Schumpeter's approach, however, competition and creative destruction precluded inter-firm cooperation. In his view, each firm competes on the basis of its own proprietary technologies, which it tries to differentiate from those of other competitors. In this sense, Schumpeter is one of the forefathers of present-day industrial economics.

Technical cooperation among firms takes place when independent enterprises put together commonly defined R&D projects, often with the help of universities and government laboratories. The spectrum of technical cooperation goes from informal collaboration (usually through the short-term exchange of research personnel, ideas, and/or laboratory material without any written contract between the parties) to strategic technical alliances (i.e. long-term – six months or more – written R&D agreements between firms aiming at the creation of new or improved products or processes). Technical collaboration thus differs both from technology transfer, and from other types of strategic alliances (i.e. commercial, manufacturing, advertising, etc.). Other types of long-term agreements between firms have very different aims: securing and linking groups of customers (marketing agreements), putting together productive assets (production alliances), or combining advertisement efforts (advertising partnerships).

Some of the building blocks for a theory of technical cooperation already exist. They are to be found in a variety of new concepts and perspectives on technology laid down in the last ten to twenty years by heterodox economists and historians of technology. The following is a brief review of these building blocks.

Evolutionary Perspectives on Economics and Technology

Evolutionary economics provides the general framework for the understanding of alliances and technical cooperation. This perspective argues that in the course of their life, firms acquire a specific set of operating practices or *routines*. Routines change slowly, but discontinuously, under the influence of changes in the economic environment and internal requirements (Nelson and Winter, 1982).

Technical alliances may thus be conceived as industrial organization routines, adopted by firms under internal and external constraints, often through a mix of imitation and in-house learning processes, and changing under the influence of a dynamic environment, and internal factors. Routines are long-term, semi-permanent sets of practices; alliances also share this characteristic with other types of routines, as the factors that explain their rapid dissemination (technological turbulence brought by the new generic technologies; economic turbulence brought by the increasing number of competitors in practically every industry; and commercial turbulence brought by the opening and globalization of markets) will not disappear overnight.

Evolutionism in managerial theories[1] also brings other fresh elements into the analysis of technical cooperation: organizational forms and routines (like technical alliances) are developed by trial and error, with variation, selection and competition as major factors explaining their change patterns (McKelvey and Aldrich, 1983).

Evolutionary economics is based on the assumption of bounded rationality of economic agents, a condition of the understanding of learning processes of all sorts, including R&D processes such as technical alliances. Learning determines variety, as the acquisition of knowledge brings specialized capabilities, and thus selection among the new capabilities and associated routines. Most important, the evolutionary perspective maintains that economics must be, like all present-day natural sciences, a historic science; that trajectories and path dependencies – including organizational and technical – matter. In other words, the nineteenth century neoclassical paradigm derived from Newtonian physics may be changed for the new scientific approach based not on an immutable universe, but on a world in perpetual change, where equilibrium is only a dimension of dynamic systems (Saviotti and Metcalfe, 1991).

The differences between evolutionary economics and biology for the analysis of technical change were pointed out by, among others, DeBresson (1987). While his remarks apply strictly to technology, they are also useful for the analysis of organizational change, like the present alliance movement. First of all, technical change (and its associated organizational change) is much more rapid than biological change, and its diffusion is usually only a matter of years or decades. Second, both technical and organizational evolution accelerate through time, as no invention (and no organizational routine) is lost, and each technical invention (or routine) multiplies the number of possible future combinations. Third, technical systems and routines (unlike species) seldom disappear entirely, and at least some of their components are preserved in the following ones. Fourth, technical systems and routines interbreed much more than species do; this is particularly true in the present triple technological revolution, where the technical and organizational spillovers from electronics, advanced materials and biotechnology are sending shock waves across the board in the overall economy. Fifth, technical and organizational change is partially reversible: it is possible to re-adopt previous techniques and organizational schemes, a situation that does not occur in nature. Finally, in evolutionary economics, the unit of analysis is unclear. There is no equivalent to species in biology. Sometimes technologies, sometimes firms, and sometimes routines are the unit of analysis. These flaws, however, do not limit the usefulness of evolutionary economics and managerial theory as a *heuristic* tool for social science and management research in the area of technical cooperation.

Institutions of a New Technoeconomic Paradigm

Freeman and Perez (1988) associate strategic technological cooperation with the emergence of a new phase in the development of technology. They classify innovations into four categories of increased complexity and systemic effects. These four categories are incremental innovations; radical innovations, changes of technology systems (or clusters of radical and incremental innovations, like the introduction of synthetic materials), and changes in *technoeconomic paradigms*. In this latter case, the changes include many clusters of technology systems, together with organizational and managerial innovations. These technoeconomic paradigms would correspond to each Kondratieff wave of prosperity. The introduction of steam power and the railway from the 1830s to the 1890s was such a change; it brought with it mass production, the first modern corporations, and favoured the expansion of electricity, steel, coal, oil and gas, and synthetic dyestuffs. The introduction of electricity, and the accompanying birth of the automobile, heavy engineering and petrochemical industries had the same effect from the 1890s to the 1940s. The corporate organization was extended to most industrial, commercial and financial sectors. Taylorism emerged and was diffused through the new large enterprises. National oligopolies and monopolies developed in North America and Western Europe. The next technoeconomic paradigm, developed since the 1940s, was linked to the automobile, the aircraft, consumer durables and synthetic materials. The assembly-line production model became generalized, the multinational corporations with their international hierarchies dominated the economy.

In the postwar period a new technoeconomic paradigm started to emerge and gained momentum in the 1980s. Freeman and Perez call it the 'information-technology paradigm'. It is characterized by the generalization of computers and numerically controlled machines, the application of optical fibres and new ceramics to the production of new electronic goods, robots and information services. New technologies also appear, namely biotechnology and advanced materials. Horizontal communication, collaborative research among independent organizations, and concurrent engineering displace the previous vertical and sequential links among organizations, and between functions within the organization. There is a massive entry of smaller innovative firms, and a rapid diffusion of technology that brings increased uncertainty and risk. Collaborative research appears as the effect of this increasingly turbulent environment, first in information technologies, then in other new technologies, and finally catches up with established firms of the previous technoeconomic paradigm.

This approach suggests that new technology has resulted in widespread organizational innovation in order to integrate technological change into efficient production systems. In a context of rapid technological change, increased complexity and massive entry of competitors, collaborative research may reduce risks, uncertainties and costs associated with R&D in information technology.

Localized Learning and Technology as a Quasi-Public Good

In neoclassical theory, technology is made of perfectly codified information, easily transmissible between independent firms. This perspective has been challenged from several angles. In several seminal articles and other papers, Stiglitz (1987) has insisted that *technological learning is mostly localized*. He argues that technology is different from science, in that it is much more specific to particular industries, processes and products. As such, technology is much more subject to obsolescence than science. Localized technological progress has little impact on (and no utility to) other industries and technologies.

It follows that R&D (a specific type of learning process) is also mostly a localized activity. From this perspective, we can deduce that cooperative research is often so specific that the results may only be applied by the partners themselves, with few potential spillovers to imitators and competitors. When a large manufacturer of central telecommunications switching systems, and a major cellular telephone producer conduct a collaborative research project to make their equipment totally compatible, the result of such a project is only useful for them (see below). The protection and appropriation of such intellectual property should be easy for members of the alliance, as few externalities and spillovers can be obtained by non-member firms.

Technology, being mostly specific knowledge, is also best characterized as a 'quasi-public' or 'impure public' good. Its transmission and diffusion depend both on the stock of knowledge of the potential buyer or imitator, and on the degree to which it is explicit, codified and incorporated into manuals, documents, drawings and blueprints. Again, several authors insist that technology is mostly implicit, tacit, and incorporated in the expertise of workers, technicians and engineers (Cohendet et al., 1992). The apparent paradox of alliances between both complementary or competing firms thus disappears: cooperative knowledge production needs close collaboration between the bearers of such knowledge: the R&D personnel of alliance members.

From Flexible Production to Flexible Innovation

One of the major contributions of the French regulation school is the analysis of the transition from Fordist mass production, predominant between the 1920s and the 1970s, to flexible manufacturing since then (Coriat, 1982, 1990). In a context of opening markets, the arrival of new industrial competitors, and increased economic turbulence, rigid large-scale production is a hindrance, while productive flexibility procures strong advantages in the market.

The same reasoning can be applied to the R&D function. In the present context of technological turbulence, with the emergence of several new competing technologies, technical alliances procure a higher level of 'flexible innovation'. Collaborative research allows for a more rapid variation from one technology to the next and, compared to mergers and acquisitions, leads to an easier incorporation of complementary knowledge, with reduced costs and risks.

New Topics

To understand collective innovation, new topics must be added to the economist's and the management scientist's agenda. They are the concepts of cooperation (versus competition), collective learning (versus other types of learning) and traded externalities (versus unintended spillovers).

Cooperation

Economic and management theory has devoted many pages to underlining the advantages of competition, and the costs of monopoly (Yoshida, 1992). But the disadvantages of competition were seldom analysed, especially as compared with cooperation. The forms and varieties of economic cooperation were not studied, and the optimal mix between competition and cooperation in different markets (products, technologies, organization, etc.) was neglected. Markets and hierarchies are only two methods for the allocation of resources. Cooperation is another, and it does not stand between the other two, but constitutes an entirely different mechanism.

Our study shows that the comparative study of the costs and benefits of competition, integration and collaboration may be useful and may bring a significant renewal to economic theory. Economic efficiency may be the result of cooperation, as well as competition, and a comparative analysis of both types of arm's-length transactions may be worth-while (Teece, 1992).

Collective learning

In 1962, Kenneth Arrow wrote a classic article on the concept of learning by doing, a concept that drew attention to productivity gains within the firm, as the workforce gains a better grasp of the newly incorporated technology. A few authors developed that basic concept to understand other types of learning in the firm: learning by searching (in-house R&D), learning by consulting, learning to invest (Dutton and Thomas, 1985; Siggel, 1987; Teubal, 1987). Johnson (1992) and Lundvall (1992) correctly pointed out that almost all cases of learning processes were interactive, social phenomena. Hence, their concept of 'interactive learning'.

It may now be necessary to develop a new concept, 'collective learning', to define this type of cooperative, which encompasses several economic units, and collective projects. The concept will be based on the study of cooperation in R&D, be it formal, as in the case of alliances, or informal.

'Collective learning' is close to 'collective invention', a concept proposed in 1983 by Allen (1983) to analyse technological developments in the British and American iron industries during the nineteenth century. As many inventions and innovations are the outcome of formal or informal cooperation, collective learning processes often take place through the interaction among independent firms and other research units. There are, however, some major differences. Collective invention was based on a free exchange of information. Collective learning is a more planned process, carefully monitored by members of technological partnerships. Collective invention made information freely available to all firms in the industry. In alliances, only the partners capture the increases in capabilities produced by the cooperative project, with the exclusion – at least during a certain period of time – of non-member firms. Collective learning is thus a particular case of interactive learning. It is the one that takes place within technical alliances.

Trading externalities

Externalities are another underdeveloped area of economic theory. 'A technological externality exists when some activity of party A imposes a cost or a benefit on party B for which A is not charged or compensated by the price system of the market economy' (Whitcomb, 1972). In economic theory externalities, be they positive or negative, are either *imposed* by one economic agent on another, or unwillingly lost by the former to the benefit of the latter. Externalities are thus spillovers, social returns, or unintended benefits that the producer cannot capture for itself (Mansfield, 1977). Or they are costs (such as environmental disruption or pollution) that one company imposes on another.

Conversely, an alliance represents a conscious search for mutual externalities by all cooperative partners. In a sense, alliances represent a purposive exchange of positive externalities between firms and other parties. They thus constitute a kind of trade in technological externalities. 'Traded externalities' are thus different from traditional 'positive externalities', the kind of spillover that economic theory of technical change has time and again dealt with in empirical analysis.

Conclusion: From Isolated to Cooperative Innovation

The prevalent theory of technological innovation was based on the assumption that knowledge is a public good and that information spillovers freely occur among corporations. Also, through the development of new or improved products and processes, individual companies were able and eager to produce durable 'special advantages' (in Hymer's terminology) or barriers to entry (Bain) against competitors. These advantages were produced in closely isolated R&D laboratories. They were seldom exchanged, or traded, and never produced by teams for actual or potential competitors, as companies tried to minimize spillovers, and maximize temporary monopoly profits. Learning by searching, learning by using, and learning by doing are in this perspective the most important forms of accumulation of intangibles; they are conducted within the corporation.

The emerging theory of cooperative innovation is based on the assumption that technology is a quasi-public good, and that learning is mostly localized. Under the new conditions of economic and technological turbulence, the shortening life cycle of products and processes, and the increasing number of competitors, companies prefer to collaborate with some rivals, in order to compete with others. Companies 'trade externalities' and develop a new form of collective learning that occurs side-by-side with previous learning processes. These learning processes are new routines that companies incorporate in their previously accumulated set of behaviours.

CANADIAN TECHNOLOGICAL ALLIANCES

The study was conducted in 1990–91, through the interviewing of some 130 firms conducting technical alliances. The firms were identified through a preliminary search across the Canadian financial press, as well as technical and scientific journals. This search allowed the identification of firms conducting alliances, either with Canadian or with foreign partners. The preliminary database showed some important characteristics. The first was that all the firms thus identified conducted R&D as a regular activity. The second was that most of the firms operated in two industries and two technologies. The industries – identifiable through SIC codes – were electronics (including the production of semiconductors, computers and parts, telecommunications equipment and other electronic equipment, but excluding consumer electronics), and transportation equipment (mass-transportation vehicles of all sorts, including aircraft, subway and railway, but excluding automobiles). The two technologies – dispersed through a wide variety of industries – were advanced materials (including metal-matrix, ceramic and polymer composites, and fibre optics), and biotechnology (including both dedicated biotechnology firms, and other firms, including chemical, pharmaceutical and agro-business, with substantial biotechnology R&D). The total number of Canadian firms with research activities in each sector was identified through Statistics Canada publications and through employers' associations and it appears in Table 6.1. A questionnaire was designed and employees from a random sample of companies was personally interviewed either by the principal investigator or one of the assistants. The results of the study are valid for the universe of companies conducting alliances in the four areas (Niosi and Bergeron, 1992; Niosi, 1993).

Table 6.1   Canadian corporations conducting R&D in four selected areas

Industry	Population of firms conducting R&D	Sample
Electronics	238	36
Advanced materials	100	36
Biotechnology	250	36
Transportation equipment	37	20

Sources: Statistics Canada, industry associations.

The concentration of alliances in the three generic technologies confirms Freeman and Perez's technoeconomic paradigm hypothesis (the link between new complex technologies and institutional arrangements), but adds something else: alliances are more frequent in the electronics industry (as argued by Freeman and Perez), but also in biotechnology and advanced materials. Thus the new technoeconomic paradigm concerns not only the information-technology industry, but all three new generic technologies. In fact the three of them are interconnected. The electronics industry is an avid consumer of new materials, like silicones, gallium arsenide, optical fibres and crystals (Forester, 1988). The new biotechnology thrives on new electronic equipment, including electronic microscopes and computers (these allowing complicated research projects, like the use of programmes for the automatic scanning files of long DNA sequences – Davis, 1991).

The Growth of Alliances

Few alliances seem to have existed in Canada before the 1980s. They include some in the most R&D-intensive industries, including chemical, nuclear, telecommunications, transportation and heavy electrical equipment. The two main aircraft producers (De Havilland and Canadair) had collaborated for decades with their turbine manufacturers and other principal suppliers (DeBresson et al., 1991). The Canadian nuclear reactor, Candu, was produced in the 1950s through the collaboration between Atomic Energy of Canada, Ontario Hydro, and several electrical manufacturers and engineering firms (Bothwell, 1988).

The largest Canadian-owned chemical firms collaborated with their suppliers and clients since their inception in the 1940s. In 1925, the pulp and paper manufacturers had organized an industry–university consortium, the Pulp and Paper Research Institute of Canada, or PAPRICAN, to conduct collaborative research. But according to both public records and our own interviews, these were isolated cases of formal technical cooperation.

The rise of technical cooperation as a regular and important activity of hundreds of firms took place in the late 1970s and 1980s. Several factors were at work. One was the widespread use of electronic components in many manufacturing industries, such as transportation equipment, machinery (electrical and non-electrical), medical and scientific equipment, etc. The introduction of the personal computer – developed in the 1970s – was a major factor in the new networking, as was the introduction of electronic telecommunications equipment in the early 1970s. Also, the design of custom semiconductors needs cooperation between the electronic producer and its user. The development of compatible standards between two or more pieces of hardware in the information-technology industry requires cooperative R&D of all parties involved.

The second factor was the rise of biotechnology in the late 1970s, which increased enormously the levels of networking between the new dedicated biotechnology firms (DBFs), with traditional chemical, pharmaceutical, and food producers, and also with universities, agricultural laboratories, hospitals and other users and suppliers.

Finally, the postwar development of advanced materials, and their increased use in several industries, starting first with defence suppliers and transportation equipment manufacturers, but then continuing with electrical utilities, telecommunications carriers, construction corporations, and machinery producers, gave a massive boost to the development of technical cooperation. Composite materials are designed to fit the specific needs of users. They also require close cooperation between user and producer.

These three generic technologies represented a great leap in complexity, and needed a qualitative increase in scientific inputs. The cooperation with universities and government laboratories became indispensable for private firms.

Time patterns of alliances show the massive increase of cooperation after 1980. Table 6.2 shows wide differences between industries and technologies. Biotechnology was a 'network technology' from the start (almost all firms existing in 1980 in the area were already conducting collaborative research), while less than half of electronic and advanced material producers, and transportation equipment corporations, were involved in alliances before 1980. Figures show that technical cooperation rapidly increased in the 1980s.

Table 6.2   Sample firms conducting R&D alliances before and after 1980

Period	Electronics	Advanced materials	Biotechnology	Transport equipment	Total
Before 1980	8	13	11	4	36
1980 and after	28	23	25	16	92
Sample companies existing before 1980	24	28	13	18	83
Sample cos in alliances before 1980 (%)	33	46	85	22	43

Characteristics of the Firms

A first characteristic of companies involved in alliances has already been mentioned: they all conduct R&D in the sense of the Frascati definition.[2] There is a second characteristic: the largest industry and niche leaders are involved in strategic alliances. The general pattern varies from one industry to the other.

Most large traditional materials producers (chemical, metal, wood) conduct collaborative R&D in the area of new materials with both large users and small innovative firms, while keeping mostly in-house the largest part of their research, in the area of processes. The university input is important in this new technology: practically all firms interviewed had developed alliances including universities in the last few years.

In electronics, all the largest firms and niche leaders are conducting collaborative R&D. User–producer alliances coexist with horizontal partnerships between rivals, and 'oriented' alliances between complementary firms. The university input was here smaller; however, more than two-thirds of the firms had developed cooperation with universities, mainly in the areas of software and coatings (materials).

In biotechnology, virtually all firms are involved in alliances. These include partnerships between DBFs and large chemical, pharmaceutical and food producers, equipment and inputs suppliers, specialized R&D biotechnology laboratories and consultants, university research centres and government laboratories. The university input here was significant, as many of the DBFs were founded by university professors, and still had intensive links with the university for the more fundamental aspects of their research.

In transportation equipment, large assemblers are the focal point of alliances, both vertical (with their own suppliers, domestic or foreign), horizontal (with foreign competitors) and 'oriented' (with complementary producers, like manufacturers of electrical and electronic equipment, and advanced materials).

Larger firms and niche leaders are making the strongest R&D effort. The alliance routine seems to appear in the more R&D-intensive firms of each sector. In the same vein, both Canadian- and foreign-controlled firms conducted alliances, but compared to domestically owned firms, foreign subsidiaries were latecomers in technical alliances, their collaborative effort was smaller (as was their R&D effort as a percentage of sales), and they participated mostly in local and national partnerships. This latter dimension will be developed in a further paper.

Management

Small firms conduct a larger percentage of their R&D effort in collaboration with other firms, universities and government laboratories. Figure 6.1 shows the general pattern.

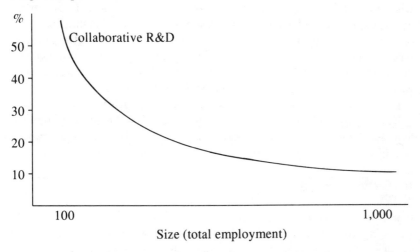

Figure 6.1   Size of firms and collaborative R&D as a percentage of total R&D effort

In smaller companies, economies of scale in R&D were important considerations in the decision to enter into technical alliances. For larger companies, economies of scope (R&D and product diversification) were more crucial. Thus, large materials producers entered into alliances with smaller firms with new advanced materials, while large chemical or pharmaceutical firms made alliances with DBFs in order to gain access to biotechnology products (mainly vaccines) and methods.

Two principal methods of coordination existed in the alliances. The simpler and most widely used was the memorandum of understanding (MOU), a legal contract linking the two parts for the duration of the project. This type of arrangement was adopted by the majority of alliances in all sectors. The second main form of arrangement, joint ventures, was adopted in a minority of cases (see Table 6.3).[3]

Table 6.3   Forms of arrangement: MOUs and joint ventures

Form/area	Electronics	Advanced materials	Biotechnology	Transport equipment	Total
MOUs	26	33	29	19	107
Joint ventures	10	3	7	1	21

Joint ventures were used in only two circumstances. The most frequent was when product development was the goal of the collaboration, and where manufacturing and marketing considerations were either included in the agreement, or were close to being included. Here, a less flexible form of organizing innovation was adopted because the stakes were higher, the budgets larger, and the time frames longer. The other situation in which joint ventures were preferred was industry–university consortia with government funding.

In the majority of cases (107/128 or 85 per cent), MOUs were adopted, that is less heavily committed governance structures. This finding confirms the hypothesis that alliances are flexible forms of organization for innovative activities.

Intellectual Property

Flexibility was also a key element in the management of the intellectual property stemming from the collaboration. Two indicators were used. The first was the use of simple schemes like collective property bestowed on all members, leader appropriation of intellectual property, and division of results on the basis of a previous division of labour (see Table 6.4). A second indicator was the reduced use of patents to protect the results of the technical collaboration (see Table 6.5).

Except in biotechnology, patents are not often used to protect collective inventions. This certainly increases flexibility. An important caveat, however, needs to be entered. These findings may be the consequence of different factors, other than the search for flexibility. First, some companies declared that the results were not patentable, as they consisted mostly of fundamental knowledge. Second, other companies declared that the alliance had not yet produced patentable results. Third, yet other companies suggested that the present patent system is not adequate to protect collective intellectual property. In this latter case, the absence of patents may be interpreted both as the consequence of rigidity in the patent system, and as a company strategy in search of flexibility.

Table 6.4   Sharing the intellectual property

Solution	Electronics	Advanced materials	Biotechnology	Transport equipment	Total
Collective property of members	14	5	26	9	54
Leader appropriation	6	15	6	5	32
Each member keeps own results	7	5	2	–	14
Other and mixed forms	7	10	–	4	21
Valid responses	34	35	34	18	121

Table 6.5   Use of patents in the protection of intellectual property of alliances

Patents/area	Electronics	Advanced materials	Biotechnology	Transport equipment	Total
Yes	11	9	17	5	44
No	25	27	19	15	84

Other respondents argued that secrecy is a better way to protect innovation in their particular area. This type of (unexpected) response also shows some kind of search for flexibility in the context of technological turbulence, a shorter life cycle of products and an increased number of competitors. It may also be an indication of localized learning: the results of the research have few applications outside the group of companies forming the alliances.

CASE STUDIES

Four case studies – one within each industry or technology – illustrate the characteristics of alliances and cooperative firms.

MacMillan Bloedel and Parallam

MacMillan Bloedel is the largest forest products company in Canada, and one of the largest in the world. Based in Vancouver, it conducts the most ambitious research programme in the Canadian forest products, pulp and paper industry. Its strategy is one of diversification through the development of new and improved products. The following is an account of its most important research project, a collaborative initiative in the area of new materials. This long-term R&D project by MacMillan Bloedel, conducted since the early 1970s and concluded in 1991, permitted the invention, development, testing, and now manufacturing of a new building material called Parallam. The material is a wood composite, made of parallel strips of wood bonded with waterproof glues. The resulting material is three times as strong as the strongest natural wood, and is used in the construction industry, shaped as beams up to 19.8 metres long. Total R&D cost, including testing, was Canadian $150 million. The research project was conducted by MacMillan Bloedel in collaboration with the German manufacturer of the new numerically controlled special presses that use microwave energy to cure the glue, and a Canadian chemical producer that developed the powerful adhesive required to hold together the wood fibres. Once the R&D project was completed, MacMillan Bloedel spent $100 million in building two Parallam plants, one in the state of Georgia, US, and one in British Columbia. The R&D allies did not participate in the new production facilities.

Northern Telecom's Alliances

Canada's largest electronics firm, Northern Telecom (NorTel) also conducts a certain number of international alliances. These are private arrangements between NorTel and foreign partners. The following are three of the many international partnerships of the Canadian multinational.

Since March 1990, NorTel has been an associate and a shareholder of the Microelectronics and Computers Technology Corporation (MCC) and is represented on its board of directors. MCC is a privately owned and financed non-profit cooperative joint venture of some twenty large American (plus NorTel) corporations, including Control Data, Digital Equipment, Martin Marietta, 3M, Motorola, National Semiconductor and Rockwell International. Founded in 1982, with headquarters in Austin, Texas, MCC conducts collaborative research on a large number of areas of computer electronics, including advanced computing technology, CAD, software technology and interconnection. Shareholder companies are those who have bought one share, participate in at least one research project, and participate in its governance structure. Associate companies are those that share the funding of at least one research project, with the priority to use the technology produced. MCC holds the intellectual property rights. Shareholders and associates have a first right to license the technology, but MCC may later (or in case of absence of interest by these) license the R&D results to third parties.

MCC is one of the earliest, largest and most widely publicized US consortia (Peck, 1986). It is not an industry–university consortium, nor it is officially linked to any government, though it has government sponsors including DARPA, NASA and the US Department of Defense.

In March 1992, a different type of strategic alliance was announced by NorTel in conjunction with Motorola, the world leader in cellular telecommunications equipment. The short-term goal of the alliance is to develop service and markets to their combined existing network technology. A second phase will add joint R&D to develop the new broad-band network technologies. In this case, a joint venture was created, Motorola NorTel Communications Inc., based in Chicago and equally controlled by the two partners. Each of them brought its technology and its marketing experience to the alliance. Manufacturing remained at the parent level. No other details were published.

In July 1992, NorTel announced another international strategic alliance, this time with Matra SA of France. Under the agreement, NorTel buys a 20 per cent stake in Matra's telecommunications subsidiary, and 5 per cent to 8 per cent of MMB's shares; MMB is the holding that controls Matra. The goal of the alliance is to combine Matra's advanced radio technology with NorTel's switching equipment technology. Two joint ventures will be created, one in digital telephone technology, the other in the area of public communications networks. The agreement has financial, manufacturing and research dimensions that were very scantily published.

BioChem Pharma

This medium-sized biotechnology company started its operations in 1986, when a group of scientists bought the pharmaceutical facilities of the Institut Armand Frappier, of the Université du Québec, in the city of Laval, north of Montreal. Soon after, IAF BioChem (the original name of the company) floated its first shares in the Montreal stock market, under the Quebec Stock Savings Plan. The company is currently controlled by its management, mainly composed of scientists, who hold 10 per cent of its shares, while two institutional investors, the Quebec Savings and Investment Fund (Caisse de dépôt et de placement du Québec) and the Solidarity Fund of the Quebec Federation of Labour hold a majority of the shares.

Through different research projects and local collaborations, BioChem has developed two new promising drugs. One is BCH-189, an anti-AIDS drug. In 1990 that drug was picked by the US National Cancer Institute in Washington as the best and most promising candidate to replace AZT, the only product presently used, known for its toxic side effects. BCH-189 was developed primarily within BioChem. The second promising drug is BCH-242, an anti-cancer product that is also less toxic and more effective than any other existing compound. Besides these future products, BioChem also produces vaccines, fine chemicals and diagnostic kits.

Early in 1990, BioChem announced a strategic alliance with Glaxo Holdings PLC, the British-based pharmaceutical multinational. The alliance gave the British corporation exclusive rights to the BCH-189 drug in the world except for the US and Canada; Glaxo paid $15 million for that right, and entered in a technical collaboration with BioChem for preclinical research. Later in November of that year the agreement between the two companies was extended to the anti-cancer drug. Glaxo would form an R&D and marketing joint venture with the Montreal-based medium-sized biotechnology firm, pay $25 million for a 10 per cent equity interest in it, and keep open a two-year option for another 10 per cent of IAF BioChem's shares. Meanwhile, in 1990, the chances of success of BCH-189 went from 25 per cent to 50 per cent as preclinical R&D progressed.

This alliance is one in which a Canadian SME with a strong R&D base (40 PhDs in its 60 R&D staff), but less than 300 employees, collaborates with a giant firm with 38,000 employees and an annual R&D budget of over $1.2 billion. The small firm puts its innovative products in the alliance, against the financial, marketing, and technical strengths of the large multinational corporation. This international alliance, as the previous ones, is an outcome – both in technological and organizational terms – of several initial collaborative projects with local partners.

Alcatel, CN and the ATCS Consortium

This railway control technology consortium was formed in 1988, under the leadership of the SEL Division of Alcatel Canada, and included the Canadian National, Motorola Canada, and Vapor Canada of Montreal. Alcatel Canada is the Canadian subsidiary of the giant French telecommunications producer, Alcatel Alsthom. Alcatel is the world's largest telecommunications equipment manufacturer, and an active partner in the French high-speed train – TGV (*train à grande vitesse*). In April 1991, Alcatel bought Canada Wire & Cable from Noranda to further its presence in Canada. The Canadian National Railways (CNR), Canada's largest railway company, was the first user involved with the partnership. The goal of the $20 million R&D project is to develop, install and test an Advanced Train Control System (ATCS) on a CNR rail line. SEL is the systems integrator, responsible for both the locomotive on-board and the central office computers. Motorola engineers the radio communication network, and Vapor Canada develops the computer displays and keypads for the locomotive cab, together with the transponders. This ATCS would be the first of its kind in North America and put the Canadian consortium in the lead over other US and Canadian competitors. The Industry, Science and Technology Canada Department (ISTC) will finance up to 40 per cent of the eligible R&D project costs, CNR will finance the installation and testing costs, with the main three partners funding the balance.

This case illustrates that technological complementarity is at the basis of technical alliances. It also shows how both electronic technology and its associated R&D collaborative organization spreads over other industries, like transportation equipment.

CONCLUSION

Our study shows an evolutionary pattern at the origins of technological collaboration. Most corporations presently conducting cooperative research started some time ago (in Canada, between the early twentieth century and the late 1970s), performing either technical quality control or occasional R&D. In due course, these operations became more substantial, as they formed the basis of permanent R&D laboratories. Later, these firms learned to transfer technology and to contract out R&D projects to external organizations. Finally, they developed cooperative activities in the area of R&D. There are, thus, evolutionary technical organization patterns, from purely internal and auxiliary activities, to more strategic and collaborative research behaviour.

While Freeman and Perez have put the accent on electronics as the core technology of the new technoeconomic paradigm, our research suggests that this paradigm also includes the two other generic, though less developed technologies, namely advanced materials and biotechnology. The three of them constitute information-intensive production systems (Willinger and Zuscovich, 1988), that is, technological change based on science as never before. This new technological paradigm is characterized by a qualitative leap in complexity, requiring an increasing number of specialized, advanced knowledge inputs from different sources.

Our study also confirms the validity of Stiglitz's (and others') approach to localized learning. Corporations keep intellectual property stemming from alliances protected through secrecy, which, among other things, implies a high level of specificity of research results, which are non-patentable, because either too specific or too fundamental.

Collective technological learning is not to be confused with Johnson and Lundvall's interactive learning. Collective learning is a carefully organized process of trading externalities within the framework of technical collaborations. Interactive learning is a more general concept encompassing all types of learning process involving any degree of social interaction. Collective technological learning is a specific case of interactive learning.

Flexibility is a key aspect of alliances both in their organizational structures (MOUs instead of joint venture) and in the use of simple ways of sharing intellectual property.

Collective innovation is different from Allen's collective invention. The latter is based on a free, uncontrolled exchange of information among inventive firms. Collective innovation is a purposeful, carefully monitored process, through which firms and other economic agents create new and improved technology within the limits, and for the benefit, of the alliance members. Among the battery of learning processes that Western firms have developed through time, collective innovation is probably the latest and the most complex. It is based on previous learning routines, and constitutes, according to us, a permanent addition to the capabilities of the most research-intensive firms. Their long-term survival is based on the permanence of the factors that brought their dissemination in the industrial organization landscape: technological turbulence determined by the three simultaneous generic and science-based technology revolutions of electronics, biotechnology and advanced materials; economic turbulence determined by the entry of new competitors in practically every industry (many of them from South East Asia); and commercial turbulence determined by the opening of markets either through liberalization or through the newly-acquired capacity of firms of all sizes to internationalize their operations.

Finally, even if our research has gathered information exclusively on Canadian alliances, comparative studies done elsewhere show that Canadian strategic partnerships are different from those in other countries, reflecting the contours of its domestic high-technology industries. As there are no large pharmaceutical Canadian-owned firms, the largest biotechnology alliances of Canadian DBF are with foreign counterparts, either American or European. Also, there is no Canadian participation in the largest strategic alliances conducted by multinational pharmaceutical firms.[4] Conversely, in the area of advanced materials, some large Canadian producers of traditional materials are looking for small innovative firms, both in Canada and abroad, to achieve economies of scope and related diversification. The absence of large numbers of Canadian users of advanced materials explains the fact that their R&D usually remains localized abroad. In electronics, the importance of Canadian telecommunications equipment producers (and the notorious absence of consumer electronics manufacturers that are critical in the Japanese electronics industry) also explains the industrial distribution and characteristics of technical alliances. In addition, the presence of only one major Canadian producer in most areas of transportation equipment (business jets, helicopters, subway cars, locomotives, aircraft engines, etc.) explains the large number of international horizontal alliances (between systems' assemblers) and the local vertical alliances between Canadian assemblers and their suppliers. In sum, Canada's strategic alliances look more like those of other small industrialized countries like Sweden, Switzerland, the Netherlands and Belgium. A small number of producers in a reduced number of industrial sectors often precludes large horizontal alliances within the national frontiers, and encourages international collaborations.[5]

NOTES

1. For a review of developments in this area see Singh (1990).
2. OECD, *The Measurement of Scientific and Technical Activities: Frascati Manual*, Paris, 1981.
3. It is thus inaccurate to identify alliances with joint ventures, as in the work of Harrigan (1987).
4. The largest of these alliances was signed in April 1993 between fifteen of the world's largest corporations in the ethical pharmaceutical industry to conduct cooperative research on AIDS. No Canadian firm was a partner in this alliance.
5. For a comparative view see Chesnais (1988), Langlois et al. (1988), Hagedoorn and Schakenraad (1991), Hakanson et al. (1993).

REFERENCES

Allen, R.C. (1983), 'Collective Invention', *Journal of Economic Behaviour and Organization*, **4**, 1–24.

Bleeke, J. and Ernst, D. (1993), *Collaborating to Compete*, New York: Wiley.

Bothwell, R. (1988), *Nucleus. The History of Atomic Energy of Canada Ltd*, Toronto: The University of Toronto Press.

Chesnais, F. (1988), 'Les accords de coopération technique entre firmes indépendantes', *STI Revue*, Paris, OECD, December, 55–132.

Cohendet, P., Heraud, J.A. and Zuscovich, E. (1992), 'Apprentissage technologique, réseaux économiques et appropriabilité des innovations', in D. Foray and C. Freeman (eds), *Technologie et richesse des nations*, Paris: Economica.

Coriat, B. (1982), *L'atelier et le chronomètre*, Paris: Bourgois.

Coriat, B. (1990), *L'atelier et le robot*, Paris: Bourgois.

Davis, B.D. (ed.) (1991), *The Genetic Revolution*, Baltimore: The Johns Hopkins University Press.

DeBresson, C. (1987), 'The Evolutionary Paradigm and the Economics of Technical Change', *Journal of Economic Issues*, **XXI** (2), 751–62.

DeBresson, C., Niosi, J. and Dalpe, R. (1991), 'Technological Linkages and Foreign Control in the Canadian Aircraft Industry', in D. McFetridge (ed.), *Foreign Investment, Technology and Economic Growth*, Calgary: The University of Calgary Press.

Dutton, J.M. and Thomas, A. (1985), 'Relating Technological Change and Learning by Doing', in R.S. Rosenbloom (ed.), *Research on Technological Innovation, Management and Policy*, Greenwich, Conn.: Jay Press.

Forester, T. (ed.) (1988), *The Materials Revolution*, Cambridge, Mass.: MIT Press.

Freeman, C. and Perez, C. (1988), 'Structural Crisis of Adjustment: Business Cycles and Investment Behaviour', in G. Dosi et al., *Technical Change and Economic Theory*, London: Pinter.

Hagedoorn, J. and Schakenraad, J. (1991), 'Inter-firm Partnerships for Generic Technologies – the Case of New Materials', *Technovation*, **11** (7), 429–44.

Hakanson, P. et al. (1993), 'Strategic Alliances in Global Biotechnology – A Network Approach', *International Business Review*, **2** (1), 65–82.

Harrigan, R.K. (1987), 'Strategic alliances and their new role in global competition', *Columbia Journal of World Business*, Summer, 67–9.

Johnson, B. (1992), 'Institutional Learning', in B.-A. Lundvall (ed.), *National Systems of Innovation*, London: Pinter, 23–44.

Kanter, R.M. (1989), *When Giants Learn to Dance*, New York: Simon & Schuster.

Langlois, R.N. et al. (1988), *Micro-Electronics. An Industry in Transition*, Boston: Unwin Hyman.

Lundvall, B.-A. (1992), 'User–producer relationships, national systems of innovation and internationalization', in B.-A. Lundvall (ed.), *National Systems of Innovation*, London: Pinter, 45–67.

Mansfield, E. (1977), *The Production and Application of New Industrial Technology*, New York: Norton.

McKelvey, B. and Aldrich, H. (1983), 'Populations, natural selection and applied organizational science', *Administrative Science Quarterly*, **28**, 101–28.

Nelson, R. and Winter, S. (1982), *An Evolutionary Theory of Economic Change*, Cambridge, Mass.: Belknap/Harvard University Press.

Niosi, J. (1993), 'Strategic partnerships in Canadian advanced materials', *R&D Management*, **23** (1), 17–27.

Niosi, J. and Bergeron, M. (1992), 'Technical alliances in the Canadian electronics industry. An empirical analysis', *Technovation*, **12** (5), 309–22.

Peck, M.J. (1986), 'Joint R&D: the case of the MCC', *Research Policy*, **15** (5), 219–31.

Saviotti, P. and Metcalfe, J.S. (eds) (1991), *Evolutionary Theories of Economic and Technological Change*, Reading, UK: Harwood Academic Publishers.

Siggel, E. (1987), 'Learning by Consulting: A Model of Technology Transfer by Consulting Engineering Firms', *Canadian Journal of Development Studies*, **VI** (1), 27–44.

Singh, J.V. (ed.) (1990), *Organizational Evolution. New Directions*, Newbury Park, Cal.: Sage.

Stiglitz, J.E. (1987), 'Learning to learn, localized learning, and technological progress', in P. Dasgupta and P. Stoneman (eds), *Economic Policy and Technological Performance*, Cambridge: Cambridge University Press, 125–53.

Teece, D. J. (1992), 'Competition, cooperation and innovation', *Journal of Economic Behaviour and Organization*, **18**, 1–25.

Teubal, M. (1987), *Innovation Performance, Learning and Technology Policy*, Madison: University of Wisconsin Press.

Whitcomb, D. (1972), *Externalities and Welfare*, New York and London: Columbia University Press.

Willinger, M. and Zuscovitch, E. (1988), 'Towards the economics of information-intensive production systems: the case of advanced materials' in G. Dosi et al. (eds), *Technical Change and Economic Theory*, London: Pinter, 239–55.

Yoshida, K. (1992), 'New Economic Principles in America – Competition and Cooperation', *Columbia Journal of World Business*, **XXVI** (4), Winter, 30–44.

7. The simultaneous shaping of organization and technology within cooperative agreements

Vincent Mangematin

INTRODUCTION

Both products and markets are redefined during the innovation process. Studies devoted to it have rapidly outgrown the framework of standard economic theory and stress the simultaneous creation of technology and markets. Yet, while the market has been the object of particular attention and studied in a particular way, it has often neglected a detailed description of the transformation of technologies themselves which are at the heart of the problem. In diffusion models (Mansfield, 1961; Metcalfe, 1988), the successive reduction of a technology to one-dimensional variables, preferably quantifiable, is a prerequisite for analysis. In the evolutionary economics approach (Nelson and Winter, 1982; Lawrence and Lorsch, 1967) and in sociology of science and technology (Callon, 1980, 1986; Latour, 1989, 1992; Callon and Law, 1987), it is the market which loses definition. From this work, we learn how designers make their choices in favour of a particular technological option and thus endow an object with a particular form. Yet we learn nothing about the details and the kind of competition between technologies (see Mangematin and Rabeharisoa, 1992). We are told that it is the environment which carries out the selection between technologies; but the nature of this environment remains a mystery, as does the way in which it operates. Either technology is studied in detail, but how the market makes its selection is neglected; or markets are analysed, but technology is reduced to one dimension.

By studying information technology (IT) (David, 1986; Arthur, 1989) or science based technology (Pavitt, 1990), economists have highlighted the links between the characteristics of a technology and the form and shaping of the market. They emphasize self-reinforcement mechanisms and irreversibility, which influence the mode of competition between technologies and thus the construction of the market. Is it possible in a similar way to establish relations between the mode of development and the characteristics of a technology? Can we envisage extending the observations made for production (Woodward, 1965; Tarondeau, 1982; Cohendet and Llerena, 1989) to the design stage?

What are the design parameters of the organizational structure? How are technical choices made? Do links between the two processes exist? If so, what are they? These are the types of question which I shall try to answer in this chapter.

These issues are the result of the study of a cooperative research agreement over a three-year period. Carminat is a joint research project between Philips, Renault, Sagem and TDF (see Mangematin and Callon, 1995; Mangematin, 1993 for details). The aim of the programme was to propose a system of road guidance based on the dissemination of the most recent road information. Each party in the contract had worked on the design of such systems for a long time. Before the contract, Philips was working on the Carin project which had two parts: improvement of the radio receiver so as to perfect the radio data system, and development of a technique for locating vehicles. Sagem was working on the design of a navigation technology within the Minerve programme while Renault and TDF were carrying out research on the acquisition and broadcasting of information and services (Atlas). In 1986, these three projects were merged into Carminat. Each partner contributed its technical skills and knowledge of guidance systems to the consortium. The different stages of the project can be summarized as follows.

As a start, the general 'architecture'[1] of the system was negotiated between the partners, who had to accept technical and organizational constraints. In view of the complementary nature of the technology they were pooling, the partners decided to distribute the work according to their own areas of specialization (see Figure 7.1). Philips was to take care of navigation, Sagem and Renault of vehicle control and diagnosis, Renault of integration into vehicles. These choices permitted each partner to develop a part of the system independently of the others. Each carried out the task entrusted to it without the need to create a shared laboratory. However, the separate design of each subsystem meant that the technology would be modular. The partners thus chose, from the many other technical possibilities, to design a system where the interface between the different subsystems would be fixed, since the subsystems themselves were to be developed independently.

The main idea of the agreement was that each subsystem be developed independently by each partner while being compatible with the full system at the same time. The partners thus rapidly decided on an overall 'architecture' for the technical system which was in keeping with their organizational choices. Interrelations between organization of cooperative work and technical choices were thus tightly knit. This paper discusses the determinants of those linkages. All the subsystems were then brought together in a test vehicle. Within this framework, the option chosen was that each laboratory would instal its modular subsystem on the test vehicle, which would then be driven to the next laboratory.

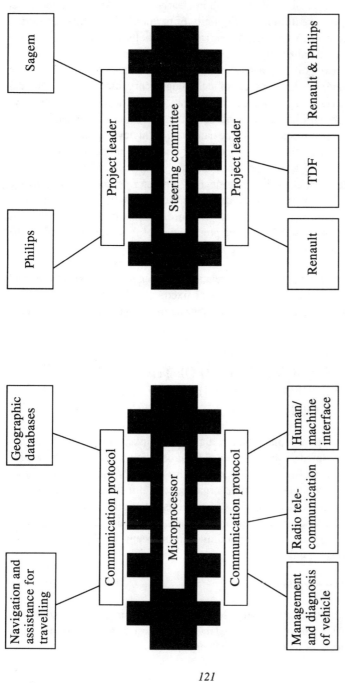

Source: Carminat cooperative agreement, pp. 39 and 40.

Figure 7.1 The central position of the microprocessor and the general organization of cooperation

How do organizational choices influence technical ones? Three elements of choice in the organization of cooperation clearly seemed to bear on technical choices: first, the institutional multiplicity of partners who decided to form a group to develop a new product; second, the nature of the technology developed by these partners; and finally, the level of trust between the partners.

I shall make two points in this paper. First, it is clear that links do exist between the way in which the development of technology is organized, and the characteristics of the resulting technological innovation. So, I shall analyse the ways in which technical choices are guided by organizational choices. Second, technology has two faces. On the one hand, technical developments have to be coordinated. On the other hand, a technology is itself a mode of coordination, as I intend to show. The joint development of a given technical innovation does not take place without posing a number of problems of coordination, as the question of the loyalty of partners adds to technical uncertainty. I intend to demonstrate that technology can be a mode of coordination when the relationships between partners are stabilized. The presentation of this paper is based on the two stages of development of the cooperative research project:

1. The process of stabilization of the relations between partners taking the overall architecture of the technical system as fixed.
2. The technological development of subsystems when the organization of the cooperation is stabilized.

SIMULTANEOUS DEFINITION OF THE MODE OF DEVELOPMENT AND THE CHARACTERISTICS OF A TECHNICAL OBJECT

Research focusing on production has highlighted links between the characteristics of manufactured goods and those of the production process. The production mode structures the firm's organization; there is thus a link between characteristics of products and corporate organization. But the links between the organization of creative activity and characteristics of products have not been analysed in the economic and sociological literature. This paper tries to throw some light on this, using concepts drawn from recent developments in both sociology and economics.

Design and Cooperation

Questioning the influence of the designer's position in the organization of cooperation, Alexander (1964) defined the product design process as the meeting between the form of a product and its context:

Every design problem begins with an effort to achieve fitness between two entities: the form in question and its context. The form is the solution to the problem. In other words, when we speak of design, the real object of discussion is not the form alone, but the ensemble comprising the form and its context (Alexander, 1964, quoted in Clark 1985, p. 236.)

It seems that technical developments depend on both the state of the technology and the context in which the product evolves. Nelson and Winter (1982) emphasize the notion of the technological trajectory in which the product is inscribed. Clark (1985), on the other hand, defines the product by its basic functions. In the automobile industry, Clark refers for example to the power of the engine, brakes, shock absorbers, etc. The designer of the product chooses between different components fulfilling the same functions according to the perception he has of the qualities expected by the user. Clark concludes that, when technical alternatives are given, the form of products will depend on the perception of qualities required by future users. These results confirm those of Von Hippel (1988). In effect, the inclusion of users in the design and development of products transforms their technical characteristics.

In pursuing Clark's analysis, one can go even further. The form of a product depends on the perception that designers have of the characteristics expected by consumers. But work on bounded rationality by Simon (1962) as much as research on the process of communication in firms shows that the perception which each member of an organization has, of both the organization and the environment, depends on his place in the organization. One can then logically infer that the perception of the consumer which the designers of a new product have depends on the place of those designers in the organization. Decisions by designers between different available technologies thus depends on the way in which development is organized. It is for this reason that numerous studies stress the necessity of links between the different corporate functions, particularly in marketing and development research (Anderson and Tushman, 1990, Xuereb, 1991). It is an opportunity to refer explicitly to the literature of different disciplines: strategy in evolutionary economics, R&D management in the management literature, and networks in the sociology of innovation.

Links Between Design Processes and Product Characteristics

This paper tries to explain systematically the links between organization of R&D and characteristics of the resulting technical innovations. After a brief definition of variables which emerge from the case study, I shall propose a typology of the different combinations of the variables.

A series of variables was identified in the case study. They were chosen by comparison with cases taken from the literature and they seem to be relevant.

However, they still have only hypothetical status. Three groups of variables are defined. The first deals with the identity of the partners, which is the result of a further three exogenous variables: the multiplicity of the partners, the nature of the technologies developed and the degree of *ex ante* mutual trust. The second group of variables defines the technical artefacts developed as a result of the cooperation: the interconnected modular technical object (IMTO); the technical object divisible into subsystems (TODSS); and the non-modular technical object (NMTO). This group is considered as endogenous to the decisions of the development consortium. The main constraint is the availability of technological alternatives. The third group of variables defines the division of labour among partners. Only two types of organization are taken into account: one based on pooling resources and the other based on pooling the developed artefact.[2] This group is also endogenous.

Exogenous variables

Multiplicity of the partners   Carminat brings into play several partners in different firms. My study is limited to inter-firm cooperative research contracts where a hierarchical settlement of controversy is not possible, even if the impossibility results from a choice made by the partners.

Nature of technologies developed by contracting parties   I define the technologies developed by each contracting party by their degree of complementarity or similarity. The technologies contributed to each of the partners are complementary, since they want know-how they do not have. The technologies contributed by each of the partners are similar, since they want a critical size.

I use the notions 'complementary' and 'similar' to describe not an agreement, but two technologies (Teece, 1990). The 'complementary'/'similar' distinction conforms to the mode of analysis adopted by the partners themselves. The definition of similarity between two technologies has in fact two dimensions: the first emphasizes technological proximity; the second stresses substitutability, from the consumer point of view. Technologies are said to be complementary if the use of the first requires the use of the second, i.e. if the utility of the sum of the combination of the two technologies is greater than the sum of the individual utilities $[U(x1; x2)>U(x1)+U(x2)]$.

Perceived degree of trust and mistrust   The degree of *ex ante* trust perceived by the partners is defined as follows: if the partners have confidence in each other from the outset, trust prevails in their mutual commitment. If suspicion prevails in the contract, each party has an attitude of mistrust *vis-à-vis* the other. The perceived degree of trust or mistrust between the contracting parties is analysed *ex ante*. Initially, I have settled for a binary variable: trust or mistrust.

It is clear that these two attitudes are the product of history (Granovetter, 1985), of past experience, and of the reputation or the capacity for retaliation of the partners. The research topic will influence this attitude.

Mistrust is likely to be less, the more definable and appropriable the output.

Endogenous variables

Characteristics of the technical artefact   Technical artefacts play a very complex role in the model. They are a compromise between technical and organizational constraints. The partners choose the characteristics of technical artefacts constrained by available technologies and influenced by the identity of their partners and their mutual trust. Technological constraints must not be underestimated. The three types of technical artefact are as follows.

Interconnected modular technical object (IMTO)   This is characterized by a modular design for the product as a whole, which permits the integration of different modules in varying numbers without changing the system's architecture. There is a high degree of interconnection between the different subsystems and the central one (the microprocessor in the case of Carminat). I define[3] 'modularity' according to two properties: a module is a subset of a larger set forming the product, and the product is said to be modular when it can function without certain modules. These are usually information or data-processing-based technologies, and telecommunications play an essential role. The Carminat system is a very good example of this kind of product. The system can work even if a component is missing.

Technical object divisible into subsystems (TODSS)   These technical objects are divisible into strongly interconnected subsystems and the presence of all the subsystems is required for the operation of the overall system. The technical failure of a subsystem leads to failure of the entire system. Similarly, the defection of one of the partners, if not replaced, leads to the overall system being abandoned. This would be the case in certain complex technologies, such as the development of a vehicle.

Non-modular technical object (NMTO)   These technical objects form a whole which is not divisible into subsystems. Developing them requires grouping together R&D activities in one place. It is outside the scope of this paper.

Division of work between partners   This is defined by the two extreme positions in the continuum of organization structure. Pooling resources defines the first type of organization. The shared laboratory and the joint venture are examples. The common characteristic is that authority is delegated to a steering committee which is responsible for the execution of work. Creation of the technical product comes under its authority. Task division among the firms involved in the cooperation is the other extreme. In this framework, separate tasks are allocated to each firm and coordination of those tasks can be hierarchical. Each development group has its own hierarchy which is completely independent of the steering committee. Work is divided according to specialism. In this case, this is not a pooling of resources but a pooling (i.e. assembling) of the developed technical product. Division of work is an endogenous variable and is mainly determined by the partners' identity and the availability of technologies determining the choice among various types of technical object.

The combination of variables: a typology

Hypothesis 1   The identity of the partners and their degree of *ex ante* mutual trust as well as the technology which they pool influence both the characteristics of the technical object and the organization of the cooperation.

I can develop this hypothesis as follows:

H1.1: If the technologies are complementary and if the level of trust is low, then the work will be divided and regrouped by specialism.
H1.2: The more the work is divided and regrouped by specialism, the more modular will be the product developed.
H1.3: The more modular the product and the more divided and regrouped by specialism the work, the less will hierarchical organization be an appropriate form of coordination; and other modes of coordination will be needed.

The forms of the technology and the organization will be the result of the extent of each partner's *trust in* the other, the complementarity or similarity of the technologies pooled during cooperation, and the internal or external nature of the cooperation. This chapter ignores the latter dimension, and is limited to cooperative research between different firms.

Table 7.1 illustrates the various combinations of the four groups of variables: trust/mistrust; complementary/similar technologies; characteristics of technical product (interconnected modular/divisible into subsystems/non-divisible; IMTO TODSS and NMTO) and division of work (pooling resources or 'pooling' (assembling) developed technical artefacts).

Situations 1 and 2   The partners trust one another and they decide to pool similar technologies. The main aim of the agreement is to attain a critical mass. The partners anticipate low risks of opportunistic behaviour. They can thus invest in the production of a non-modular technical artefact. The strong interconnection of the different subsets does not present an *a priori* problem, considering the degree of *ex ante* trust between partners. They can decide on the pooling of R&D resources, whether these are in the form of a joint laboratory (essential in the case of non-modular technical objects) or the distribution of tasks by specialism if the technical product is divisible into subsystems).

Table 7.1   Division of work according to the partners' identities

	Exogenous variables		Endogenous variables	
	Trust/ mistrust	Complementarity/ similarity	Technical artefact	Division of work
1.	Trust	Similar	TODSS	Resources pooled
2.	Trust	Similar	NMTO	Resources pooled
3.	Trust	Complementary	IMTO	Possibility of pooling resources by specialism
4.	Trust	Complementary	TODSS	Resources pooled
5.	Trust	Complementary	NMTO	Resources pooled
6.	Mistrust	Similar		No cooperation
7.	Mistrust	Complementary	IMTO	'Pooling' (i.e. assembling) of developed technical product
8.	Mistrust	Complementary	TODSS	'Pooling' (i.e. assembling) of developed technical product with high incentives for cooperation

Situations 3, 4 and 5   The partners trust one another; they have decided to pool their complementary technologies. This type of partnership may lead to any type of technical object. Concern about risks of opportunism is reduced due to the initial trust of the partners. If the partners decide to pool R&D resources by establishing a joint laboratory, they have more chance of ending up with a technical product which is divisible into interconnected subsystems or with a non-modular technical object, since the grouping of research resources at the same place creates little incentive for modularity.

Situation 6   If the partners are suspicious of one another, cooperation on the basis of a similar technology has little chance of taking place. In this case potential partners are competitors. Risks of opportunism are all the greater as the partners are suspicious. The pooling of research resources is necessary for R&D on a critical scale, the basis of the agreement in this case. If it is possible to specify the results and to distribute the work by specialisms, cooperative research may take place. This will favour the development of a modular technical object, with each of the partners being able to work internally on a part of the final product.

Situation 7   If the partners are suspicious of one another and if each of them has a complementary technology at its service, then the choice of an alternative technology will favour modular technical objects interconnected to a basic component. In this case, each of the partners will try to limit the risks of opportunism. This attitude will lead them to define the scope of interdependence between technical systems. In fact, each will develop modular subsystems independently. The technical product as a whole, the aim of the cooperation contract, will be designed to function even if one of the components is missing, although performance will be reduced. The technology thus limits the advantages of opportunism for the cooperators. The division of work is carried out by specialism and large investments must be made in coordination mechanisms. If cooperation does not lead to the establishment of a joint laboratory, a hierarchical organization is not likely to appear to manage the cooperative work since each of the partners will maintain its independence. The pooling or assembly of the developed technical product demands a precise definition of the interface between the subsystems, as I shall demonstrate below.

Situation 8   If it proves impossible to develop a modular technology, a division into subsystems is possible on condition that there are sufficiently powerful incentive mechanisms for a contract to be agreed.

As I have said, the form of the technical product influences the organizational form the cooperation takes. It seems logical that the number of partners, i.e. the basis of the organization, also influences the form of the technical artefact. During the partners' research, particularly where they contribute complementary technologies, each potential contracting party has for its part carried out research on a subsystem. Value from the investment in this preliminary research is obtained through the very modularity of the final technical product and the way in which the general architecture of the system integrates initial developments. I can thus hypothesize that the products resulting from cooperative research will be modular.

Similarly, when trust between the partners is low, they delay specifying how much will be invested and exactly where it will go, so as to maximize their chances of obtaining value from their work if one of the partners defaults or behaves opportunistically. Thus, the complementary nature of subsystems is combined with the aim of rapidly redeploying the technology at moderate costs. Doubts about the loyalty of partners therefore orientates technical developments towards highly modular technologies.

These propositions need to be tested using detailed case studies where each technical choice as well as rejected alternatives are analysed according to Table 7.1.

This approach requires details which are outside the limits of my analysis of Carminat.

Hypothesis 2   The more modular the technology, the more feasible is incremental innovation.

The Carminat case is of course too recent to make such a hypothesis possible from observation. It does however offer us an example of the opposite. The project was completed even though the initially planned technical developments could not be achieved. These technical dead-ends led to the specifications of the final product being relaxed, but they did not challenge the project itself. This observation suggests that the modularity of the technology allows for the incorporation of new developments which were not initially planned. Thus, if it is possible to incorporate subsystems which can function without all their components, one may suppose that so too is the integration of subsystems with additional components. Langlois and Robertson (1992) emphasize, taking the example of microcomputers and electronic components, the role of the modularity of the technology in incremental innovation, which tends to confirm my hypothesis.

Advantage of Cooperative Research Agreements

Highlighting the influence of the identity of partners and their degree of mutual trust on the characteristics of the technology which is developed, leads us to question the nature of research alliances. Models of strategic management treat decisions to form alliances as based essentially on cost/benefit analyses. The firm will take the decision to do something or have someone else do it, depending on the respective development costs. Yet this decision will affect the characteristics of the technical product developed and thus the development of its market.

Undertaking cooperative research is not only a decision to minimize costs; it is also an approach based on industrial logic. One of the participants of the CEC (Commission of the European Community) DRIVE programme affirmed that 'in the final analysis, the European subsidy did not compensate for the costs involved in obtaining it, but that the principal advantage of European programmes lies in the framework of cooperative work which they allow'.

The final question relates to which partners are to be integrated in the development of the product. On this point sociologists of science and technology contribute a number of convergent responses. It is necessary to enlist the support of potential partners for them to adopt an innovation.

Going into partnership for the development of a technology also means choosing one's allies, i.e. the different developers of the technology. If the idea is accepted that potential adopters of a technology are all more or less the same, it can be recommended that firms include, from the design stage, representatives of each group of potential users.

The link between the traditional diffusion model and the shaping of the supply side of technology is thus made. Integrated into the technology design process are representatives of users who inscribe within the technology the technical characteristics they want and which are accepted by the designers of the technology.[4] As the project advances, their role slides slowly from that of designer to developer. The technology will then be diffused by an epidemic-like process among similar users.[5]

This model has the particular merit of taking the historicity of the process back to the design stages. It allows for the process of recruitment of users to be an endogenous one, as is the degree of substitutability or decisions about hybridization.[6]

THE ROLE OF THE TECHNOLOGY AS A MODE OF COORDINATION

Highlighting the advantages of cooperative research as a form of development poses the problem of coordinating the agreements. If I show that innovation is a process of simultaneous formation of the organization of cooperation, the technology and the future users, it is necessary to ask questions about both the parameters of organizational design and the ways in which such research agreements are managed.

To start with I analysed the parallel creation of the technology and the organization. This study enables us to show that the level of trust and form of the technical product are linked. I emphasized, in particular, that if the number of partners is high and trust is low, then the need for coordination is great. How are the different types of cooperative research projects coordinated? Coordinating a project means ensuring the coherence of the means employed for achieving its aim. During Carminat's development, several stages are worth distinguishing. I focus particularly on the mode of coordination of a project based on 'pooling' or assembling the technical product which is developed. The modes of coordination of the project based on pooling resources have been left out of this analysis. I have already shown the role of the technology as a parameter for organizational design, when the relations between partners are stabilized. Coordination of the project is based on the management of points of stability which change over time.

I shall first show that technology gradually replaces hierarchy as a mode of coordination. After analysing the conditions in which this mode of coordination can be expressed, I shall see how the different risks inherent in a cooperative research project are dealt with.

Coordinating – Finding Points of Stability

A negotiation phase precedes the development period as such. This stage is characterized by negotiations between the contracting firms. They decide on the
technical contribution of each of the members and on the general organization
of the project. During this period, the technology is considered as stable, once
the general architecture of the project has been determined. This first phase of
the agreement is devoted to the negotiation of the financial clauses of the contract.
The financial and corporate management of each contracting firm are mobilized
by the programme managers of each firm participating in this negotiation. What
is fixed and what is in negotiation can be summarized as in Table 7.2.

Table 7.2   Variables of the precontractual phase

Fixed	In negotiation
The characteristics of the future product are defined in terms of functions, target price and range	Partners negotiate the elements integrated into contract
The technology of each subsystem is defined	
The general architecture of the system is fixed and serves as a base for division of work between partners	The division of risks and the guarantee systems are at the centre of discussion. At any moment a partner can default
Authority is still internal to each firm	
A steering committee is constituted by the programme directors of each firm who defend their respective interests	
Coordination based on hierarchy	

Once the contract has been signed, specialist work groups are formed. The
steering committee activates or deactivates the different groups. The system under
development is then distributed within the firms, keeping the organization in
work groups constituted by specialism. Finally, the technical products in development form a link between the groups. The system's main instrument of
cohesion is its modular architecture. The different subsystems are united by a
microprocessor, just as coordination between the different work groups is

provided by the steering committee. Within the technical system this ensures compatibility between the different functions of Carminat without entirely determining the technology of each subsystem. The only requirements are compatibility of communication protocols and interfaces.

Each subsystem can then be developed autonomously by the work group on condition that it is compatible with the microprocessor. The need for adjustments between the partners is thus reduced, since such adjustments will have been integrated into the specifications at the start of the project. Similarly, the microprocessor represents a rule whose effectiveness requires no further coordination. In this sense, the microprocessor is a disembodied and decentralized authority which reduces the gradual erosion of the hierarchy.

It is not the steering committee or one of the partners who determines whether the quality of the developments is good or bad or whether they conform to specifications, but the microprocessor. If the development produces the required functions and is compatible with the microprocessor and communication protocols, the subsystem is integrated into the product.

The integration phase of the different subsystems is not fully understood by the steering committee. An examination of its minutes confirms that technical discussions are totally absent during debate. The steering committee manages the progress of the different work groups, but not the content of their work. It does not decide in favour of any particular group in case of conflict and leaves the line managers to negotiate the outcome of controversy themselves. Once the prototypes of subsystems have been designed and developed, they are mounted on test vehicles[7] and travel from laboratory to laboratory, from Eindhoven to Paris, via Rennes and Cergy Pontoise. These vehicles are accompanied by the development engineers for the relevant subsystems. Thus the adjustment of the different parts of the system and their link to the microprocessor is carried out by technicians within the test vehicles. The technical product itself appears to be the lowest common denominator, the link which unites. This central characteristic of coordination by the basic technology is confirmed by other case studies. Dubreil (1991), who led the development of the X06, the Twingo, emphasizes the role of technology as the element of accord between technicians:

> Two draughtsmen, looking at the same drawing, see a different object. That is why, in the bodywork design department, we see small cardboard models; people communicate better with physical objects. Different departments rail at each other with bits of paper, but this is rarely the case with physical objects; objects dissolve opposition. The best language is that of objects. It is this property that we wanted to use systematically.

Weil and Moisdon (1992) also describe this adjustment by technicians amongst themselves, using the technical product under development. Their description of the work of design unit draughtsmen shows that agreement between technicians is reached via competition between alternative technical artefacts and the process of making interfaces compatible. The technology itself is what appears to establish the coherence of the project and therefore to be the true mode of coordination.

The technology thus appears, from both sides, to be a parameter of organizational design and a method of coordination of work between the partners. In a cooperative research programme where the level of trust between partners is low and where the work is distributed by specialism, the technology appears to be a method of coordination which progressively replaces hierarchical control. In the Carminat project the steering committee's prerogatives were weak. Once the rules of cooperation had been set and published officially in the contract, negotiations took place at the most decentralized level, that of the technicians who conceive the subsystems. At this stage of the project's development, the questions were mainly technical. Thus, for the technology to be a method of coordination, a network of designers must be established, the borders around the agreement must be clearly defined and the rules and conventions governing the agreement must be sufficiently integrated to become implicit. Table 7.3 outlines the development phase.

Table 7.3   Variables of the development phase

Fixed	In negotiation
The general architecture of the product is set	Minor changes can be made by technicians who negotiate between themselves integration of final product into subsystem
Functions, interfaces and communication protocols are set	The subsystem is being developed
The division of risks is fixed in the contract as well as the systems of guarantee and the general organization of the cooperation	
The steering committee provides coordination between the different work groups	Different subsystems are grouped in test vehicles. Technical objects serve as a common language for technicians
	Technology supplants the steering committe as a mode of coordination

Coordination by the technology appears thus as a complementary mode of coordination to that of the hierarchy. It provides for coherence between the methods established and the developments implemented when the hierarchy cannot ensure that function. What are the advantages of this type of coordination? What are its limits?

Influence of Technical Artefacts in Development on Organization

Organization of the Carminat project is instructive in several ways. In particular it shows how the partners chose to manage the risks inherent in cooperative research: opportunism, technical uncertainty, commercial uncertainty and learning.

After briefly presenting the method of managing risks in the Carminat project, I shall define the interaction between the different methods of coordination and risk management.

Response to opportunism

The struggle against opportunism at the centre of the Carminat contract is based on two principles related to its organization: task partitioning between technical functions and representation functions; and task partitioning between work groups and firms. Technical functions are the prerogative of work groups and are decentralized up to the development engineers' level. Technical problems do not go as far as the steering committee. The only demands to which engineers and technical managers are subject are those of compatibility and meeting deadlines. The steering committee manages all external relations and appears as a necessary intermediary between the 'market' (for the transfer or sale of the technology) and the development engineers who do not fully understand the market.

This principle of separation is accentuated by the distinction between a working group and a firm. The modularity of the system permits the progressive and independent creation of specific complementary assets which are barely redeployable. Until their integration into the test vehicles, value can be obtained independently from each of the developments by the firm responsible. Nevertheless, the complementarity of subsystems, in the implementation of the Carminat system, led the cooperators to conform to certain constraints, notably compatibility. Thus, during independent development, each partner conceived his product so as to grasp an opportunity for joint assembly.[8]

These two principles allow for considerable independence of developments while guaranteeing the partners a possible way out if one of them should default, and an incentive to cooperate as long as the terms of the contract are respected. They allow for flexible management of the appropriability of the technology. In developing modular products, the partners ensure that they do not lose everything if one of them opts out. This modularity is also a strong incentive for cooperation.

Response to technical uncertainty

Part of the response to technical uncertainty will be the same as that for opportunism. Opting out by one of the partners may be due to opportunism or to a genuine technical impossibility. The independence of systems favours limiting technical uncertainty and decentralization to work groups. Development areas have been created for each subsystem, the link with the outside being the interface. Dissociation between the different functions (managerial and technical) prevents the confusion of problems. Work group managers appear as operators of 'translation'.[9] The steering committee only controls 'management' variables; it never enters directly into the technology. On the other hand, the dissolution of a work group signifies that the task has been executed and that the technology is stabilized. Similarly, bringing a work group on stream indicates the presence of a problem to be solved. For the steering committee, the work group is a black box: its choices of action are the activation or deactivation of work groups. The modularity of the system ensures the division of tasks, a source for limiting technical uncertainty. Furthermore, work groups which cut across divisional boundaries guarantee the integration of subsets and possibly the redesign of the system capable of functioning without all its components.

Response to competitive uncertainty

The separation between technical and managerial functions makes competitive uncertainty even greater. The project is carried out in a competitive sector where dynamic guidance appears as one of the strategic advantages of the automobile industry in the future. However, taking into account competitive uncertainty is without doubt one of the weak points of Carminat's organization. This weakness cannot be imputed to the organization itself but rather to the composition of the steering committee in which technical prevails over marketing thinking.

Management of externalities and learning

How are links between the different subsystems managed? How are independent developments coordinated? Does the Carminat research programme produce synergy? On the whole, it can be said that the organization of the project and management of learning or externalities are almost contradictory.

Dodgson (1992) and Hamel (1991) show clearly that alliances are often where learning takes place. They even stress that they can be an arena for what amounts to a learning race. The case of cooperative development which I have examined does not support this conclusion. The organization and the technology were conceived and thought through to minimize links between firms and maximize zones of private appropriation, both of technology and of learning. No structure was set up to facilitate simultaneous learning; no formal arrangement described the accumulation of experience and know-how. Neither of these two dimensions was measured or even mentioned during the steering committee's discussions or in its reports.

Management of the Carminat project was thus driven by the need to limit the risks of opportunism among the partners. The method of coordination adopted, based essentially on ways of dealing with technical uncertainty, could – with a few adjustments – also have made possible the management of market uncertainty. In practice, however, market uncertainty was under-emphasized as a result of the technical outlook and orientation of the steering committee members. In contrast, the method of coordination was inappropriate for the management of learning and of externalities from the start. Management of the Carminat programme highlighted the terms in which decisions were made. By emphasizing division of work by specialism, and coordination based on technical interfaces, the programme's partners were not able to take advantage of the learning process, identified by Hamel as an important benefit to be obtained from cooperation.

Table 7.4 Different methods of coordination

Technical product	Non-modular	Divisible into subsystems	Interconnected modular
Project coordination	Little division of work; hierarchical coordination; constitution of a common laboratory; dominant role of the head of the laboratory; important role of partners in strategic orientation of the laboratory	Division of work by speciality; work can be done in the contracting firms, great need for coordination due to incomplete modularity of the system. Contract law and hierarchy are complementary to possible financial incentives to co-operation. The technology permits coordination of work by grass-roots technicians	Distribution of tasks by speciality and by firms. The technology is a mode of coordination. Modularity of the object protects the contractants against opportunism and encourages the partners to cooperate. The dual hierarchical and *ad hoc* link of grass-roots technicians are complementary to the technology as a mode of coordination

Table 7.5   Response to risks

Modularity	Opportunism	Technical uncertainty	Commercial uncertainty	Learning	Integration of new partners
IMTO	Independence of technical developments guarantees against opportunism	Can function without certain modules; partial loss of value	Separation of design and product functions	No collective learning	Easy; need only ensure compatibility of interfaces
TODSS	Strong interdependence of subsystems; necessity for a strong hierarchy to maintain group cohesion	Failure of a subsystem leads to failure of entire system	Unknown	No collective learning unless pooling resources	Easy if general architecture permits it
NMTO	Legal and financial arrangements	Very high due to indivisibility of technical product	Dynamic management taking technical uncertainty into account	Much collective learning	Problems of approachability; difficult to manage; technical difficulties if partners complementary

Although the contracting firms had great weight in the negotiation of the contract, modes of coordination evolved during the course of cooperation. During the development of the technical product, the technology appeared as an essential mode of coordination. For it to play this role, it was essential that overall organization of cooperation limited the risks of opportunism and that it provided satisfactory answers to technical and competitive uncertainty. In the case of a modular project, the independence of modules can play this role of a guarantee against opportunism. However, in contrast, in the case of a technical product divisible into subsystems, other mechanisms must be found. Dubreil (1991) sees internal contracts as an additional mechanism to that of hierarchy for ensuring the viability of the project. Different methods of coordination are shown in Table 7.4.

Each organization responds in a different way to the problems which I have identified: opportunism, technical uncertainty, competitive or market uncertainty, learning, and integration of new partners (see Table 7.5).

CONCLUSION

Following a development research project very closely enables the multiple facets of the technology to be highlighted. Technical choices are influenced by the identity of the partners (the number and the technology which they decide to pool) as well as their respective levels of trust. These parameters enable them to determine both the organizational form chosen to develop the technology and the characteristics of the technical product developed. These characteristics are of course also determined by technological constraints. But the decisions of partners are expressed in the choice between the different available technical options. Technical choices and organizational choices are thus defined together.

During the development of the technical object, the multiplicity of partners and the organizational choices made condition the methods of coordinating the activity. If the modular nature of the technology and the absence of a common laboratory permit the effective control of opportunism and technical uncertainty, in no way are there guarantees against competitive or market uncertainty. It seems, moreover, that this organizational choice is incompatible with the accumulation of learning within firms. In this organizational configuration, the technology seems like a mode of coordination which replaces the hierarchy. The latter is not an effective mode of coordination considering the few prerogatives conferred on the steering committee. The limits to its powers are however logical if one considers the mistrust which reigns within the consortium. Nevertheless, for the technology to be a true mode of coordination, it is necessary for all the rules and conventions governing relations between the partners to be defined and stabilized. By taking a common analytical approach to the links between the partners, the characteristics of the technical products and the mode of coordinating R&D agreements, it is possible to envisage several ways of constituting a typology of R&D agreements or collaboration between laboratories. If this approach provides a conceptual framework which seems coherent, numerous empirical problems still remain. How can the degree of trust between partners be grasped, for example? In the Carminat project, a range of convergent signs (numerous references to the contract in the minutes of the steering committee, the absence of specific finance for the steering committee, etc.) lead us to conclude that there is a high level of mistrust. But the definition of external indicators of trust remains to be found. Similarly, if at first approximation it is possible to define a modular technology and a non-divisible technology, the precise outlines of the boundaries remain to be drawn.

This case was studied in an actor-network perspective. Using an interdisciplinary micro-study, I have attempted to throw some light on the linkages between characteristics of technical products and the way in which they are designed and developed. It provides an interesting framework, but one which needs further development.

NOTES

1. 'Architecture' means the general arrangement of the technical system.
2. I use the term 'pooling the developed technical product', in the sense of 'assembling the developed technical subsystems'.
3. I do not use Tarondeau's definition of modularity. He identifies 'two interchangeable products as two functionally identical products [.....]. The concept of modularity surpasses and includes that of interchangeability. Whilst an interchangeable product can be intended for one use only, a 'module' is an interchangeable product intended for multiple uses' (Tarondeau, 1989, pp. 2371 and 2372).
4. After negotiations which can be lengthy, as is shown by sociologists of science and technology.
5. See Mangematin and Callon (1995) for a presentation of the hypothesis of this model.
6. Details are to be found in Mangematin and Callon (1995).
7. The different subsystems are grouped into categories and mounted on to vehicles.
8. The utility of each subsystem can be divided into the intrinsic utility of the subsystem and its functions; and the option value corresponding to possible integration of the subsystem into Carminat. This option value can be estimated by considering the costs for development and additional tuning necessitated by the cooperation, from which is subtracted the part covered by the public authorities. When the independent developments are complete, the realization of the option proves to be the least costly solution considering the complementarity of subsystems and the costs of redeploying the technology.
9. This concept refers to actor-network theory, in particular to Callon's work.

REFERENCES

Alexander, C. (1964), *Notes on the Synthesis of Forms*, Cambridge, Mass.: Harvard University Press.
Anderson, P. and Tushman, M.L. (1990), 'Technological Discontinuities and Dominant Designs: A Cyclical Model of Technological Change', *Administrative Science Quarterly*, **35** (4), 604–33.

Arthur, B. (1989), 'Competing technologies, increasing returns and lock-in by historical events', *Economic Journal*, **99**, 1131–46.

Bijker, W.J., Hughes, T.P. and Pinch, T. (eds) (1987), *New Directions in the Social Studies of Technology*, Cambridge, Mass.: MIT Press.

Callon, M. (1980), 'The State and Technological Innovation: A Case Study of the Electric Vehicle in France', *Research Policy*, **9**, 358–76.

Callon, M. (1986), 'Éléments pour une sociologie de la traduction. La domestication des coquilles Saint Jacques et des marins pêcheurs dans la baie de Saint Brieuc', *Année sociologique*, **36**, 169–208.

Callon, M. (1993), 'Variety and Irreversibility in networks of technique conception and adoption', in C. Freeman and D. Foray (eds), *Technology and the Wealth of Nations*, London: Pinter.

Callon, M. and Law, J. (1987), 'The Life and Death of an Aircraft: A Network Analysis of Technical Change', Paper presented at the International Workshop on the Integration of Social Historical Studies of Technology, Twente University, the Netherlands.

Clark, K. (1985), 'The Interaction of Design Hierarchies and Market Concepts in Technical Innovation', *Research Policy*, **14**, 235–51.

Cohendet, P. and Llerena, P. (1989), 'Productique et gestion', in *Encyclopédie de gestion*, Paris: Economica.

David, P.A. (1986), 'Understanding the Economics of QWERTY: The Necessity of History', in W.N. Parker (ed.), *Economic History and the Modern Economist*, Oxford: Basil Blackwell, 30–49.

Dodgson, M. (1992), 'Strategy and Technological Learning: An Interdisciplinary Micro study', in R. Coombs, P. Saviotti and V. Walsh (eds), *Technological Change and Company Strategies,* London: Academic Press, 136–63.

Dosi, G. (1982), 'Technological Paradigms and Technological Trajectories: A Suggested Interpretation of the Determinants and Directions of Technical Change', *Research Policy*, **11**, 147–62.

Dubreil, Y. (1991), 'Comment réussir un projet impossible', seminar on Business Life, Report on session, ed. M. Berry.

Eymard Duvernay, F. (1989), 'Conventions de qualité et formes de coordination', *Revue économique*, **40**, 329–59.

Granovetter, M. (1985), 'Economic action and social structure: the problem of embeddness', *American Journal of Sociology*, **91** (3), 481–510.

Hamel, G. (1991), 'Competition for Competence and Interpartner Learning with International Strategic Alliances', *Strategic Management Journal*, **12**, 83–103.

Joly, P.B. and Mangematin, V. (1994), 'Profile of laboratories, industrial partnerships and organization of R&D: The dynamics of relations within industry in a large research organization'. Paper presented at European Network on the Economics of Technological and Institutional Change conference, Strasbourg, October.

Kidder, T. (1982), *Le projet Eagle*, Paris: Flammarion.

Koenig, G. (1990), *Le management stratégique*, Paris: Nathan.

Langlois, R. and Robertson, P. (1992), 'Networks and Innovation in a Modular System: Lessons from the Microcomputer and Stereo Components Industries', *Research Policy*, **21**, 297–313.

Latour, B. (1989), *Science in Action, How to Follow Scientists and Engineers Through Society*, Cambridge, Mass.: Harvard University Press.

Latour, B. (1992), *Aramis ou l'amour des techniques*, Paris: La Découverte.

Lawrence, P. and Lorsch, J. (1967), *Environment and Organisation*, French translation *Environment et Organisation*, Editions des Organisations 1972.

Mangematin, V. (1993), 'Recherche coopérative et stratégies de normalisation', thèse de doctorat, Université Paris IX Dauphine.

Mangematin, V. and Callon, M. (1995), 'Technological Competition, Strategies of the Firms and the Choice of the First Users: The Case of Road Guidance Technologies', *Research Policy*, **24** (3), 441–58.

Mangematin, V. and Rabeharisoa, V. (1992), 'New Ways for Bridging Technology Studies and Economics of Technical Change', 4S/EASST Joint Meeting, Gothenburg, Sweden, August.

Mansfield, E. (1961), 'Technical Change and the Rate of Imitation', *Econometrica*, **29**, 741–66.

Mansfield, E. (1968), *Industrial Research and Technological Change*, New York: Norton.

Metcalfe, J.S. (1988), 'The Diffusion of Innovation: An Interpretative Survey', in G. Dosi et al. (eds), *Technical Change and Economic Theory*, London: Pinter, 560–88.

Nelson, R.R. and Winter, S.G. (1982), *An Evolutionary Theory of Economic Change*, Cambridge, Mass.: Harvard University Press.

Pavitt, K. (1990), 'What We Know about Strategic Management of Technology', *California Management Review*, Spring, 17–26.

Simon, H. (1962), 'The Architecture of Complexity', *Proceedings of the American Philosophical Society*, **106** (6), December, 941–73.

Tarondeau, J.C. (1982), *Produits et technologies*, Paris: Dalloz.

Tarondeau, J.C. (1989), 'Produits', in *Encyclopédie de gestion*, Paris: Economica, 2357–74.

Teece, D. (1990), 'Innovation and the Organisation of Industry', CCC Working Paper no. 90–6, University of Berkeley.

Von Hippel E. and Urban, G. (1988), 'Lead User analyses for the Development of Industrial Products', *Management Science*, **34** (5), 569–82.

Weil, B. and Moisdon, J.C. (1992), 'Groupes transversaux et coordination technique dans la conception d'un nouveau véhicule', *Cahier de Recherche*, no. 3.

Wolff, S. (1992), 'Accords inter-enterprises et flexibilité', thèse de doctorat, Beta, Strasbourg.

Woodward, J. (1965), *Industrial Organisation: Theory and Practice*, London: Oxford University Press.

Xuereb, J.M. (1991), 'Une re-définition du processus d'innovation', *Revue Française de gestion*, July.

8. The technoeconomic network: a socioeconomic approach to state intervention in innovation

Philippe Larédo and Philippe Mustar

INTRODUCTION

The paper explores the outcome of some major EC programmes whose stated aims have been the encouragement of European technological competitiveness through the support of 'precompetitive' cooperative R&D.[1] The empirical work on which this paper is based is a survey of over 1,000 French industrial, academic and government research laboratories and their participation in EC programmes between 1983 and 1988.

This evaluation exercise chose not to address only the direct economic benefits which individual participants derived from the EC support but to take as the central focus of its analysis the two assumptions which underlie EC intervention: the collaborative pattern and the pre-competitive aim of the work undertaken. The two major findings of the research concern the nature and organization of the cooperative research carried out as a result of these programmes.

We use the term 'basic technological research' to reflect the nature of the research – technological because a majority of teams (not just the industrial teams) were taking part on the assumption that a new commercial product or process would evolve out of their work; and basic because a large majority of all teams (not just the academics) placed a great deal of importance on outputs normally regarded as associated with academic work, such as publications in refereed journals and the production of PhDs. This led us to re-think the conventional difference between 'fundamental' and 'applied' or 'industrial' and 'academic' research, and describe 'basic technological research' as a new form of research activity.

The organizational forms that were developed to carry out the cooperative research and gain maximum benefit from it, involved the building of links between a variety of heterogeneous actors, including university laboratories, technical research centres, financial organizations, users, public authorities, etc. These are organized relations that mobilize various types of intermediaries and coordination mechanisms, which did not limit themselves to research, but embraced all elements and actors of the innovation process. We have proposed to call these arrangements 'techno-economic networks' and the paper argues that the TEN is a new form of economic actor.

In analysing these phenomena, the paper draws together ideas from the sociology of innovation, notably the actor-network approach developed at CSI, some recent developments in the economics of technical change, particularly those which focus on inter-firm cooperation, and the work of science policy analysts concerned with government and EC policy instruments intended to promote technological competitiveness.

R&D POLICY AND THE RISE OF 'TECHNOLOGICAL PROGRAMMES'

Public policies for supporting, stimulating or orienting research have been profoundly modified in the course of the past few years. They no longer limit themselves to the development of a public scientific and technological potential by creating and supporting research organizations or agencies. Neither do they consider that focusing on 'large' projects (such as the Apollo programme) is enough to promote innovation. In the wake of what has been termed by politicians 'technological competitiveness', a new type of state intervention has spread in most industrialized countries and has very fast become a major R&D policy instrument: acronyms like ESPRIT or RACE illustrate the rise of the 'technological programme' (Rip, 1988).

Whatever form they may take, technological programmes have in common three main features (Callon et al., 1989):

1. They constitute an engagement of limited duration – it may go on for several years, but there is a definite endpoint.
2. The technological programme is directly inserted in the pre-existing competitive milieu: it does not aim to create *ex nihilo* a new market but rather draws on a given economic environment and supports the efforts of its actors to improve their international standing.
3. It is not aimed at supporting individual actors as such but rather at developing an economic environment, and so the technological programme does not focus directly on marketable products; it rather seeks to develop the key skills for the realization of new products and thus the creation of competitive advantage.

These various characteristics lead us to propose a more general definition of a technological programme that brings out the central feature of its operation: the encouragement of heterogeneous actors (scientific research laboratories, technical research centres, industrial companies) often in competition with each other (two companies or two laboratories) to collectively identify for particular geopolitical areas (regions, nations, Europe, etc.) those skills that will become strategic in the future, and to develop programmes enabling their development and application.

Such an approach explains why the evaluation of their effects face serious difficulties. First there can no longer be any direct connection with traditional approaches of measuring economic benefits (sales, employment, profits and so on): one has to question the economic and social theories which underlie science policy assumptions. We shall see how much these new patterns of state intervention relate to recent results in both the economics of technical change and sociology of science/innovation. At the same time, this raises the question of the effective outcomes of such public intervention. Through an empirical analysis of EC programmes, we argue that they simultaneously promote a new type of research activity – basic technological research – and a new organizational arrangement crucial to innovation processes – the technoeconomic network.

LESSONS FROM THE ECONOMICS OF TECHNICAL CHANGE AND THE SOCIOLOGY OF INNOVATION

Science policy has long been based on one main assumption derived from neoclassical economics: the consideration of science as non-appropriable information. The use of the technological programme as a policy instrument requires us to re-think the assumptions underlying state intervention in R&D, to use the recognized OECD terminology. This will be done by focusing on four main directions: challenging the idea of science as a public good; questioning the linear model of innovation; underlining the importance of dependency paths and initial phases; and the crucial role of collaborations. We shall simultaneously consider research results from the economics of technical change and from the sociology of science/innovation.

Science as a Public Good

First, the definition of technological programmes breaks with the traditional model of science as a public good. In this model, there is a strict barrier between 'fundamental' and 'applied' science (recall the UK debate on science policy at the beginning of the 1970s). Fundamental science is defined both by its mechanism of production (curiosity-driven) and by the fact that its results cannot be appropriated at the individual level. Thus nobody has an interest in developing it on their own and it is the role of the state(s) to organize the production of this collective good and to make it available to all its constituents. In such a scheme, research results can be considered as gathered on the shelves of a huge supermarket in which everybody can come and freely pick up what they require for their own activities. Private efforts (and indeed public ones for the other collective goods for which they are directly responsible) focus on applied R&D which is directly connected to market objectives and is appropriable, the patenting system being the public organization for the respect of individual property rights.

The nature of research as a public good, which was for a long time a debate between economists and has been made the object of many empirical studies showing how much social benefits supersede private ones (e.g. Arrow, 1962; Griliches, 1964), has again been at the forefront of discussions since the beginning of the 1980s, from both the economic and sociological angle. Economic analysis focuses on the multiple barriers to access to this supposedly publicly available knowledge; it underlines that heavy human investments are required to enable companies to follow the dynamics of science and to absorb its results (Mariti and Smiley, 1983; Teece 1986). Watkins (1991) proposes to extend Williamson's transaction costs theory from the marketing and producing aspects to technological information: 'technological communications costs' are the main factor limiting this 'absorptive capacity' (Cohen and Levinthal, 1989) and, for instance, explain the movement of large multinational companies towards the creation of in-house basic research laboratories. Seen from the 'other side', science studies have demonstrated how much 'tacit knowledge' was involved in the building of new knowledge (Collins, 1974) and thus in its circulation and the ability of firms to capture it in their innovations. And many studies on innovations (Hughes, 1983; Latour, 1989, to name only a few) have pointed to the importance of (human and financial) investments required for the connection of adequate economic and academic interests.

In such an environment, technological programmes appear as a means to promote direct links between selected public 'scientists' and private 'engineers' in order to make the construction of relevant knowledge and its effective circulation possible.

From the Linear to the 'block-building' Model of Innovation

Innovation has long been described as a linear process going from one step to another once the initial decision is made. This initiation could either come from the engineers – technology push – or from demand – market pull. Typically large public programmes such as the space one could be classified in the first category while incremental innovations adapting existing products would correspond to the latter. Having said this, it is easy to go to the next step and define one role for state intervention: to support these technological pushes, all the more since any such technical advance would be considered as bringing progress to society. Technological programmes, by focusing on existing markets and actors, and at the same time trying to anticipate the next generation of technology, obliged us to question these relations. Again, recent economic and sociological findings have helped in strongly reshaping these connections. Kline and Rosenberg (1986, 1986) opened the black box and revealed the role of the multiple links which had to be developed within the firm and the iterative process which this implied between the different units of the innovating firm. Von Hippel (1988) added outside units to this chain-link model by showing the role of the 'lead users' in this process. In this approach research activities are still seen as one homogeneous step similar to production or marketing. This conception was challenged by sociologists studying cases of breakthrough innovations. Akrich et al. (1987) in their synthesis also focused on the iterative dimension of the innovation process; but at the same time they underlined the numerous actors who participate in this process, making the innovative firm the actor who crystallizes in the innovation all the stabilized links agreed upon by these heterogeneous actors. The innovation is thus described as an iterative process which drives the potential innovation to gain progressively its definite shape through all the adaptations and transformations it undertakes in order to acquire more and more allies: the invention actually turns into an innovation when new alliances no longer compel the transformation of the artefact.

A first modification of the innovation model was thus identified: one could no longer establish nice clean borders between different phases, research activities and development, for instance. In other words, there were no longer clear-cut attributions between phases and actors: at any moment in the innovation, lead users or scientists could be called upon to help solve a problem. As lead users were the representatives of future customers, the question rapidly arose about the intervention of scientists in the process: science was no longer only seen as information and required direct connections with public laboratories. So what should the innovating company internalize? How could it develop 'specific assets'? What should it share and what should it strictly appropriate? Some economists tended to separate 'technology' and 'innovations', seeing the former as 'not fully appropriable' (Bozeman et al., 1986) or an area 'where research results are non rival' (Watkins, 1991) or dedicated to 'knowledge production activities' (Mytelka and Delapierre, 1988). Some authors even went to the point of considering that technologies were non-rival in consumption (Von Hippel, 1987).

Implicitly these analyses draw upon what could be termed a 'block-building' model of innovation, whereby skills and knowledge about bricks can be shared between competing firms. These firms then develop a competitive edge in the market thanks to their in-house engineering abilities to assemble and transform these shared bricks into products and processes. In turn, this model clearly addresses long-standing policy issues: how to help in the organizing of such bricks? French 'centres techniques' whose funding is based on specific professional taxes have been a postwar answer to bridge the technical gap. And this, as all the surveys on ESPRIT, RACE and Eureka programmes show, is the main aim of technological programmes, i.e. collective skill building and cost sharing of what may be termed, following the UK debate in the 1970s on strategic science (for a recent review see Senker, 1991), 'strategic competencies'.

The Role of Initial Phases and Dependency Paths

The problem is then to anticipate these strategic competencies. Recent 'evolutionary' theories (see e.g. Arthur, 1988 or Foray, 1990) have shown that 'two technologies or products performing the same function' have unpredictable but unequal chances of sharing the market; it depends on the initial 'small events' (such as the early choice by the US marines of the light water nuclear reactor – Cowan, 1990) which favour one against the other. Through 'learning by using' (Rosenberg, 1982), economies of scale in production (Metcalfe, 1988), information dissemination and its effects on future adoptions and network externalities (Chandler, 1977), a self-reinforcing mechanism operates and produces 'lock-in effects' often up to a technological monopoly. Such situations studied by economists have their equivalent in historico-socio-philosophical studies of science (Latour, 1987) which show similar initial choices resulting in the discarding of potential theoretical orientations, a movement strongly reinforced with the rise of large instruments (such as CERN) and 'big' science. Many examples of such a situation can be found in the recent scientific advances in superconductivity or the debate on cold fusion. Both groups of analysts emphasize the role of initial phases in this process.

This problem is at the core of technological programmes: by operating a 'strategic co-programming' (through an 'orchestration' model – Nederhof, 1990) and by driving all interested partners to collectively determine long-term research axes and strategic developments (through foresight exercises – see Irvine and Martin 1989), they try to offer an answer while formalizing the process which should produce these 'small events'.

The Role of Inter-Firm Collaborations

If science is no longer only information and requires direct connections between researchers and engineers; if technologies are non-rival in consumption; and if collective anticipation is crucial to their identification and development, we cannot be surprised to see collaborations between numerous actors being a key feature both of innovation processes and of technological programmes. Inter-firm collaborative ventures have been a growing field of analysis for economists of technical change, cooperative arrangements in industrial R&D being seen as 'a middle ground between the two primary foci of economic theory to date: markets and hierarchies' (Watkins, 1991). Most surveys insist on the growing importance of technological agreements in collaborative ventures (Chesnais, 1988; Mytelka, 1990; Hagedoorn and Schakenraad, 1990). Why is it so? First, such technological collaborations make it possible to obtain the same advantages as with the hierarchical organization of firms but without losing flexibility: spread risks, gain economies of scale, achieve a critical mass of skills, avoid duplications. Second, they make it possible to exploit 'systems properties of new technologies' and to favour their diffusion through 'cross-disciplinary alliances in applications-specific markets' (Mytelka, 1990): this gives an impetus both to a reduction of lead times for the introduction of new technologies and in a wider spectrum of applications.

The context of such analyses has to be noted here, since most of them draw on 'evaluations' of recent research policies: the US National Cooperative Research Act (Scott, 1988), the Japanese and the EC programmes (Ouchi and Bolton, 1988; Mytelka, 1990; Hagedoorn and Schakenraad, 1990, Watkins, 1991). This makes the link with most science policy and sociological studies, which focus on the role of such programmes in fostering links: evaluations like those of Alvey (Guy, 1991) or of EC research programmes have all pointed to the numerous and durable connections which derive from them and associate heterogeneous actors: university laboratories, company laboratories and so on.

State Intervention in Perspective

The four main attributes which characterize technological programmes appear thus strongly related to recent results both in the economics and the sociology of innovation. It is, from our point of view, an interesting result to see that a policy instrument could be developed (even if it has been in a clearly localized international setting) at the same time as changes were occurring. Up to now studies dealing with them have focused on two main aims: first to identify and illustrate this movement; second to justify such state intervention either through non-appropriation motives (Ouchi and Bolton, 1988; Mansfield, 1990) or through 'impure public goods' approaches (Watkins, 1991). In all these studies, little has been said about the so-called 'consortia' thus built and the concrete production to which they lead. To get a better insight was the main object of our empirical study of the effects of the EC programmes (taken as a whole) on the French scientific and technological fabric (Larédo and Callon, 1990). We shall focus on two main aspects.

'Techno-economic networks' (TENs)

The creation of collective knowledge and skills does not necessarily only mean inter-firm cooperation: most analyses of European programmes have forgotten that half the participants are not industrial companies but public laboratories. Could it be that programmes were completely dual-oriented? This is a difficult hypothesis to prove. Furthermore if 'technologies are non-rival in consumption', one can easily argue that public participation is yet another way to lower costs while at the same time reinforcing the nature of research as a public good and thus justifying state intervention. We shall even see that universities play a central role in developing the firms' absorptive capacity through the PhD students and their embodied knowledge. This enlargement is not fortuitous or undifferentiated, one public laboratory being equivalent to another; on the contrary, the search for adequate laboratories and the establishing of specific connections (often through ex-graduates and PhDs) are key ingredients of such collaborations. This corresponds to a different reality from the one described by the 'consortia' terminology. A later section will use our results to make a first attempt to analyse the composition and structure of these 'techno-economic networks' (TENs).

Basic technological research

The content which helps in the emergence and construction of TENs we propose to call 'basic technological research'. We have already differentiated between strategic competencies and engineering skills. Is it enough to qualify the type of works performed in such emerging TENs? Is it not too loose a definition to enable us to get a better insight of TENs dynamics? Again, the empirical study makes it possible to answer these questions in part and offers a clearer definition of the actual content of the relationships built up.

Before presenting the results which drive us to these conclusions, we review the method which we used to gather the relevant information and which determined the size of our 'sample'. The reader will have thus a clearer view of which industrial activities and settings are concerned and what technological programmes represent for them.

EC Programmes and the French Science and Technology Community

We used a mailed survey[2] for the collection of four major sets of information about research actors: identification and characterization of participating teams; type and degree of involvement in EC programmes; their visions of EC programme objectives; the hoped-for outputs classified in two categories: direct (articles, theses, patents, innovation projects, etc.) and new collaborations with other research actors. It addressed all French teams financially supported by EC programmes between 1983 and 1987. Two aspects are of relevance for the analysis.

First, the survey deals with a large sample of the French S&T community: over a thousand teams were concerned, 25 per cent being 'industrial' and the others belonging to public research organizations or universities. It would thus be quite restricting to consider only private industrial research laboratories collaborations since it would exclude three partners out of four in such networks.

Altogether the sample represents a quarter of the relevant public S&T potential,[3] equally split between 'academic' institutions (universities and CNRS) and 'mission-oriented' research organizations.[4] It also involves more than half of the French industrial research effort.[5] It is interesting to note that, apart from the pharmaceutical industry, nearly all main manufacturing activities are significantly covered (over a third of the national potential), some even being heavily involved (over two-thirds of the national potential), mainly in electronics, computers, telecommunications and transport.

Second, EC funding represents on average a quarter of total funding,[6] this figure being quite similar for all types of participating teams (see Table 8.1). These figures (which are not commonly available for research teams and have been verified through random checks afterwards) demonstrate that public intervention through technological programmes is not a marginal phenomenon; it has to be considered, even just at the financial level, as a strong element in R&D strategy building for larger companies which have developed specialized research laboratories.

Table 8.1 Origin of funds of teams participating in EC programmes

	Average for all participating teams (%)	Average for all industrial teams (%)	Average for all public research teams (%)
Own resources	43	45	43
Public contracts			
National	19	13	20
EC	23	24	23
Clients and other			
sources	15	18	14
Total	100	100	100

Source: Larédo and Callon (1990).

ONE MAJOR OUTPUT: BASIC TECHNOLOGICAL RESEARCH

When asked about the 'direct' results teams were expecting from their participation, we were struck by the interchanges which took place in what are considered the traditional roles of public and industrial scientists. We observed that both shared simultaneously in the academic outputs generally associated with 'fundamental' research and in the commercial hopes usually associated with 'applied' research. We also noted the limited importance of traditional outputs linked to industrial research (patents, norms, prototypes etc.) and the emergence of a new type of production, method and software, all elements which drove us to propose the concept of 'basic technological research' to grasp this new focus for research activities.

Numerous 'Academic' Outputs

As expected in 'fundamental' research, publications and PhDs were highly cited. Three teams out of four intended to publish articles in international journals (and in English: remember that we are dealing with French teams!). The common idea which links industry participation to secrecy does not seem to be confirmed: teams belonging to programmes such as ESPRIT intended to produce as many publications as teams participating in SCIENCE, which can be considered as the archetype of the academic programme. And within such programmes, industrial researchers are no less productive than their university colleagues (five articles instead of seven per project!). PhDs were a second commonly cited output, mentioned in large numbers (on average three PhDs per supported team) by two-thirds of the teams and more than one industrial team out of three.[7]

Clear Commercial Goals

All this goes along with the fostering of 'basic knowledge' which two-thirds of respondents expected from the EC programmes: are we then facing a situation whereby, thanks to EC funding, basic research activities would also be undertaken by large firms having developed central laboratories (and chasing, like IBM researchers, after Nobel prizes)? It is an open question. Still, we have clear indications of a different nature: more than half the teams participating in these programmes expect a new commercial product or process to evolve directly out of their work, and in most cases less than five years after the end of the action. In these programmes, public teams are as numerous as industrial teams in giving a positive answer: when a public team participates in such a programme, it joins a 'club' (Callon et al., 1989) which has commercialization as one of its objectives. On the other hand, negative answers are not the specialty of public teams since nearly four industrial teams out of ten cannot directly link their work with a forthcoming identified commercial output.

Methods Rather Than Patents or Commercial Products

Applied research is usually linked upstream with patents and downstream with 'industrial development', embedded most of the time in prototypes or 'large-scale' pilots.

Clearly none of these outputs is of significance for participating teams: less than one out of twenty mentions patents. The same figure applies for pilots and prototypes. One may hope for commercialization and yet produce other outputs than these. Preliminary interviews had made us conscious of this potential gap, so we had offered teams another possible answer:[8] 'methods'. And it gathered a significant percentage of answers: they are cited by one team out of three as one of their expected outputs and they account for two-thirds of the remaining answers (apart from basic knowledge).

From 'Precompetitive Research' to 'Basic Technological Research'

Important academic outputs, high hopes for commercialization, a major role for 'methods' – all shared by academic and industrial teams: does not it point to the rise of a new form of research? In the following paragraph we shall explain why we propose to name it 'basic technological research' (BTR).

Let us analyse the content of this research activity: it is largely devoted to the elaboration of new methods, often linked to feasibility studies and a large share of its output consists of computer models and the simulations which go with them. This establishes a new relation between theoretical work and experimental activities: instead of realizing complicated and costly experiments on pilots or prototypes, the validation of the concept and the design studies are carried out through the development and use of mathematical models. This results in two complementary types of output: first, new knowledge which needs to be evaluated as such by peers (creation of models and formal definition of physical and chemical mechanisms on which they rely); and second, measures and information specific to a given productive activity, which are localized in participating companies and which they may use in their in-house innovative efforts. This explains the double nature of this type of research: it is technological because it is geared towards a specific industrial activity and the new skills it requires; and it is 'basic' as it aims to create new knowledge of generic interest. Such research is thus characterized by two sets of constraints, often seen as contradictory, and by the two corresponding evaluation mechanisms: the production of certified knowledge (hence the numerous publications in international journals mentioned) and the insertion in in-house innovation processes (hence the high expectations for future commercial activities).

This combination of research activities generates a type of knowledge which large terminologies such as 'skills' or 'knowledge base' do not adequately describe; in the 'block-building' model of innovation, it only deals with part of the bricks (see Figure 8.1 for a tentative positioning of this type of research). And the label of 'precompetitive' research, often referred to by policy analysts when speaking of such collaborative schemes, does not seem adequate to describe this reality either. First, it strongly refers to the public good model, thus not taking into account the localized benefits which explain why industrial

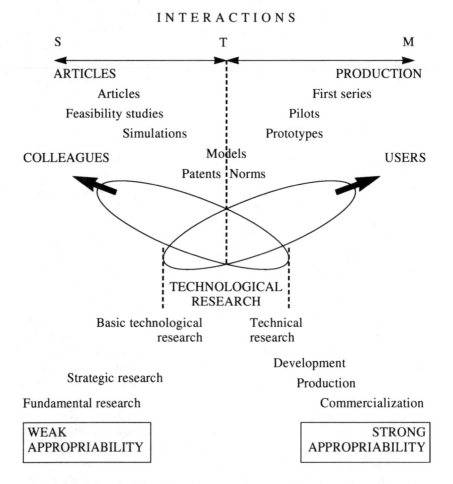

Figure 8.1   Interactions between articles and production

firms share in such activities. Second, it seems to establish barriers, even frontiers, between two separate worlds, and all the evidence gathered goes against it. What we see, as in the plays by Marivaux, is a permanent interchange of roles: university researchers act as industrialists and hope for commercialization while industrial engineers taste the supposedly forbidden pleasures of academic publication! Such a situation clearly relates, at a different level, to organizational architectures described by Wakasuki (1988) in his consideration of the Japanese Opti-electronic research association and go further than the simple 'exchange of technological information' supposed to be connected to joint R&D projects as long as they do not develop specific infrastructures. This drives us directly to the second and inseparable dimension to this new type of research activity: it establishes new durable connections between institutionally heterogeneous actors.

TOWARDS A NEW ECONOMIC ENTITY: THE TEN

When qualifying the type of research undertaken under the umbrella of technological programmes, one is thus referred to the organizational dimensions underlying the emergence of BTR. In this last section we shall examine the relations so developed and propose, through the concept of TEN, an enlargement of the 'chain-linked' model of innovation (Kline and Rosenberg, 1986) and the 'intra-firm cooperation' model described by Aoki (1989) by taking into account cooperative organizational architectures (Foray, 1990) which do not limit themselves to inter-firm arrangements such as those analysed in the 'umbrella consortia' approach (Watkins, 1991) when studying the effects of the ESPRIT and EUREKA programmes. First we present the main findings on which such proposals are based in order to make the point about TEN clearer.

Numerous New Actors

Abbing and Schakenraad (1990), using the MERIT-CATI database which enables a comparison of private cooperative agreements with those promoted under EC programmes, arrives at the conclusion that most of them (with the possible exception of SMEs) existed before EC action. This may be true with inter-firm cooperative patterns of large firms but our study shows very different conclusions, especially for a programme like ESPRIT. In this programme, participants have met, on average, seven new partners (we must recall that, again on average, an ESPRIT participant participates in more than two projects) and, for a third of them, they think this new link will go beyond the end of the programme.

Universities at the Core of these Collaborative Arrangements

Who are these new partners? Two points here are of interest. The first cited partners are nearly always homologues (companies first cite other companies; public research laboratories other public research laboratories etc.). The technological programmes seem to be the occasion to link with competitors from other EC countries, thus organizing the initial small events previously mentioned so that coordination for similar activities may operate at the future single-market level. The other interesting feature deals with university laboratories: for all types of participating actors, they are the most cited type of new partner. There is a strong convergence in the answers to many different questions which indicate their central position in the construction of BTR. One can see three reasons for this: academic publication; embodied knowledge in PhDs as a sure means of integrating this newly built basic research; and last but not least, it is well known that universities depend quite strongly on their industrial links (both to ensure adequate positions for their ex-students and as a source of research funds[9]). There is a fourth reason which sociologists would rank first: such collaborations between heterogeneous partners are not easily built and developed and they often require a recognized mediation which organizes communication, through meetings and exchanges. Universities are well placed to play this role and foster this cooperative learning process.

The Intensity of Exchanges and the Change in R&D Practices

How do these consortia work? We got only limited, though valuable, information on this. For instance, in ESPRIT projects, people meet once a month on average: this is far too often if people only exchange technological information and it incurs significant organizational costs (indeed underlined in the evaluations performed both for ESPRIT and BRITE, some interviewees even saying that EC money just covered these organizational costs). Asked about internal practices, nearly one participant out of two mentioned that these collaborations drove them to adopt new working methods. The further evaluation of EC 'concerted actions' in medical research (Larédo et al., 1992) illustrates this aspect: the harmonization of laboratory practices and the systematic comparisons of experimental results, the exchanges of samples, reagents, software, computer programmes, the construction of common tools such as databases or unique analytical tools, the recognition of leading teams on specialized aspects – all this points to the progressive construction of 'common' specializations. If such collaborative arrangements enable participating firms to internally mobilize the results obtained, they do not enable one actor alone to further develop them without the others; even when acquiring the specific competences he lacks, such an actor would have difficulty in rebuilding the whole process of internal 'harmonization' created during the collaboration and which renders individual activities in different settings both comparable and aggregative. In saying this, we are employing dimensions used to describe the 'industrial district' (see Foray, 1990) and its positive sum game (Klein, 1988), but taking into account a larger set of partners than only firms.

From Inter-firm Consortia to TEN

In the chain-linked model, the 'downstream integration of crucially complementary activities' considers research as a homogeneous phase to be integrated with the other internal steps of the production process (development, test, design and marketing). Inter-firm cooperation patterns add to this model of organizational design to share 'technologies'. In such a situation, not only do resources acquire supplementary qualities through integration, but flexibility can be maintained through an adequate equilibrium of internal and external activities. These analyses, however relevant, lack, in our opinion, at least two complementary and paradoxically similar approaches. 'Downstream', one may question the internalization of 'markets' through 'marketing activities'. Von Hippel has underlined the role of 'lead users' in the innovation process, with very similar findings made by sociologists about the innovation process (see Akrich et al., 1987). And we have just shown, 'upstream', a similar situation by which science can no longer be considered as undifferentiated and requires direct connections in order to stimulate firms' absorptive capacity. This double aggregation of specific actors in the traditional object of analysis of economists, the firm, can no longer be assimilated in any type of public good or externality since its benefits are strictly localized (even when locally shared). We are thus facing an emerging new economic actor, no longer built on an informal assimilation between the 'economic' firm and the 'legal' companies, but on a flexible and reversible arrangement of heterogeneous actors with different institutional backgrounds. We have proposed to name them 'techno-economic networks' (Callon et al., 1992).

What we define as a TEN is a coordinated set of heterogeneous actors – laboratories, technical research centres, financial organizations, users and public authorities – which participate collectively in the development and diffusion of innovations, and which organize, via numerous interactions, the relationships between research and the market-place. A network is not just defined by the actors that make it up. A whole set of intermediaries circulates between them which give material contents to the links uniting the actors: they can be written documents (scientific articles, reports, experimental data, patents etc.), incorporated skills (researchers changing laboratory, engineers moving between companies), money (contracts for cooperation, subsidies and grants, financial loans, initial purchase by a client), and support materials (samples, reagents or

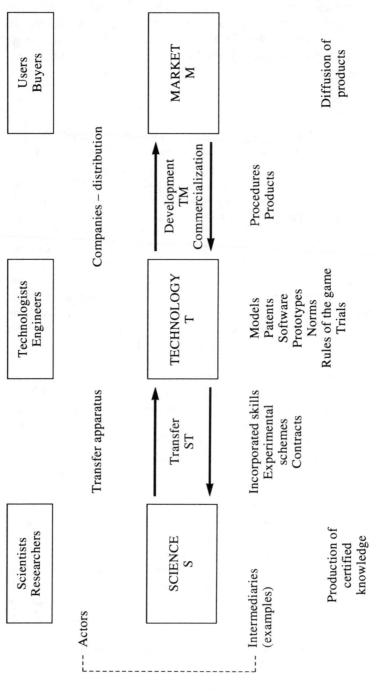

Figure 8.2   The technoeconomic network

reference materials), technical artefacts (software, prototypes, machines etc.). We have proposed that a TEN is built around five major poles out of which three are the supporting pillars. The scientific pole (S) is characterized by the production of certified knowledge (most of the time through articles in refereed journals). The technical pole (T) corresponds to the conception, elaboration and transformation of material objects that have their own coherence (assuring them durability and reliability) and capable of rendering services (i.e. contributing to the realization of certain programmes of action). The market pole (M) corresponds to the universe of users; it is not the market as defined in economic theory as the place where supply meets demand, but this terminology draws heavily on the practitioners' definition of the market: identity of users, nature of their 'needs', information on their expectations, hierarchy of preferences, forms of organization etc. There is no *a priori* equivalence between those pillars and their output, for instance between certified knowledge and a technical object. Coherence between the two is progressively constructed, step by step, by trial and error.[10] If it turns out that the results obtained by a given laboratory are transformed into innovations, this is not the fruit of some miraculous happenstance. There has been a deliberate process of engendering and nurturing of these different activities, and by successive iterations this has permitted a progressive co-adaptation and complementarity between the one and the other. If one wants to describe the network as a whole, then two further mediating poles need to be added. What we call the development – commercialization pole consists of production and distribution activities that mobilize technology to create/satisfy needs (TM). The transfer pole (ST) specializes in connecting science and technology.

If we speak of a network, it is, on one hand, to underline the heterogeneity of actors and activities, the flexibility of arrangements and the diversity of coordination mechanisms; but it is also to point to the existence of a new 'actor' capable of a collective attitude and strategy and able to build a clear differentiation (even if it changes over time) between itself and the outside world.[11] Figure 8.2 illustrates this definition connecting it to the major groups of actors who intervene and to the main intermediaries that circulate.

Technological Programmes and the Emergence of TENs

All the evidence gathered shows the role of EC intervention in the intermediation between the scientific and technical poles: in supporting and developing BTR and the corresponding cooperations between actors, they contribute to the emergence of TENs and to their upstream consolidation.

The main justification for state intervention lies in the cost of establishing such networks. Technological programmes help marriages, all the more difficult as they deal simultaneously with five or more partners who know little about each other, who live in distant worlds and who do not necessarily have the same projects or attitudes. How many trials and errors before arriving at the right combination! How many lost investments before each partner is paid back by the created synergies and before network externalities are such that a university professor, an industry engineer, a marketing man and a user take advantage of the collaboration and prefer it to individual action! Once these relations have been established, then it is time for public authorities to withdraw their support: localized positive feedbacks and externalities are such that everybody has an interest in collaborating and maintaining the established TEN. Characterizing the two main types of outcomes deriving from technological programmes, we are then sent back to a new set of assumptions justifying state intervention, its roles and limits.

CONCLUSIONS

Using results from economists of technical change, sociologists of innovation and science policy analysts, we have shown that technological programmes, which are newcomers as policy instruments, are strongly connected in their conceptual framework to recent results in social sciences. For both, science can no longer be considered as a public good. Both reject the linear model to implicitly develop a 'block-building' model of innovation which differentiates between the 'knowledge base' and 'engineering skills'. Both recognize the importance of the early stages in the innovation process and the role of what may be termed small initial events. Both think that 'technologies are non-rival in consumption' and thus can be developed on a collective base which justifies the growing importance of inter-firm collaborations.

Economic and science policy studies of these programmes have underlined their effective role in inter-firm collaborations; most of them link such developments to three complementary approaches: an impure public good model where benefits cannot be fully appropriated, state incentives thus being necessary and inter-firm collaboration the best way to minimize costs; an enlargement of the transaction costs theory to technological communications costs which, on the contrary, focuses on all the organizational forms necessary to develop the absorptive capacity of firms and, thus, their ability to adapt to new emerging technological potentialities; and an industrial localization model which leads to cost and competence sharing on 'bricks'.

All three underline the growing importance of inter-firm coordination, outside the market and outside hierarchies, on the upstream side of R&D activities. Staying within the strict boundaries of competing firms, they ignore a large portion of the picture: our survey of the impacts of all EC programmes on the French S&T

community shows the importance of public research teams (and especially university teams) in these booming 'consortia'. A more in-depth analysis of the content of such collaborations points to the emergence of a new type of research activity we name 'basic technological research' (BTR). Focusing on methods and on computer models, it builds up a corpus of new knowledge at the same time which has to be evaluated by peers within the research community. The outcome and information may be specific to a given productive activity, which will be internalized in the participating companies, and used by them in their in-house innovative efforts.

Such research activities establish connections between heterogeneous actors which go far beyond the simple exchange of technological information and can be characterized by similar concepts to those used for the localized positive feedback derived from intra-firm collaborations or the positive sum game associated with the industrial district.

This features 'upstream' a similar transformation of relations to the 'environment' as Von Hippel's results feature 'downstream' with the role of lead users. No longer can science and markets be taken as undifferentiated entities: competing firms establish direct relations with identified scientists, and users create a new type of composite economic agent. Coupling these results to those previously obtained, we propose to extend the analysis by considering the collaborating actors as a whole: TENs are thus at the core of a contextual transformation of innovation activities, and their creation and emergence are the central preoccupation of technological programmes. One could even argue that the concept of TENs can contribute to a revised theoretical approach which is consistent at both the micro (firm, laboratory) and macro (industry, national economy, European) level of analysis and be a key unit in the emerging analysis of 'systems of innovation', be they local, national, European or global.

Our survey suggests that, while focusing on the BTR level, technological programmes (here at the EC level) are very active in promoting this institutional and economic reorganization.

NOTES

1. EC research policy is decided on a four-year basis and inscribed in the 'framework programme', which is in turn implemented through 'scientific programmes'. ESPRIT, the largest one, deals with information technologies. BRITE deals with manufacturing technologies, robotics and new materials; RACE with telecommunications technologies; and NNE with renewable energy sources and energy savings. All these programmes have in common fixed terms at the end of which they are evaluated before the next stage can be implemented. We were in 1993 in the third ESPRIT round, the fourth NNE (now labelled JOULE) and the second BRITE.
2. See Larédo and Callon (1990) for a full presentation of the methodology adopted.
3. Covering what is usually labelled 'exact sciences', i.e. not including humanities and social sciences as well as the life sciences.

4. See Irvine and Martin (1989) for related definitions.
5. A tenth of the companies doing research under the Frascati definition, but, owing to the concentration of research efforts on a limited number of large firms, more than half of the French S&T potential.
6. The notion of total funding has different meanings depending on the institutional background. For all academic teams and half of the teams dependent upon public research institutions, the reference is only to 'marginal funds' (excluding salaries of permanent researchers) while for the other half (e.g. teams belonging to CEA, the French atomic research organization) and for industrial research laboratories, 'total costs' refer to classical definitions (with salaries and equipment amortizations). Since we are only searching for costs that teams are responsible for, and within them, for the role of 'outside' funding, this difference in definitions does not change the meaning of the results and thus these can be compared.
7. We even calculated that nearly one PhD out of eight in France in the 'exact' sciences received some kind of financial support through an EC programme.
8. One must remember the limitations of any mailed questionnaire for this has a relevance for the preliminary interviews, the objective of which is to draw a map of possible answers (here 80 interviews). The mailed questionnaire will then weigh the different opinions, non-answering rates or answers to the 'other reasons' items being strong indicators of an unsatisfactory spread of possible answers. In this case both conditions were matched to give a clear significance to the relative weights observed.
9. This is well illustrated by the results obtained: university laboratories are those who are most dependent for their research funds on private 'clients', far more than any other type of public laboratory and even more than industrial companies.
10. See Vinck and Larédo in Larédo (1992), for examples of such dynamics promoted by the EC medical research programme.
11. In our study of the networks of the EC medical research programme we have shown how this differentiation goes with the establishment of internal rules which cover a whole range of practices and behaviours.

REFERENCES

Abbing, M.R. and Schakenraad, J. (1990), 'Joint R&D Activities of Firms in European Cost-Sharing Programmes', MERIT, mimeo.

Akrich, M., Callon, M. and Latour, B. (1987), ' A Quoi Tient le Succès des Innovations', *Gérer et Comprendre*, (11 & 12).

Aoki, M. (1989), 'Global Competition, Firm Organization and TFP: a comparative micro-perspective', *OECD Seminar on Science, Technology and Economic Growth*, Paris: OECD.

Arrow, K.J. (1962), 'Economic Welfare and the Allocation of Resources for Invention', in National Bureau of Economic Research (ed.), *The Rate and Direction of Inventive Activity: Economic and Social Factors*, Princeton: Princeton University Press.

Arthur, B. (1988), 'Competing Technologies: an Overview', in G. Dosi, C. Freeman, R. Nelson, G. Silverberg and L. Soete (eds), *Technical Change and Economic Theory*, London: Pinter.

Bozeman, B., Link, A. and Zardkoohi, A. (1986), 'An Economic Analysis of R&D Joint Ventures', *Managerial and Decision Economics*, 7.

Callon, M., Larédo, P., Vinck, D. and Mauguin, P. (1989), *L'Évaluation des Programmes Publics de Recherche, le Cas du Programme Communautaire Enérgies Non Nucléaires*, Namur: Presses Universitaires de Namur.

Callon, M., Larédo, P. and Rabeharisoa, V. (1992), 'The Management and Evaluation of Technological Programmes and the Dynamics of Techno-Economic Networks: the Case of the AFME', *Research Policy*, **21**, (3).

Chandler, A. (1977), *The Visible Hand*, Cambridge, Mass.: Harvard University Press.

Chesnais, F. (1988), 'Technical Cooperation Agreements between Firms', *STI Review*, **4**.

Collins, H.M. (1974), 'The TEA Set: Tacit Knowledge and Scientific Networks', *Science Studies*, **4**.

Cohen, W.M. and Levinthal, D.A. (1989), 'Innovation and Learning: the Two Faces of R&D', *Economics Journal*, **99**.

Cowan, R. (1990), 'Nuclear Power Reactors: a Study of Technological Lock-in', *Journal of Economic History*, **L** (3).

Foray, D. (1990), 'L'Économie des Rendements Croissants et l'Économie de la Firme Innovatrice: Perspectives sur le Changement Technique', paper presented at the OECD Conference on Technology and Competitiveness, Paris, 24–27 June.

Griliches, Z. (1964), 'Research Expenditures, Education and the Aggregate Agricultural Production Function', *American Economic Review*, **44**.

Guy, K. (1991), *Evaluation of the Alvey programme for advanced information technology*, London: HMSO.

Hagedoorn, J. and Schakenraad, J. (1990), 'Inter-Firm Partnerships and Cooperative Strategies in Core Technologies', in: C. Freeman and L. Soete (eds), *New Explorations in the Economics of Technical Change*, London: Pinter.

Hughes, T.P. (1983), *Networks of Power, Electrification in Western Society 1880–1930*, Baltimore: Johns Hopkins University Press.

Irvine J. and Martin, B.R. (1989), *Research Foresight: Priority Setting in Science*, London: Pinter.

Klein, B. (1988), 'Luck, Necessity and Dynamic Flexibility', in H. Hanusch (ed.), *Evolutionary Economics*, Cambridge: Cambridge University Press.

Kline, S. and Rosenberg, N. (1986), 'An Overview of Innovation', in H. Landau and N. Rosenberg (eds) *The Positive Sum Strategy*, New York: National Academy Press.

Larédo, P. and Callon, M. (1990), *L 'Impact des Programmes Communautaires de Recherche sur le Tissu Scientifique et Technique Français*, Paris: La Documentation Française.

Larédo, P., Kahane, B., Meyer, J.B. and Vinck, D. (1992), *The Networks Built by the Fourth Medical and Health Services Research Progamme*, Brussels: CEC.

Latour, B. (1987), *Science in Action*, Milton Keynes: Open University Press.

Latour, B. (1989), 'Joliot, l'Histoire et la Physique Mêlées', in M. Serres, *Elements d'Histoire des Sciences*, Paris: Bordas.

Mansfield, E. (1990), 'Academic Research and Industrial Innovation', *Research Policy*, **20**.

Mariti, P. and Smiley, R.H. (1983), 'Cooperative Agreements and the Organization of Industry', *Journal of Industrial Economics*, **31**.

Metcalfe, S. (1988), 'The Diffusion of Innovation: an Interpretative Survey' in G. Dosi, C. Freeman, R. Nelson, G. Silverberg and L. Soete (eds), *Technical Change and Economic Theory*, London: Pinter.

Mytelka, L.K. (1990), 'New Modes of International Competition: the Case of Strategic Partnering in R&D', *Science and Public Policy*, **5**.

Mytelka, L.K. and Delapierre, M. (1988), 'The Alliance Strategies of European Firms in Information Technology Industry and the Role of ESPRIT', *Journal of Common Market Studies*, **26** (2).

Nederhof, A.J. (1990), 'Between Accommodation and Orchestration: the Implementation of the Science Policy Priority for Biotechnology in the Netherlands', *Research Policy*, **19**.

Ouchi, W.G. and Bolton, M.K. (1988), 'The Logic of Joint Research and Development', *California Management Review*, **30**.

Rip, A. (1988), 'Contextual Transformation in Contemporary Science', in Andrew Jamison (ed.), *Keeping Science Straight. A Critical Look at the Assessment of Science and Technology*, Gothenburg: Department of Theory of Science.

Rosenberg, N. (1982), *Inside the Black Box: Technology and Economics*, Cambridge: Cambridge University Press.

Senker, J. (1991), 'Evaluating the Funding of Strategic Science: Some Lessons from British Experience', *Research Policy*, **20**.

Scott, J.T. (1988), 'Diversification versus Co-operation in R&D Investment', *Managerial and Decision Economics*, **9**.

Teece, D.J. (1986), 'Profiting from Technological Innovation: Implications for Integration, Collaboration, Licensing and Public Policy, *Research Policy*, **15**.

Von Hippel, E. (1987), 'Cooperation Between Rivals: Informal Know-how Trading', *Research Policy*, **16**.

Von Hippel, E. (1988), *The sources of Innovation*, New York: Oxford University Press.

Wakasuki, R. (1988), 'A Consideration of Innovative Organization: Joint R&D of Japanese Firms', Seminar of the Schumpeter Association, Vienna.

Watkins, T.A. (1991), 'A Technological Communications Costs Model of R&D Consortia as Public Policy', *Research Policy*, **20**.

9. Understanding 'strategic alliances': the limits of transaction cost economics

Mo Yamin

INTRODUCTION

Transaction cost economics (TCE) is rapidly growing in influence and is regarded by many as the general theory of economic organization. One of the main preoccupations of TCE relates to the question of the organization or governance of the relationships between firms. There are a number of alternatives for governing such relationships: the price system; contractual arrangements (e.g. a licensing contract or a franchising agreement); the creation of a distinct entity that two or more firms jointly own and control (i.e. a joint venture charged with the responsibility of carrying out some activities on behalf of its multiple parents); and, of course, the merging of two or more legal entities into one.

The problem that firms face is to choose the efficient governance mode from the above list. TCE argues that there is a systematic relationship between some characteristics of transactions, in this case the particular type of relationship or interdependence between firms, and efficient organizational modes. In particular, Williamson (e.g. 1985) stresses the crucial relevance of asset specificity. If the consummation of a transaction requires commitment of significant resources that have no or little value outside that transaction, then 'arms-length' methods such as the price system or a contractual agreement will incur, at least partially avoidable, costs and hence be inefficient relative to the more hierarchical arrangements.

It is therefore not surprising that the TCE has had a significant though varying influence on many of the studies concerned with the rapidly growing phenomenon of strategic alliances (see, among others, Pisano, 1990, 1991; Pisano et al. 1988; Mitchell and Singh, 1992; Tapon, 1989; Hennart, 1988, 1991; Terpstra and Simonin, 1993). These studies all adopt an organizational choice or, more narrowly, a 'make or buy' perspective in their analysis of strategic alliances. Hence their reliance on the TCE as the theoretical framework dealing with questions of organizational choice and the boundaries of the firm. Superficially, at least, the TCE seems a highly relevant theoretical perspective and its influence in this field of application may well grow.

The aim of this paper is to argue that the TCE is not necessarily a suitable theoretical framework for analysing strategic alliances. My basic argument is that, when dealing with strategic alliances, organizational choice may, to a large extent, be illusory rather than real. Obviously the existence of organizational choice is logically and practically prior to the efficiency or optimality of a given organizational arrangement.

For organizational choice to exist, it is necessary that the transaction does not change as it is shifted from one organizational mode to another. This does not mean that all details remain unaffected by the change in the organizational mode but that whatever constitutes the core purpose of the transaction is not affected by the change (Dow, 1987). In the present context, if the main reason for cooperation between two firms is inter-firm learning, then only organizational arrangements that can allow effective communication of firm-specific and hence implicit knowledge can be considered for the governance and management of such a relationship. This limits organizational choice and could conceivably rule it out altogether.

The rest of this paper is divided into two sections. The first deals primarily with some definitional issues. It considers those features and purposes, as indicated by the gradually accumulating stock of information and data on strategic alliances, that may render alliances meaningfully 'strategic'. Two points emerge. One is that 'strategic alliances' have much more to do with *creating* capabilities than with exploiting already existing capabilities. Second, individual alliances between any two firms are usually part of complex and interlocking network involving a large number of participants.

The second section considers the relevance of these features for the applicability of the TCE. With regard to creating capabilities, the TCE does not seem to give sufficient attention to the organizational requirements for learning as such. Inevitably, of course, there is increasing recognition of the implicit and inarticulate nature of much individual and organizational knowledge, a feature that is relevant not only in the transfer of existing knowledge (which is where it has received much attention) but also in the process of creating new knowledge. I shall argue that these characteristics of the learning process limit the usefulness of the notion of transaction costs and in the limit may make it irrelevant.

With regard to the second characteristic of strategic alliances, it seems clear that the concept of a 'transaction' cannot be so stretched as to cover a whole network of inter-corporate links. At the same time we must, at the very least, allow for the possibility that a network is more than the mere sum of a number of individual transactions or alliances. The broader context, defined as the potential or actual network of alliances, may have a significant influence on how any one alliance is seen by the respective parties.

THE NATURE OF STRATEGIC ALLIANCES

Strategic Versus 'Traditional' Alliances

Recent years have witnessed a rapid growth in the number of various types of inter-firm collaborative links. For example the MERIT–CATI databank has information on over 10,000 such links virtually all of which were formed in the 1980s with over half being formed in the period 1985–89 (Hagedoorn and Schakenraad, 1992,1990). Other, less extensive data sets also point to a very rapid growth of collaborative arrangements (Terpstra and Simonin, 1993; Dunning, 1993). These recent collaborations are commonly regarded as of strategic significance, although this is not defined in any precise way, if at all, or related to any particular underlying concept of strategy (one possible exception is Porter and Fuller, 1986; see also the appendix in Hagedoorn and Schakenraad, 1990).

However, it is universally agreed that the new wave of inter-firm links is qualitatively different from that which took place in the 1970s, 1960s or earlier. By highlighting some of the key differences between the new wave and the older, more 'traditional' alliances it is possible to appreciate that the new alliances do serve broader or higher-level and hence more 'strategic' corporate purposes.

Perhaps the most obvious difference is the overwhelming concentration of the new alliances in a small number of technologically dynamic fields. For example, 42 per cent of all alliances in the MERIT database are in information technology (Hagedoorn and Schakenraad, 1992, p. 163). Most of the rest are in biotechnology and new materials. By contrast most alliances in the 1970s or earlier were probably in those industries or activities with a fairly mature technology and standardized product line. Another clear difference is that the new alliances are, virtually exclusively, between firms from the 'triad' countries in Western Europe, North America and Japan, whereas the earlier alliances were, most often, between partners from developed and developing countries and were usually located in the latter (Dunning, 1993).

Strategic alliances also differ from traditional alliances in terms of underlying motives. Thus traditional alliances, particularly those that took place across national borders, were often a substitute for direct foreign investment as a method of entry into particular country markets. Strategic alliances are not a substitute for direct investment or a method of entry in the narrow sense, but seem more intended to give the firm capabilities that it does not possess already. Of course this capability acquisition may relate to the need to enter, or to enter more rapidly, a major or strategic market such as the US. For example, many of the alliances in the telecommunications field have taken place in order to give participating firms the technical and or marketing capabilities to enter and operate in the US market (Pisano et al., 1988). Similarly, an alliance may give the firm an opportunity to 'test the technical and market waters' of new /emerging technical fields before full entry. This has apparently been the strategy behind many alliances in the US medical diagnostic and imaging industry (Mitchell and Singh, 1992). The point is that whilst traditional alliances (and direct foreign investment) were a vehicle for utilizing the firm's *given* capabilities in new markets and locations, strategic alliances are aimed at gaining new capabilities.

Related to the above, and analytically the most significant distinction between strategic and traditional alliances, is that the underlying *relationship* between the partners in the new alliances is probably different and considerably more complex compared to that in the earlier type of alliances. Thus the new or strategic alliances are typically between firms that are actual or potential competitors in many markets. This was not usually the case for the earlier type of alliances. Of course there could be and often was a conflict of interest between, for example, a Western pharmaceutical company and its licensees in developing countries, over the distribution of costs and benefits emanating from the licensing agreement, but there would be little or no competition between the firm and its licensees in third-country markets (licensing contracts typically incorporated the prohibition of exports by the licensees).

Strategic alliances are more complex as, whereas they are formed by potential or actual rivals, they may nevertheless involve a much greater degree of cooperation than was typically the case with traditional alliances. In fact, the term 'alliances' is probably applied too loosely to cover a rather heterogeneous spectrum or range of inter-firm link-ups. At one end of the spectrum may be those links that 'merely' involve the *transfer or the exchange* of well packaged and articulated knowledge. These probably call for relatively little 'cooperation' between the partners so far as the *process* of the exchange itself is concerned. Cooperation, understood as 'mutual forbearance' and refraining from 'cheating' (Buckley and Casson, 1988, p. 21) may be necessary if the relationship is to endure or develop in new directions, but is not necessarily critical to the exchange itself.

At the other end of the spectrum are those relationships in which firms may to some degree combine each other's embedded knowledge or capabilities. Here we may be leaving the realm of exchange or transactions altogether.[1] The process involved is one of learning rather than exchange as such and the *need* for cooperation may be dictated by the requirements of the learning process: by the impracticality, if not the impossibility, of contractual 'solutions' to the problems that arise in the learning process and *independent* of the characteristics or the intentions of the partners. The latter will naturally be ambivalent, reflecting the fact that the partners are also competitors. Not surprisingly, within strategic alliances one may well observe both a significant degree of cooperation as well as attempts by parties to learn *faster* than their partners (Hamel, 1991).

We are not suggesting that strategic alliances can dispense with contracts altogether. But whilst contracts may be necessary or even crucial for the proper management of alliances (Badaracco, 1991), they have a different role from that assumed in the TCE. Thus contracts are likely to be regarded as a provision against the *failure of the relationship*, rather than as central to the process of cooperation or learning as such. To the extent that parties consciously act according to the contract, the relationship may have actually failed.

Nor are we suggesting that *all* strategic alliances necessarily require an atmosphere of intimate cooperation between the parties. For example many technology partnerships in the MERIT–CATI databank are 'technology exchange agreements' and 'one-directional technology flows' (Hagedoorn and Schakenraad, 1990, table 1). This description suggests that these are essentially exchange transactions, albeit exchange involving knowledge. It would not be surprising if such arrangements did not involve a great deal of cooperation between the partners or if the relationship was primarily contractual. In fact some, indirect, evidence suggests that this is the case. Thus both Terpstra and Simonin (1993) and Pisano et al. (1988) found that unless a partnership was primarily for product development it was likely to be organized around a formal contract.

On the other hand, product development partnerships involving cooperation in R&D, production and marketing and therefore including considerably more than exchange of knowledge, were much more likely to be organized as joint ventures. It does seem that product development projects are a very large and, possibly, the single most frequent type of collaboration. Thus, for example, joint product developments were by far the largest category of partnership, accounting for 41 per cent of the total in Terpstra and Simonin's sample of 658 alliances (1993, table 1 and p. 13).[2]

Strategic Alliances as Networks

We have suggested that the underlying rationale for strategic alliances is that firms are increasingly forced to learn from each other. But why should such alliances be part of a network? How does this fact (see below) relate to the 'strategicness' of alliances? These questions have not, to my knowledge, been examined in any depth as yet. However it is possible to put forward an argument for the existence of a network of alliances that is at least consistent with learning and capability extension as the primary motive of strategic alliances.

The argument relies on the ever-increasing degree of specialization of knowledge. Badaracco (1991, p. 25) reports that whereas in the 1940s there were only about 54 scientific specialities, in the 1970s there were about 900. Today there are probably considerably more than that. In relation to this increase any firm, even those with the largest technological resources, can develop only a fairly narrow range of 'core competences' (Prahalad and Hamel, 1990). Moreover, within any broad technological area, such as 'information technology' or 'biotechnology', there is a large and probably increasing number of sub-specialisms, implying a large number of quite small and highly specialized firms with *unique* capabilities unobtainable from any other source. Larger firms seeking to broaden their capabilities need to have access (or absorb?) to a wide range of such specialisms, within as well as across broad technology areas, making it necessary for them to develop a cooperative network of links with the smaller specialist firms.

Research by Hagedoorn and Schakenraad (1990, 1992) leaves little doubt that an important feature of strategic alliances is that they are usually part of a network. These authors have analysed the structure of alliance clusters in terms of network density and stability in information technology, biotechnology and new materials. For all three core technologies they find 'a large number of strong partnerships between many of the leading companies' (1990, p. 28). The density of networks does vary across the technologies, being much less for biotechnology compared to information technology (ibid. p. 24).

Hagedoorn and Schakenraad's most extensive research concerns information technology. Their analysis focuses on 45 firms with the largest numbers of alliances in five information technology sectors (computers, microelectronics, telecommunications, industrial automation and software). Taking information technology as a whole their data indicate a high and rapidly rising degree of network density. The value of their network density index rose from 23 to 40 per cent during the 1980s. As they put it, 'one can speak of a very intensive, dense network in information technologies' (1992, p. 183). Their data also point to a significant degree of network stability during the 1980s. They find that while the networks are 'open' – there is some entry and exit – the ranking of the core firms did not change significantly. In other words it appears that in all sectors of information technology, except software, there is at least a moderate degree of domination by firms that have a nodal position in the networks.

THE LIMITED RELEVANCE OF TRANSACTION COST ECONOMICS

The characteristics of individual strategic alliances and the existence of fairly dense and stable networks of alliances raise two questions for the relevance of the TCE:

1. Are 'transactions' a useful unit of analysis so far as strategic alliances are concerned?
2. Is there as much organizational choice as the TCE assumes?

The Transaction as the Unit of Analysis

Networks versus transactions
Let us accept, for the time being, that the kind of relationship embodied in individual alliances can be described as a transaction in the sense that Williamson has defined and others have applied this term. Even so, as we have seen, the underlying purpose for strategic alliances is a *programme* of broadening and enhancing the firm's capability, and this may require a complex network of inter-corporate links. It is obvious that such a programme and the resultant network cannot be construed as a transaction, even if each pair of links in *isolation* could be so construed. Clearly it is, to say the least, questionable to ignore, as all those studies applying the TCE to strategic alliances do, the fact that each alliance may be part of a larger network of transactions. Looking at each alliance in isolation, as a free-standing transaction, will not necessarily unravel the important reasons for its formation or for its eventual fate. Regarding the latter, in a study of the dissolution rates of alliances Kogut (1989) found that the overall network of ties in which a joint venture was embedded was the most important factor influencing the probability of dissolution. As he concluded, this finding 'provoca-tively, ... challenges a contrary tendency to analyze governance issues as restricted to the economic properties of a transaction. An implication of these results is that an analysis of the governance of a transaction must include the network of ties among the partners' (p. 195).

The reasons for the formation of any single alliance are also likely to strongly reflect influences emanating from the broader setting of existing or emerging networks. These influences may well be more important than, and may well counteract, the characteristics of the individual transaction (such as asset speci-ficity) but some of them, at least, are likely to be overlooked if the individual transaction is to be the focal point of the analysis.

Consider the otherwise very careful empirical investigation of the (biotech-nology) R&D 'make or buy' decision by Pisano (1990). He is aiming to explain why a high percentage (47 per cent in 1986) of biotechnology R&D projects are undertaken in-house, even though biotechnology has proved 'competence-destroying' and has significantly undermined the traditional approach to drug discovery within established firms.

To explain this, his paper 'develops and tests transaction cost hypotheses for R&D procurement at the *project* level' (Pisano, 1990, p. 154, my emphasis). He finds support for the hypotheses in as much as 'the small number' and 'appro-priability' problems do seem to explain the tendency towards in-house R&D.

Whilst these may be relevant considerations, his analysis ignores simpler and potentially more powerful explanations for the unexpectedly high frequency of in-house R&D.

The majority of specialist biotechnology firms are of very recent origin, with little or no history or a credible record. A network of relationships that could have provided relevant information does not exist or is not very strong.

As Langlois (1992) has argued, the degree of vertical integration (or disintegration) depends on the balance between internal and *external* capabilities of individual firms. Vertical disintegration requires a measure of external capability by the firm, including the ability to assess reliably what the 'market' is capable of doing for it. This is why the firm's networks of ties and contacts with other firms may be an important *asset*. The lack of a strong network of existing or even emerging links may be important in explaining the high incidence of in-house biotechnology R&D. Developments in biotechnology, whilst destructive of internal capabilities, cannot necessarily generate external capabilities!

Strategic alliances versus transactions

Our earlier consideration of the nature of strategic alliances has suggested that the relationship embodied cannot necessarily be viewed as a transaction. Here we consider this issue more explicitly.

First, however, we must note that the notion of uncertainty plays a fairly minor role in the TCE.[3] Uncertainty in the TCE is essentially of a 'strategic', or even a 'contrived' variety, rather than a structural type: each party may be uncertain about the intentions and plans of other participants in a transaction, but the information structure of the environment itself is stable. Even 'strategic' uncertainty is present only to an 'intermediate degree' (Williamson, 1985, pp. 56–60, 80; see also Englander, 1988). This is necessary for the TCE as, otherwise, the *ex ante* attribution of characteristics to transactions would become problematic. For example, in an uncertain or highly changing environment the notion of asset specificity becomes rather ambiguous. The flow of services from any asset is not something that can be known *ex ante*. Strictly speaking, the specificity of assets, implying a known, specifiable flow of services, is not consistent with uncertainty. It is therefore not surprising that Williamson (1985, p. 143) remarks that 'the introduction of innovation plainly complicates the earlier-described assignment of transactions to markets or hierarchies based entirely on an examination of their asset specificity qualities'. He adds that 'indeed, the study of economic organization in a regime of rapid innovation poses much more difficult issues than those addressed here'. Those who have applied the TCE to the analysis of strategic alliances do not seem similarly cautious, even though the issues of innovation and technical change are central to strategic alliances.

The main problem is that strategic alliances, particularly those concerned with joint creation and commercialization of technology, cannot be viewed as having

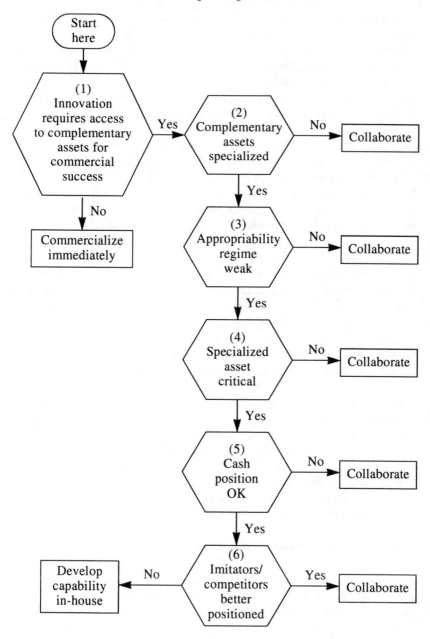

Figure 9.1   Flow chart for integration versus collaboration decision

known or stable transactional characteristics. The risks that the parties may be exposed to is largely a function of the pattern of learning that develops within the alliance. Those that learn more slowly may end up in a situation of total dependence on their partner(s). This may appear, in its effect, to be similar to asset specificity. The important difference is that unlike the situation of asset specificity, asymmetric learning has no obvious *contractual/governance* solution. As Hamel has found in his detailed investigation of a number of alliances, 'the legal and governance structure may exert only a minor influence over the pattern of inter-partner learning and bargaining power' (Hamel, 1991, p. 87).

Sometimes alliances may be a 'post-innovation' strategy. Here the TCE approach suggests a focus on the characteristics of the complementary assets. Following this approach, Teece (1986) and Pisano et al. (1988) point out that an innovator should collaborate with other firms in order to commercialize its innovation if a number of conditions hold. Their suggested flow chart for the integration versus collaboration decision is shown in Figure 9.1.

The problem with this kind of approach is that many firms may not be able to appreciate the ramifications of their own innovations and hence do not ask the 'right' questions. Furthermore, of course, the answer to the question, once asked, may not be obvious or clear. The problem may be particularly severe for 'architectural' innovations, those that create a new linkage among existing concepts and components (an example is the jet aircraft – see Henderson and Clark, 1990). Radical innovations that change a core design concept may have radical but *obvious* implications in that the firm may quickly recognize the inadequacy of its existing skills and organization. The need for new skills and possibly new relationships for commercialization may thus be correctly assessed and acted on. With architectural innovation, by contrast, 'the organization may mistakenly believe that it understands the technology' (Henderson and Clark, 1990, p. 17) and hence is unlikely to grasp the need for, among other things, changing relationships with complementary asset holders, or appreciate fully key capabilities that such relationships should provide for it. Once again, therefore, the relationship is surrounded by too many ambiguities or uncertainties to be regarded as a transaction.

Is There as Much Organizational Choice as the TCE Assumes?

The basic assumption of the TCE is that various governance arrangements are *feasible* alternatives for organizing any particular transaction, implying that while they may involve greater or lesser costs, any one of them can be employed for organizing the transaction. The various governance structures are regarded to be qualitatively similar in being, to varying degrees, 'like markets', or are 'contract-like'. Thus Williamson notes that 'one of the attractive attributes of the transaction cost approach is that it reduces, essentially, to a study of contracting' (1986, p. 197). Even firms are not so much a means of *suppressing* markets (as with Coase) as a means of *internalizing* them: substituting internal markets for external ones (Kay, 1992). It is their essential similarity that makes the various governance structures feasible for organizing any transaction.

As we noted in the introduction the validity of this assumption requires that the purposes of a transaction remain unaffected by the particular mode chosen to organize it. From our point of view the key question is whether the various organizational modes will allow, even though at varying costs, a similar pattern and degree of learning. This is not, admittedly, easy to determine empirically. But, by the same token, it undermines much of the evidence that is usually cited in favour of the TCE as such 'evidence' simply ignores the question. For example, Hennart (1988) regards the following observation as supporting the TCE analysis of joint ventures: 'There is also a good deal of evidence that joint ventures are used to transfer a *different* technology package than licensing. Joint ventures are used to communicate both patent rights and tacit knowledge, while licensing is limited to patent rights' (1988, p.366, my emphasis).

Hennart interprets this as reflecting cost differences between the two modes for transferring tacit knowledge. Yet it seems clear that it may sometimes be *impossible* to incorporate know-how, at any cost, in a (licensing) contract, because those who possess it cannot make it articulate, or convey it through formal instructions. 'Know-how' is an obvious example of what has been called 'procedural' rather than 'descriptive' knowledge (Metcalfe, 1992, p. 229). Its transfer may require an essentially non-contractual or cooperative relationship permitting a process of close interaction and dialogue between individuals (Hedlund, 1992). Within this relationship the transferee can understand the know-how without it being made highly articulated or explicit. Thus, to the extent that a joint venture makes the transfer of implicit know-how possible while a licensing contract does not, the two modes cannot be regarded as feasible alternatives for each other in organizing a transaction whose main purpose is to effect the communication and transfer of implicit knowledge.

In practice, the ease or difficulty of the transfer of knowledge depends not only on the degree to which knowledge is implicit but also on the general technical or absorptive capacity of the transferee. Thus paradoxically, the transfer or exchange of knowledge between developed firms may encounter fewer obstacles overall and hence be more easily organized through formal contracts than that between developed and developing-country firms. For alliances that are primarily concerned with exchange and transfer of knowledge between developed-country firms, some degree of organizational choice may well exist, both formal contracts and joint ventures may be possible forms, although the latter may have redundant features if the transfer does not require much interaction between the firms.

However, those alliances that aim at joint product development, and not mere transfer or exchange of technology, do not enjoy a significant degree of organizational choice. That such alliances cannot be organized in purely contractual form should be clear. The obstacles are similar, and probably operate with much greater force, to those that prevent the transfer of existing know-how through a licensing contract.

Alliances versus acquisitions

It might be argued, however, that a firm always has the freedom and at least some capability for 'doing things for itself' which, in the present context, can include acquisition of other firms in order to broaden its own technological capability. Thus, it would seem that another alternative to forming an alliance is acquisition.

However, there are strong reasons for believing that, to the extent that acquisition can be a tool for corporate learning at all, it reflects a very different learning strategy compared to forming an alliance. The two are not effective substitutes for each other. This may be particularly true so far as *international* strategic alliances are concerned.

Foreign direct investment (FDI), including FDI through acquisition, may now be increasingly used by firms to undertake research and production activities in locations that are regarded as major sources of technological advances in particular industries of a type that may be complementary to the advance in the firm's 'home' country. An example is investment by German chemical firms in the US which is apparently motivated by such considerations (*Survey of Current Business*, July 1989). In this way the firm can enhance its capacity to absorb knowledge spillovers from competitors and knowledge that may be in the public domain (publicly funded research by universities and research institutions – see Cohen and Levinthal, 1989). The fact that most of the recent flow of FDI is intra-industry, and that much of it is directed to the US provides suggestive evidence for this (Cantwell, 1989). However this seems to be a strategy for 'learning from the environment', rather than from a particular competitor. What seems to be critical here is active *presence* in a foreign environment rather than linkage with competitors as such. Once located in a foreign environment, and such location may be more quickly and more cheaply obtained through acquisition, the firm learns on its own.

By comparison, alliances are a strategy for much more *focused* learning and involve working on a more clearly delineated programme with partners having complementary or different expertise. It is generally agreed that the acquisition of a partner is likely to be inappropriate so far as this type of learning objective is concerned (see Badaracco, 1991; Pisano, 1991). Pisano feels that acquisition may be 'a dangerous policy' because it is difficult 'to guarantee that the key assets of the company, the people, will stay' (1991, p. 248). But even apart from this problem, acquisition is likely to prove self-defeating: it creates 'negative synergy' in that the embedded knowledge of the acquired firm, access to which is presumably the purpose of the whole arrangement, may be suppressed and/or destroyed. Pisano acknowledges that acquisition may be incompatible with preserving the atmosphere necessary for keeping the 'key people on board', but does not seem concerned that this point may undermine the relevance of transaction costs. But surely if acquisition cannot achieve an effective *combination* of the knowledge bases of two or more firms and if such combination requires some degree of organizational autonomy (see Hedlund and Rolander, 1990) then, for this particular purpose, alliances and acquisitions are not feasible substitutes.

CONCLUSION

In forming alliances firms are not 'choosing' among a number of feasible organizational alternatives. In a sense, alliances are 'forced' on firms precisely because, as vehicles for learning, both contractual modes and acquisition are at best only an imperfect substitute for *alliances*. The fact that many alliances are often dissolved through acquisition by one of the parties (Kogut and Chang, 1991, Kogut, 1991) lends support to this contention. As a vehicle for *utilizing* capabilities rather than learning, acquisition is probably superior to forming an alliance. Thus once the learning has taken place the alliance has probably served its purpose and its natural fate is dissolution through acquisition. Thus, as Hamel (1991) has also noted, alliances are essentially a transitional organizational mode.

NOTES

1. If, following Williamson, a transaction is defined as a process in which 'a good or a service is transferred across technologically separable interfaces' (1981, p. 1544), then the kind of organizational learning that is often at the core of strategic alliances can hardly be described as a transaction. See below.
2. Hagedoorn and Schakenraad (1990) do not seem to include a category for joint production agreements. Their focus appears to be purely on technology agreements. Their data do include 'joint venture and research cooperations' which seem to be entities charged with joint research activities rather than with product development.
3. This has not always been the case. His earlier work (Williamson, 1975) put greater emphasis on uncertainty. Englander (1988) traces the evolution of Williamson's ideas.

REFERENCES

Badaracco, J. (1991), *The Knowledge Link: How Firms Compete Through Strategic Alliances*, Boston: Harvard Business School Press.

Buckley, P. and Casson, M. (1988), 'A Theory of Cooperation in International Business', in F. Contractor and P. Lorange (eds), *Cooperative Strategies in International Business: Joint Ventures and Technology*, Lexington, Mass.: Lexington Books.

Cantwell, J. (1989), *Technological Innovation and the Multinational Enterprise*, Oxford: Basil Blackwell.

Cohen, W. and Levinthal, A. (1989), 'Innovation and Learning: The Two faces of R&D', *Economic Journal*, **99**, 569–96.

Dow, G. (1987), 'The Function of Authority in Transaction Cost Economics', *Journal of Economic Behaviour and Organisation*, 1, 13–38.

Dunning, J. (1988), *Explaining International Production*, London: Unwin Hyman.

Dunning, J. (1993), *Multinational Enterprise and the Global Economy*, Wokingham: Addison-Wesley.

Englander, E. (1988), 'Technology and Williamson's Transaction Cost Economics', *Journal of Economic Behaviour and Organisation*, 3, 339–53.

Hagedoorn, J. and Schakenraad, J. (1990), 'Inter-firm partnerships and cooperative strategies in core technologies', in C. Freeman and L. Soete (eds), *New Explorations in the Economics of Technological Change*, London: Pinter.

Hagedoorn J. and Schakenraad, J. (1992), 'Leading companies and networks of strategic alliances in information technology', *Research Policy*, **22**, 163–96.

Hamel, G. (1991), 'Competition for Competence and Inter-Partner Learning Within International Strategic Alliances', *Strategic Management Journal*, **12**, 83–103.

Hedlund, G. and Rolander, D. (1990), 'Action on Heterarchies – New approaches to managing the MNC', in C. Bartlett, Y. Doz and G. Hedlund (eds), *Managing the Global Firm*, Basingstoke: Macmillan.

Hedlund, G. (1992), 'Organisational Requirements for Global Knowledge Management', *Proceedings of the European International Business Association*.

Henderson, R. and Clark, K. (1990), 'Architectural Innovation: The Reconfiguration of Existing Product Technologies and the Failure of Established Firms', *Administrative Science Quarterly*, **35**, 9–30.

Hennart, J. (1988), 'A Transaction Cost Theory of Equity Joint Ventures', *Strategic Management Journal*, **9**(4), 361–74.

Hennart, J. (1991), 'A Transaction Cost Theory of Joint Ventures: An Empirical Study of Japanese Subsidiaries in the United States', *Management Science*, **37**(4), 483–97.

Kay, N. (1992), 'Markets, False Hierarchies and the Evolution of the Modern Corporation', *Journal of Economic Behaviour and Organisation*, **3**, 315–33.

Kodoma, F. (1992), 'Technology Fusion and the New R&D', *Harvard Business Review*, July/August, 70–78.

Kogut, B. (1989), 'The Stability of Joint Ventures: Reciprocity and Competitive Rivalry', *Journal of Industrial Economics*, **2**, 183–98.

Kogut, B. (1991), 'Joint Ventures and the Option to Expand and Acquire', *Management Science*, **37**, 19–33.

Kogut, B. and Chang, S. (1991), 'Technological Capability and Japanese Foreign Direct Investment in the United States', *The Review of Economics and Statistics*, August, 401–9.

Langlois, R. (1992), 'Transaction cost economics in real time', *Industrial and Corporate Change*, 1, 99–129.

Metcalfe, S. (1992), 'Competition and Collaboration in the Innovation process' in A. Bowen and M. Ricketts (eds), *Stimulating Innovation in Industry – The Challenge for the United Kingdom*, London: National Economic Development Office Policy Issue Series.

Mitchell, W. and Singh, K. (1992), 'Incumbents' Use of Pre-Entry Alliances Before Expansion into New Technical Subfields of an Industry', *Journal of Economic Behaviour and Organisation*, August, 347–72.

Pisano, G. (1990), 'The R&D Boundaries of the Firm: An Empirical Study', *Administrative Science Quarterly*, **35**, 153–76.

Pisano, G. (1991), 'The Governance of Innovation: Integration and Collaborative Arrangements in Biotechnology', *Research Policy*, **20**(3), 237–50.

Pisano, G., Russo, M. and Teece D. (1988), 'Joint Ventures and Collaborative Arrangements in the Telecommunication Industry', in D. Mowery (ed.), *International Collaborative Ventures in US Manufacturing*, Cambridge, Mass.: Ballinger.

Prahalad, C. and Hamel, G. (1990), 'The Core Competence of the Corporation', *Harvard Business Review*, May/June.

Porter, M. and Fuller, M. (1986), 'Coalitions and Global Strategy', in M. Porter (ed.), *Competition in Global Industries*, Boston: Harvard Business School Press.

Tapon, F. (1989), 'A Transaction Cost Analysis of Innovations in the Organisation of Pharmaceutical R&D', *Journal of Economic Behaviour and Organisation*, **19**(2), 196–213.

Teece, D. (1986), 'Profiting from Technological Innovations: Implications for Integration, Collaborations, Licensing and Public Policy', *Research Policy*, **15**(6), 285–306.

Terpstra, V. and Simonin, B. (1993), 'Strategic Alliances in the Triad: An Exploratory Study', *Journal of International Marketing*, 1, 4–25.

Williamson, O. (1975), *Markets and Hierarchies: Analysis and Antitrust Implication*, New York: Free Press.

Williamson, O. (1985), *The Economic Institutions of Capitalism*, New York: Free Press.

Williamson, O. (1986), *Economic Organisation: Firms, Markets and Policy Control*, Brython: Wheatsheaf.

10. Dynamics of cooperation and industrial R&D: first insights into the black box II[1]

François Leveque, Christophe Bonazzi and Christian Quental

INTRODUCTION AND SUMMARY

This paper attempts to explain why there are variations in technological coop-eration in terms of the number of agreements established and organizational forms adopted. Why, for instance, did the rapid growth in the number of agreements in information technology, biotechnology and new materials decline at the end of the 1980s? Or why are minority equity investments and research contracts, which characterized the cooperation in DNA recombinant technology between small firms and large pharmaceutical companies at the beginning of the 1980s, now being replaced by more traditional customer–supplier relations?

Despite a growing amount of literature dedicated to the topic of co-operation, and especially technological cooperation (Mowery, 1988; Chesnais, 1988; OECD, 1992), there is no ready-to-use analytical framework for understand-ing cooperation dynamics. As Barbanti et al. (1992) have pointed out, one finds no sound theoretical hypothesis to explain the evolution of inter-firm agreements and technological networks. In our opinion, this situation is due to an heuristic weakness: the economic literature ignores largely what is going on within the firms' research centres. By 'black-boxing' the internal R&D of firms, economists have ignored a crucial relationship between technological coop-eration and the dynamics of differentiated oligopolies.

This paper aims therefore to demonstrate that variations in technological coop-eration should be analysed in relation to the firms' internal R&D process and its evolution according to industrial competition dynamics. It focuses mainly on inter-firm R&D cooperative agreements.[2] The model employed in this demonstration distinguishes three modes of industrial R&D. To each firm cor-responds a specific mix of these modes and to each mode corresponds a particular pattern of technological cooperation. The dynamic relationships between the R&D cooperation variations and the differentiated oligopoly evolution is studied in depth in the case of biotechnology. It enables us to explain why the number of technology agreements is currently declining.

The second section begins with the description of two main trends: the growth in the number of technological cooperation agreements and the emergence of new organizational forms of cooperation. Then it is argued that the organizational forms of cooperation could be studied according to a structural axis and a temporal axis. Along the structural axis, organizational forms are distributed according to a spectrum from pure internalization to pure market relationship. The temporal axis represents the distribution of the organizational forms according to different phases of the technological and industrial evolution. The conclusion emphasizes the need to go inside the black box II in order to link these two dimensions.

The third section introduces the industrial R&D theory. The three modes – exploratory R&D, exploitation R&D and imitative R&D – are distinguished. Emphasis is put on the distinctive features of these modes with respect to cooperation. The dynamic relationships between the R&D modes are then discussed. Two implications for cooperation are analysed: first, the theory establishes that the pattern of collaboration reflects the pattern of the internal R&D activities undertaken by firms. Second, it shows how technological cooperation depends on the competition taking place in the differentiated oligopolies. These implications are illustrated and partially validated in the case of biotechnology.

FACTS AND THEORIES

Two main trends have been observed and analysed concerning the development of technological cooperation. First, a very large increase in the number of technology agreements has been noticed since 1980 in the field of information technology, as well as biotechnology and new materials (see Table 10.1). Second, new strategic forms of technical cooperation agreements have appeared (Chesnais, 1988). Inter-firm alliances are no longer based only on cross-licensing and joint ventures as before. Currently, technological cooperation encompasses a very large variety of agreements in terms of the number of partners, competitive stage of technology, equity, scope, and so forth. These trends have been analysed in several sectoral or multi-sectoral empirical studies (see in particular Mowery, 1988; OECD, 1992; Hagedoorn and Schakenraad, 1990). The basic explanation concerns the transformation of the world economy and/or the contemporary developments in science and technology. Technological cooperation development is viewed as a reaction of firms to global competition, financial and economic uncertainty, and rapid and radical technical change. As pointed out by Chesnais (1988), new forms of agreements offer firms a high degree of flexibility in their operations and the possibility of pooling limited R&D resources to face rising costs.

Table 10.1   *Increase in number of inter-firm agreements by form of cooperation, 4-year periods, absolute numbers and percentages*

Modes of cooperation	Before	1973–1976	1977–1980	1981–1984	1985–1988	Total
Joint ventures research corporation	83 53.2%	64 41.8%	112 22.6%	254 20.8%	345 17.8%	858 21.6%
Joint R&D	14 9.0%	22 14.4%	65 13.1%	255 20.9%	653 33.7%	1009 25.5%
Technology exchange agreement	6 3.8%	4 2.6%	33 6.7%	152 12.4%	165 8.5%	360 9.1%
Direct investment	27 17.3%	29 19.0%	168 33.9%	170 13.9%	237 12.2%	631 15.9%
Customer–supplier relationships	5 3.2%	19 12.4%	47 9.5%	133 10.9%	265 13.7%	469 11.8%
One-directional technology flow	21 13.5%	15 9.8%	71 14.3%	259 21.2%	271 14.0%	637 16.1%
Total	156 100% 3.9%	153 100% 3.9%	496 100% 12.5%	1223 100% 30.9%	1936 100% 48.8%	3964 100% 100%

Source: J. Hagedoorn (1990).

However, the forms of cooperation present different evolution patterns over the last two decades (Hagedoorn, 1990). The forms that showed the greatest growth were joint R&D and mutual technology exchange agreements. Joint ventures and research corporations lost participation, while direct investments peaked during 1977–80, declining afterwards. How can we explain these variations in technological collaboration?

Moreover, the growth rate of new technological agreements levelled off at the end of the 1980s. How can we explain this fact? Is it a new trend? Does it reflect that 'collaborative relations are bound to decrease in scale and scope as the technology matures and as higher degrees of vertical integration are established in the industry' (Barbanti et al., 1992)? This raises an important question: is inter-firm technological cooperation a transient phenomenon (Walsh, 1991)? The answer is not obvious owing to the limited scope of literature addressing cooperation dynamics.

Organizational forms of R&D cooperation are studied in the literature on two axes: structural and temporal. Along the former, organizational forms are arranged according to a continuum from pure internalization to pure market relationship. Along the latter, the organizational forms are distributed according to different phases of technological and industrial evolution.

The structural axis provides a conceptualization of inter-firm cooperation. For the transaction costs theory, cooperation occurs when neither market nor hierarchies are completely satisfactory. Collaboration is viewed as an efficient governance structure when transactions are surrounded by special circumstances, such as uncertainty and the specificity of assets (Williamson, 1975). Cooperation reflects the contradiction between the efficiency of the coordinating mechanisms of price and the need to economize on the costs of using the market (Foray, 1991). Several publications have dealt with make-by-cooperate decisions for R&D within this framework. They emphasize theoretical aspects (Tapon, 1989; Teece, 1988; Pisano, 1990, 1991) or more strategic ones (Teece, 1986; Pisano et al. 1988). These authors studied the effects of several factors influencing the R&D boundaries of the firm such as appropriability, location of know-how and complementary assets, and the tacit dimension of technology.

A tentative alternative to the transaction cost theory which provides an analytical framework to explain technological collaboration has been derived from Richardson (1972) and Gaffard (1990). Cooperation is conceptualized as the resolution of the contradiction between the human resources constraint, which calls for the integration of activities in order to render them specific, and the financial constraint, which avoids the irreversibilities. Different forms of cooperation are viewed as a compromise between the need to integrate resources – condition for technical change – and the need to leave them on the market – condition for reversibility (Foray, 1991). Within this second theoretical approach, the forms of R&D cooperation are also distributed along a continuum from internal R&D to contractual R&D.

A strong opposition between the two theories rests on the question of the substitutability between internal and external R&D. As Foray and Mowery (1990) have pointed out, perfect substitutability between them is a prerequisite of the transaction cost theory. This assumption ignores the dual role possessed by the internal R&D: proposing innovation and improving the absorptive capacity (that is to say, the ability of the firm to exploit knowledge from the environment – Cohen and Levinthal, 1988), and the learning function that is associated with the innovation function considered. It ignores, consequently, any technological creation process within the firm. In other words, the transaction costs theory requires a universe of technological tranquillity (Foray, 1991). On the contrary, somewhat close to the evolutionary theory, the second theory states a non-substitutability between internal and external R&D, based on the dual function of R&D activities stated above. However, although emphasis is put on learning, this alternative approach to transaction costs also 'black-boxes' the internal R&D. It remains very vague and abstract about how a technological resource entering the firm acquires new qualities and changes its nature.

None of the theories proposes a taxonomy of different forms of cooperation – they just suggest a spectrum. Moreover, they leave aside the dynamics of cooperation as well as the dynamics of competition between firms.

The second axis refers to the temporal variations in the forms of technological cooperation. The literature is clearly less theoretical (compared to the literature mentioned above). It consists of empirical studies in which the evolution of R&D cooperation is not investigated in its own right, but where temporal variations are incidentally observed and argued. In this literature, the changes in R&D cooperation are the result of technological factors and/or firm strategies. For Orsenigo (1989) and Barbanti et al. (1992), the cooperation patterns are closely related to the technology. The evolution of the forms of cooperation depends on the specific nature of the technology and the evolution of the technological regime in terms of knowledge base, technological opportunity, cumulativeness and appropriability. According to Pisano and Teece (1989) and Pisano et al. (1988), cooperation evolution is driven by the creation and accessibility of complementary assets. The main variation factors are the sources of know-how, appropriability and transfer costs of technology. Hamilton (1990) accomplishes a synthesis between these two approaches in considering cooperation as an element of the technological strategy of the firm. R&D cooperation is expected to decrease over time as technological uncertainties decrease and firms operate their integration strategies. Moreover, R&D cooperation is also expected to change in nature over time: from equity alliances in research to contractual R&D and marketing agreements. Two major criticisms could be made of these different attempts to explain temporal variations in cooperation. First, they are very deterministic regarding technological or strategic change. Second, they leave as exogenous variables the evolution factors, such as the technology diffusion process and the appropriability or the forces of competition.

As Barbanti et al. (1992) have pointed out, one finds no sound theoretical hypothesis for explaining the dynamics of R&D cooperation. From our point of view, this situation is due to an heuristic weakness: when focusing on R&D cooperation, the literature considers the firm as a global entity, ignoring largely what is going on within their research centres. Although R&D cooperation undoubtedly involves the firm, it concerns especially its research centres. Paradoxically, this 'black-boxing' attitude is shared by authors who emphasize the concept of learning and those who put a strong emphasis on the concept of complementary assets. From this point of view, first insights into the internal R&D may be fruitful for making progress on the question of complementarity and substitutability between internal and external R&D. Moreover, black box II is where R&D and industrial dynamics are connected. Entering it enables us to observe the key relationships between technological cooperation and the dynamics of differentiated oligopolies.

THE INDUSTRIAL R&D PROCESS THEORY AND ITS IMPLICATIONS FOR COOPERATION

The Three Modes of Industrial R&D

Generally speaking, industrial R&D refers to the R&D activity developed by firms. It includes the internal capacities of the firm as well as its external R&D in relation to universities or other firms (Foray and Mowery, 1990). Within our model, it refers more specifically to the R&D activities which take place in differentiated oligopolies (Sylos-Labini, 1965). Differentiated oligopolies gather science-based industries such as the pharmaceutical industry, the seed industry or the electronics industry. In these sectors, competition is based on product differentiation, and R&D is the key activity in generating new products. Industrial R&D is therefore defined as a firm's activity dedicated to making propositions of new temporary monopolies by mobilizing science and technology. A minimal objective is also associated to this function: in order to ensure the long-term viability of the firm, industrial R&D needs to produce at least a constant flow of temporary monopolies evaluated in terms of expected discounted value. Industrial R&D is characterized by two variables: its intensity, measured by the level of R&D expenditure of the firm (including external R&D); and the nature of industrial R&D, defined by its research assets and specified according to three modes: exploitative R&D, exploratory R&D and imitative R&D.

Definition of the three modes

The taxonomy is based on three major criteria (see Table 10.2). We start with exploitative R&D. The basic pattern of its goals is similar in every company. It targets the largest markets. The consequence of this homogeneity in the objectives and the capacities is that economies of scale and of scope are the main means of success in the competition, which is very harsh, and generates an important time pressure, reinforced by the fear of imitation. It shares many economic characteristics with a regular production process. Although it is organized on the same technical basis in every company, it is specific, for it is also based on the companies' past success stories. Every company tries to build and defend a technological tradition based on a few products in a precise market segment, in a solid temporary monopoly position. Finally, exploitation R&D aims to maximize in the long term the irreversible R&D investment profitability.

Table 10.2   Definition of the three types of industrial R&D

	Exploration	Exploitation	Imitation
Definition	Search for the continuity of the innovation: feeding exploitation with reliable technologies	Search for the innovation in the continuity: obtaining new products out of well known methods	Innovation in copying: taking advantage of competitors' innovations
Competitive advantage	Learning capacity	Scale and scope	Speed
Financial logic and competitive behaviour	Preparing and evaluating the open options for future irreversible investments Option value	Long-term maximization of the irreversible R&D investment profitability Discounted expected value	Short-term maximization of irreversible R&D investment profitability Cost + margin

Imitative R&D is a similar activity, as it is based on the same techniques, often the same people, as exploitative R&D. The difference is that it has to be driven by information on competitors' successes (and failures), gathered and analysed by specialists. Within an oligopoly, a new product bound to have a commercial success gives birth to as many imitative research programmes as there are competitors able to build a task force on the matter quickly enough. There is often no room in the market for the late followers. So the main quality required to imitate is speed, or more generally flexibility and timing. From a technical point of view, imitation uses the same equipment as exploitation.

Exploratory R&D is very different from the two previous modes. Its objective is not to build temporary monopolies straight away with new products, but to keep the company able to undergo, or even to generate large technological changes. In this respect, this R&D mode is typical of the innovative firm (Amendola and Bruno, 1990), whereas the imitative R&D and to some extent the exploitative R&D are more on the passive side, helping the firm adapt to its environment, rather than creating this very environment. To achieve its mission, exploratory R&D has to test and learn by using the emerging technologies. From the firm's point of view, it works on the border of its knowledge. This R&D preserves the firm from being trapped in its own previous irreversible R&D investments. Its economic logic cannot be explained by the direct benefit it brings. Exploratory R&D may have no apparent result for years, without being useless. Only option value (Henry, 1974) can justify its existence, by giving a value to the long-term flexibility it provides.

The diversity of the activities found under the general R&D heading is not a sequence in time, but clusters of parallel activities, found within the firm, and explained by the competition dynamics of the firm in a particular industry, at a given period.

The relationships between the three modes
The viability of the firm requires that the three modes be integrated within it. There are firms, however, which manage only one of the three modes of R&D. This paradox needs to be explained. We argue in this section that the interdependency between the three modes is fundamentally based on dynamics: exploratory R&D opens the gate to exploitative R&D, which itself renders possible imitative R&D. In a long period, there is no continuous exploitative R&D without exploratory R&D within the firm, nor imitative R&D without exploitative R&D within the firm, except in a world of technological tranquillity.[3]

New biotechnology firms (NBFs) are a typical example of firms specialized in exploratory R&D. When Genentech succeeded in producing human interferon and insulin, it had neither capability in screening pharmaceutical molecules, nor in managing economies of scale and scope, which characterize the exploitative R&D of large established pharmaceutical companies. Similarly, these latter – with a few exceptions, such as Eli-Lilly or Dupont, which have rapidly developed DNA recombinant technology internally – possess only exploitative R&D capability. There are several examples of 'me-too' producers in the pharmaceutical and in the seed industry, firms whose research is only dedicated to imitation. Considering the companies where the three modes of R&D are internalized, we observe that the combinations of the three modes are specific to each of them. In the agrochemicals industry, Ciba-Geigy is very well known for its strong ability in imitative research. When a competitor finds a new chemical family of pesticides, it can be sure that 20 to 100 researchers of Ciba are investigating chemical analogues that are not dependent on its patent. On the other hand, Monsanto is very well known for putting emphasis on exploratory research even if it continues in parallel fashion to invest in the traditional process of screening. To sum up, we can say that at a given state the R&D is specific to each firm according to the amount of its expenditure and their allocation among the three modes (a formalization of this statement is given in the Appendix).

The relationship between exploitative R&D and imitative R&D In general, imitative R&D and exploitative R&D are integrated in the firm. The forces that lead to their integration are twofold: economies of scope and transaction costs. Imitative R&D uses basically the same assets as exploitative R&D (equipment and human resources). Its specific resources and skills are limited to a team of experts in analysing competitor's patents and to a special ability to organize rapidly a task force of researchers. Moreover, it is faster to gather internal assets for copying than to obtain the resources required externally. Finally, due to the appropriability and opportunism issues, costs of contracting are very high (Teece, 1986). Bonazzi (1993) observes that, in the agrochemicals industry, the better-performing firms in imitative R&D are those which own the larger capacity in exploitative R&D. They can shift rapidly a high number of chemists from exploitative projects to an urgent imitative project (without endangering the former), and so work faster in designing the imitative products. The advantage for firms which mainly dedicate their research to exploitative R&D in maintaining a minimum capacity in imitative research is based on the probabilistic aspect of the success of the former. When, by chance, the exploitative R&D does not discover interesting new products, imitative R&D can limit the decrease of the flow of expected temporary monopolies that the research of the differentiated oligopoly must ensure. Imitative R&D uses, and regulates, the activity of exploitation. The long-term survival of firms specialized only in imitative R&D is very problematic. It depends on the innovations of the competitors and, above all, on weak intellectual property rights. Moreover, such firms suffer more than any other from the industry concentration, and the reduction in the number of new products due to this concentration. This latter factor explains why one encounters such a high number of imitative small firms in the seed sector. It is worth noting that these firms were also previously involved in exploitative R&D. As Jullien (1992) has pointed out they were progressively led to specialize their exploitation research in imitative tasks. Their market performances were too weak to invest in carrying out the economies of scale and scope related to exploitative R&D.

The relationships between exploitative R&D and exploratory R&D   These two modes are not so strongly linked by shared resources as in the previous case. In essence, exploratory R&D is based on new knowledge and techniques, whereas exploitation is based on specialized assets. Because they do not use the same technology, they can even be located in different places. Several established firms of the pharmaceutical industry have created special buildings for implementing their biotechnology laboratories. As the exploratory R&D is not generating technological discontinuities that can be used to transform the exploitative R&D, its results can remain outside the firm, or just disconnected from the internal exploitative R&D. In this context one can encounter firms specialized in exploratory R&D. On the contrary, in the case of an expected technological discontinuity, close relationships between both are required.

Briefly, exploratory R&D possesses the ability in the new technology but not the organizational capability of managing research (and development which is far more time- and money-consuming than research) as an industrial productive process, whereas the exploitative R&D does not own the new technological capability, but is experienced in standardizing and scaling up research projects. Sometimes exploratory R&D regenerates the exploitative R&D. That occurs when competition on price is increasing within the differentiated oligopoly.

The three modes and the dynamics of the differentiated oligopoly
There are two pitfalls for a firm belonging to a differentiated oligopoly. The first is encountered when for a given segment of the market (e.g., antibiotics in the pharmaceutical industry) there is intense competition on price, due to product similarity. The second pitfall is met when the product is very different from what already exists, but there is no demand or no sales. There is a permanent tension within the firm between the attempt to follow successful strategies of competitors and the attempt to take lonely avenues. The former comes from the imitative and exploitative modes employed by firms; the second involves the exploratory mode. These behaviours drive the dynamics.

Exploitative R&D is exhausted when it does not enable the firm to differentiate. The temporary monopolies derived from the research become smaller and smaller. First, over time the capacity and the ability of firms in exploitative R&D become very similar. They use the same techniques and invest the same amounts. Then, what makes the difference is only the speed. Several firms are able to produce a new antibiotic or a new herbicide for wheat crops. Among them however some still have a competitive advantage in R&D due to their rapidity in developing and registering.[4] Second, the products which are already on the market can be difficult to surpass. The improvement of new analgesics or new herbicides is based on secondary characteristics such as the way to ingest them and spray them, not on primary functions which are already saturated: all the analgesics suppress the pain and all the herbicides kill the weeds. Both factors lead to increased competition on cost between the firms of the oligopoly. For each segment of the market, the number of similar products increases, introducing a demand elasticity to price. When all the herbicides for wheat crops or all the antibiotics have the same characteristics (in the sense of Lancaster, 1979), the consumer can choose on price basis. The differentiated oligopoly can then evolve in several ways. It can become an oligopoly in which the competitive advantage is based on cost. Or it can remain a differentiated oligopoly but based on marketing: innovation is achieved by adding services to the products, not via research. Both ways lead to a drop in R&D activity. Finally, it can regenerate itself by changing its exploitative R&D. A transition phase starts and the exploratory R&D changes into the new exploitative R&D.

At this stage of our analysis, we have attempted to demonstrate that:

1. To each firm corresponds a specific intensity and nature of industrial R&D.
2. The industrial R&D evolves over time according to the dynamics of the differentiated oligopoly.

These statements have two implications regarding cooperation.

Implication I: The Pattern of Cooperation Reflects the Pattern of Internal R&D

In this section we suggest that the diversity in the organizational forms of cooperation is based on the diversity of the industrial R&D undertaken internally by the firms. As such, different firms will have very particular cooperation portfolios, as they have very specific combinations of internal R&D. This can be observed not only for firms dedicated to a single R&D mode but also for firms that perform the three modes, but with different intensities.

Characteristics of cooperation in each R&D mode

One of the most striking differences in cooperation between the three R&D modes is that the number of agreements and their frequency diminish from exploratory R&D (where they are many) to exploitative R&D (where they are few), to imitative R&D (where they tend to zero). Other descriptive characteristics for the first two modes are depicted in Table 10.3. The differences arise from the particular mission and logic of organization of each R&D mode; cooperation reflects the internal activities.

Exploitative R&D   This mode corresponds to the 'production' side of R&D activities. It exploits a proven method to achieve identified technical/commercial objectives.

  Cooperation aims to enhance the profitability of the irreversible assets. It can do so through the reduction of costs and risks: reduction of costs is achieved through economies of scale and scope (the major source of performance in exploitative R&D) enabled by the additional capacity provided by the partner, and through the reduction of lead times; reduction of risk is achieved through the avoidance of competition implicit in cooperation – partners avoid the risk of being overtaken or imitated by a quick competitor.

  Collaboration in exploitative R&D is thus supposed to occur when partners have or are trying to develop similar competencies, at least where methods are concerned, so that economies of scale can act; but have complementary product lines and markets, so that economies of scope can be better exploited and lead times shortened.

Table 10.3   Characteristics of cooperation according to the different R&D modes

	Exploratory R&D	Exploitative R&D
Number of agreements	Many	Few
Number of partners/ agreements	Vary: can be many	Few
Complementarity of partner	Technological (including methods)	Product line/market
Technology exchanged	More tacit, embodied in people	Less tacit, embodied in artefacts or texts
Human resources involved	Scientists/ fundamentalists	Engineers
Assets involved	Generic and flexible	Specific and rigid
Linkage with universities	Many and stronger	Few and weaker
Specific forms used	Research grants minority equity	Customer–supplier technology exchange agreements
Common forms used (1)	R&D contracts Joint R&D Joint ventures Licensing	R&D contracts Joint R&D Joint ventures Licensing
Position in the market– hierarchy spectrum	In the middle	Near the extremes

Moreover, as the task of exploitative R&D is to generate innovation propositions that will involve the whole company, strong linkages between R&D and production and marketing activities of the firm are needed. The extreme importance of information, coordination and control channels demands that cooperation, when concerning the process of innovation itself, be very close to the internal organization, or, when the activity in question can be detached from the process of innovation, that the interface between the organizations involved be standardized and cooperation be similar to market transactions.

These features are translated into the descriptive characteristics depicted in Table 10.3. R&D cooperation will lead to few agreements, with few partners, generally possessing complementary product lines and/or markets, and involving already codified technology. These agreements will tend to be near the extremes of the spectrum hierarchy – market.

Joint ventures are, thus, one of the most characteristic forms of cooperation in this mode. An example is the announcement by Pasteur-Mérieux, number one in the world vaccine market and Merck, number two, of their intention to form a joint venture to, apart from commercializing the products of both firms, develop new products together. The development of multiple vaccines (single dose providing immunization to several diseases), provides a field for joining their complementary experiences and products.

On the other hand, linkages that imply more unilateral flows of technology tend to be one-off, providing more standardized inputs, generally embodied in artefacts or blueprints for example, universities transferring molecules to the industry, NBFs supplying specific biological inputs (such as antibodies licensed to be used by the established firms in their own diagnostic kits). These outputs can be used in products which are then marketed. Technology exchange agreements, very common in the pharmaceutical industry, although bilateral, follow the same principle, as it concerns codified technology.

Exploratory R&D   The task of exploratory R&D is to prepare new irreversible investments. As such, the function of cooperation is to access new knowledge and internalize and specify what seems promising.

The main source of performance in exploratory R&D is its learning capacity, and cooperation facilitates this task through the enhanced learning implied by the greater involvement of the partners (as compared to arm's-length market transactions), that permits easier access to the partners' competences and skills.

Cooperation also heightens the entry barriers to this activity, keeping other firms away from some of the sources of relevant knowledge. Should the project bear fruit and the firm decide to continue on that path, this may assure it some advantage on the learning curve.

The exploratory R&D mode conditions cooperation mainly through its uncertain character: it works closer to science, where the issues to be accounted for are very heterogeneous and the scope of the relevant knowledge is not defined *a priori*, in a context of uncertainty. We can expect, thus, several relationships to be established, with partners that possess scientific knowledge or intend to develop it and that these relationships will be reversible (limited time horizon or possibility of being broken).

The translation of these features into more descriptive characteristics gives us the configuration in Table 10.3: many agreements, with a varying number of partners (frequently universities) characterized by technological complementarities (generally scientific versus industrial in the case of universities and NBFs, and technologies previously related to different applications in the case of other established firms).

Research grants to universities and minority equity investments, coupled with contract R&D, and with NBFs, are among some of the most typical forms of technological collaboration. Monsanto, for example, at the beginning of the 1980s sponsored programmes within the Harvard Medical School, the Rockefeller University and Washington University. It also maintained minority positions in Biogen and Genentech (with which it established research contracts), Collagen and Genex (Horwitch and Sakakibara, 1986).

Not only the established firms but also their partners undertook several agreements, for instance Genentech. Among its stock-holders were not only Monsanto, but also Lubrizol, Fluor and Corning Glass. And different research projects were carried out with many firms such as Eli-Lilly, A.B. Kabi, Sumitomo Chemical and also Hoffman-Laroche, which finally bought it (see below).

Cooperation in exploratory R&D can also be undertaken with other established firms. An example is the project on artificial seeds, part of the Eureka Programme, that joined Limagrain, Nestlé and Rhône-Poulenc to generate basic know-how. In this case, it covered different but complementary fields, where one of the partners is a specialist: Limagrain for embryogenesis and plant selection, Nestlé for plant cell and embryo culture in fermentators, and Rhône-Poulenc for polymers (Guignard, 1992).

Imitative R&D   A firm that only pursues imitative R&D would rarely cooperate. The internal availability of the resources needed by the innovation, and the absence of technical risk reduce the incentive to cooperate. Above all, with speed as its main criterion of performance, cooperation would clearly be short-term and one-off and the object of transfer standardized, thus subject to market transactions.

Cooperation between exploitative and exploratory R&D modes

Is any cooperation possible between a firm that operates only in the exploratory mode, as most NBFs, and a firm that operates only in the exploitative mode? Only to a certain extent. There must be some overlapping of the knowledge bases and of the R&D modes for cooperation to work. For example a big pharmaceutical company must be involved in exploratory R&D when it sets up a joint R&D agreement with an NBF, even if it is limited to the small group in charge of cooperation – Monsanto, for example, had only twelve scientists in its first two years of involvement in biotechnology (according to Robert Horsch, Monsanto's manager). Similarly an NBF must be involved in exploitative R&D when it establishes a joint venture with a pharmaceutical firm intending to launch into production.

If there is no such overlapping of knowledge bases, then any commercial transaction must take place closer to the market place, for example, the licensing for production of products emerging from exploitative R&D, and agreements to supply specific biological products directly from exploitative R&D activities.

The relationship between exploratory and exploitative R&D discussed earlier is also relevant as regards cooperation. As long as technological discontinuities are not being generated, exploitative and exploratory R&D can be quite distant – establishing relations through arm's-length market transactions. But when technological discontinuities are being generated, close relationships are necessary to match the 'new technology' with the 'productive process'. When this occurs, either the exploratory R&D partner or the exploitative R&D partner (or both) will have to step into the other R&D mode to assure the necessary matching of capabilities.

Implication II: The Evolution of R&D Cooperation Follows the Dynamics of the Differentiated Oligopoly

We can now answer the initial question of the paper: why are the number and the forms of R&D cooperation changing over time? First we shall consider the deductive demonstration from industrial R&D theory. Then we shall provide some empirical evidence in the case of biotechnology.

Implication II is deduced from the connection between the three modes of R&D and the oligopoly dynamics we have established earlier, i.e. the relative intensities of the three modes at the industry level depend on the stage of the competition process within the oligopoly; and Implication I discussed earlier: to each R&D mode corresponds a specific pattern in R&D cooperation.

When the oligopoly recreates its capacity of differentiation based on a new technology, cooperation increases tremendously. The dominant organizational forms of R&D cooperation are concentrated in the middle of the spectrum of market–hierarchy; minority equity investments coupled with R&D contracts are very frequent. When the differentiated oligopoly is exploiting its irreversible research investments, cooperation is less developed. The dominant forms of R&D cooperation are then close to the market or to pure integration; customer–supplier relations and joint ventures are frequent. The decline in the number of R&D agreements can therefore be explained as the approaching end of the transition phase during which exploratory R&D is changing into exploitative R&D.

The empirical demonstration emphasizes the case of the pharmaceutical industry where the oligopoly evolution is simple to describe. In the literature, the decreasing trend in biotechnology alliances is explained by the decrease in the needs for cooperation owing to the integration processes which have been occurring both for NBFs and established firms. A vertical division of labour between NBFs and established firms initially characterized the biotechnology industry. The biotechnology industry emerged as a market for R&D, with NBFs on the supply side and established chemical and pharmaceutical enterprises on the demand side (Pisano, 1991). But while both continue to engage in cooperation agreements, there has been a trend towards forward integration by NBFs (into manufacturing) and towards backward integration by established enterprises (into biotechnology R&D).

In our opinion, the change in R&D cooperation between the NBFs and the established firms relies basically on horizontal integration, i.e. a transition process between exploratory R&D and exploitative R&D in connection with the increasing competition within the pharmaceutical oligopoly which has reached the point of being mainly on price. Two basic figures summarize this trend. In 1989 (Leveque, 1990b), 40 per cent of the world market was represented by products launched more than fifteen years before (most of them were therefore out of patent protection). Between 1955 and 1980 the number of new active ingredients discovered per year was halved whereas the R&D expenditures were increased eightfold (in constant dollars – Leveque, 1990b).

To summarize the evolution of R&D cooperation in relation to the oligopoly dynamics, three periods can be distinguished. During the first, from 1976 – the creation of Genentech – to 1981, when the number of annual creation of NBFs peaked, biotechnology used the exploratory R&D mode. But it was disconnected from the existing exploitative R&D in the pharmaceutical industry. NBFs were the main place where such research was located. Only a few established firms had an in-house biotechnology programme and when they had one, it was located in new buildings and involved new scientists. A greater number of large firms were involved in biotechnology exclusively through relationships with NBFs via R&D contracts, equity investments and joint R&D. In exchange for their support, they received rights to specific technologies or products that emerged from the exploratory research. The Cati–Merit database (Hagedoorn and Schakenraad, 1990) confirms this cooperation context: the number of the agreements increased steadily, reaching 80 per year in 1980, most of them (66 per cent) involving long-term positioning.

During the second period, from 1981 to 1987 – the year when the number of new agreements starts to decline (see Table 10.1) – biotechnology was entering the transition phase. The first products (recombinant human insulin and growth hormone) were launched on the market. And above all, completely new products (such as the recombinant t-PA), involving new markets, were in development or registration stages. Clearly, biotechnology then appeared as a new and successful source of commercial products. The growth in the number of new agreements was therefore accelerating. All the established pharmaceutical firms were making alliances with NBFs in order to develop or reinforce in-house exploratory R&D. According to the Office of Technology Assessment (1988), in 1988 96 per cent of the 53 established enterprises it surveyed conducted 'at least some' biotechnology R&D in-house. During this period, the investments in biotechnology were no longer disconnected from the exploitative R&D assets as before. The task of the R&D managers was to cross-fertilize and match DNA recombinant techniques and the exploitative R&D skills. We observe also some changes in the relative importance of different forms of cooperation. Minority equity investments and joint R&D agreements gradually decreased whereas joint ventures rose (Cati–Merit database, 1993). Furthermore, strategic objectives for cooperation shifted from long-term positioning to cost economizing (Hagedoorn and Schakenraad, 1990).

In 1987 the number of agreements started to decline, suggesting that the transition phase was near the end. Biotechnology is definitively taking the exploitative R&D mode. Biotechnology units of the pharmaceutical companies have no longer clear boundaries within the research centres. In less than ten years the industry has changed from a situation where 'big companies were seriously interested in cooperating with young start-up companies in biotech' to a situation where 'small research firm desperately seeks a large buyer'. The minority sharing and research contracts, which characterized the cooperation in DNA recombinant technology between small firms and large pharmaceutical companies at the beginning of the 1980s, are now being replaced by customer–supplier relations where small firms are simple subcontractors. A large number of NBFs closed down. The best ones have been bought out by larger firms.

CONCLUSION

This paper has attempted to deal with R&D cooperation within an industrial R&D theory, and to deduce implications from it, instead of departing from theoretical frameworks related to technology, or cooperation theories, like the transaction costs theory. Furthermore, the industrial R&D we have designed emphasizes two aspects traditionally left in the dark by literature: what is going on within the firms' research centres; and the relationships between the R&D activity and the competitive process. This approach does not invalidate most of the results obtained by Pisano and Teece (in particular, the role of complementary assets and appropriability regimes in shaping cooperation agreements), by Walsh or by Foray and Mowery. The main interest of the industrial R&D theory is that it enables us to adopt a dynamic point of view, and to explain theoretically the temporal and structural variations in the organizational form of R&D cooperation.

Furthermore, it gives some new insights about the permanent/transient feature of R&D cooperation. Our general answer is that only inter-firm cooperation involving on both sides exploratory R&D, or exploitative R&D (or in a rarer case imitative R&D) is permanent. When the agreements between the firms connect different modes of industrial R&D, collaboration is intrinsically transitory. It will last only during the change of exploratory R&D into exploitative R&D (i.e. the redifferentiation phase of the oligopoly). In the case of biotechnology, for instance, the permanent collaborative relationships which remain nowadays are only those which correspond to gains in economies of scale or scope.

NOTES

1.   This term is an humorous wink at the weak inclination of most economists to observe and take account of the internal organization of the firm which has been considered for a long time as

a black box. It emphasizes the necessity to investigate inside companies' research centres in order to understand the economics of technological changes. It obviously refers to Rosenberg, (1982).

2. This paper adopts the definition of Chesnais (1988): 'cooperation agreements between two or more companies providing for a certain degree of collaboration between them (and) involving equity participation or the creation of new companies (as well as) non-equity agreements'.

3. In this respect our R&D theory is not a linear model. We do not assume that projects start in exploratory R&D, go to exploitative R&D for market specification and improvement, and then finally to imitative R&D. There are obviously instantaneous flows of information, equipment and researchers between the three modes, but there is no basis to characterize the interdependency.

4. Ellul (1991) shows that the average length of development varies from one to five years between the ten pharmaceutical firms.

REFERENCES

Abernathy, W. J. and Utterback, J.M. (1978), 'Patterns of industrial innovation', *Technology Review*.

Amendola, M. and Bruno, S. (1990), 'The behavior of the innovative firm: relations to the environment', *Research Policy*, **19**.

Barbanti, P., Gambardella, A. and Orsenigo, L. (1992), 'The evolution of the forms of collaboration in biotechnology', Paper presented at the colloquium, 'Les accords de coopération pour la recherche développement en biotechnologie', Grenoble, SERD/INRA.

Bonazzi, C. (1993), 'R&D industrielle et concurrence, le cas de l'agrochimie et de la pharmacie', thèse de doctorat de l'ENSMP, CERNA.

Chesnais, F. (1988), 'Technical cooperation agreements between firms', *STI Review*, 4.

Cohen, W. and Levinthal, D. (1988), 'Innovation and learning: the two faces of R&D', ISS Congress, Siena.

Ellul, E. (1991), 'Réduire les délais de développement d'un produit pharmaceutique', *Annales des Mines*, July–August.

Foray, D. (1991), 'The secrets of industry are in the air: industrial cooperation and the organizational dynamics of the innovative firm', *Research Policy*, **20**(5).

Foray, D. and Mowery, D.C. (1990), 'L'intégration de la R&D industrielle: nouvelles perspectives d'analyse', *Revue Economique*, 3.

Gaffard, J.-L. (1990), *Economie industrielle et de l'innovation*, Paris, Dalloz.

Gort, M. and Klepper, S. (1992), 'Time paths in the diffusion of product innovations', *Economic Journal*, **92**.

Guignard, P. (1992), 'Analyse et présentation de l'accord de recherche EUREKA sur les semences artificielles', Paper presented at the colloquium 'Les accords de coopération pour la recherche développement en biotechnologie', Grenoble, SERD/INRA.

Hagedoorn, J. (1990), 'Organizational modes of inter-firm cooperation and technology transfer', *Technovation*, **10**(1).

Hagedoorn, J. and Schakenraad, J. (1990) 'Inter-firm partnership and co-operative strategies in core technologies', in: C. Freeman and L. Soete (eds) *New explorations in the economics of technological change*, London: Pinter.

Hamilton, W. F. (1990), 'The dynamics of technology and strategy', *European Journal of Operational Research*, **47**.

Henry, C. (1974), 'Investment decisions under uncertainty: the 'irreversibility effect', *American Economic Review*, **64**(6).

Horwitch, M. and Sakakibara, K. (1986), 'The changing strategy–technology relationship in technology based industries', *Research on technological innovation, management and policy*, **3**.

Jones, S. (1992), *The biotechnologists*, London: Macmillan.

Jullien, E. (1992), 'Imitation et appropriation dans les dynamiques industrielles, le cas des semences', thèse de doctorat de l'ENSMP, CERNA.

Lancaster K. (1979), *Variety, Equity and Efficiency*, New York: Columbia University Press.

Leveque, F. (1990a) 'Les produits biotechnologiques à l'épreuve du marché', *La Recherche*, **21**(217), January.

Leveque F. (1990b), 'Pharmacie: L'Ère des géants', *Espace Social Européen*, 64, 4 May.

Leveque F. (1990c), 'The Logic of Growth', *Bio/Technology*, **8**(8), August.

Link, A. and Bauer, L. (1987), 'An economic analysis of co-operative research', *Technovation*, **6**.

Mowery, D. (ed.) (1988), *International collaborative ventures in US manufacturing*, Cambridge, Mass.: Ballinger.

OECD (1992), *Technology and the economy*, Paris: OECD.

Office of Technology Assessment (1988), *New Developments in Biotechnology: US Investment in Biotechnology* (Part 4), Washington DC: US Government Printing Office.

Orsenigo, L. (1989), *The emergence of biotechnology*, London: Pinter.

Pisano, G.P. (1990), 'R&D boundaries of the firm: an empirical analysis', *Administrative Science Quarterly*, **35**.

Pisano, G.P. (1991), 'The governance of innovation: vertical integration and collaborative arrangements in the biotechnology industry', *Research Policy*, **20**.

Pisano, G. and Teece, D.J. (1989), 'Collaborative arrangements and global technology strategy: some evidence from the telecommunications equipment industry', *Research on technological innovation, management and policy*, **4**.

Pisano, G.P., Shan, W. and Teece, D.J. (1988), 'Joint ventures and collaboration in the biotechnology industry', in: Mowery (1988).

Richardson, G. (1972), 'The organization of industry', *Economic Journal*, **82**.

Rosenberg, N. (1982), *Inside the Black Box: Technology and Economics*, New York: Cambridge University Press.

Sylos-Labini, P. (1965), *Oligopolo y progresso tecnico*, Barcelona: Oikos-Tau.

Tapon, F. (1989), 'A transaction cost analysis of innovations in the organization of pharmaceutical R&D', *Journal of Economic Behavior and Organization*, **2**.

Teece, D. (1986), 'Profiting from technological innovation: implications for integration, collaboration, licensing and public policy', *Research Policy*, **15**.

Teece, D. (1988), 'Technological change and the nature of the firm', in: G. Dosi, C. Freeman, R. Nelson, G. Silverberg and L. Soete (eds) *Technical change and economic theory*, London: Pinter.

Walsh, V. (1991), 'Inter-firm technological alliances: a transient phenomenon or new structures in capitalist economies?' in: A. Amin and M. Dietrich, *Towards a new Europe?* Aldershot: Edward Elgar.

Williamson, O. (1975), *Markets and hierarchies*, New York: Free Press.

APPENDIX   METHODOLOGICAL CONSIDERATIONS TO MEASURE TECHNOLOGICAL COOPERATION

One of the most mentioned methodological problems when working empirically on cooperation is the unsurmountable bias implicit in databases: as they use specialized publications as their source of information, the agreements listed will be only those that the firms were interested in divulging and the press interested in publishing. Still, these practices vary a great deal among industries and countries and there is much personal judgement in the classification of the agreements from frequently incomplete news (Chesnais, 1988).

But few authors mention a central and previous problem: the definition of cooperation itself. Empirical studies on collaborative agreements adopt very different definitions, depriving the object of the analysis of its specificity.

Existing theory does not help much. It defines cooperation as a spectrum of organizational forms going from pure internalization to pure market, but does not propose a taxonomy. And from this point on, different interpretations and different objectives of research lead to the most different classifications possible.

For the limits of this spectrum several empirical approaches have already been adopted. Acquisitions and fusions are normally left outside this continuum, identified as internal organization. But there are some databases (such as LAREA/CEREM) that include them as collaboration. The inclusion of licences is also problematic as some kinds of licences are considered market transactions, but others are not (Chesnais, 1988).

The descriptive categories used to identify the organizational forms in this continuum vary immensely, reflecting the adoption of different concepts/variables to order it. Pisano and Teece (1989) use the financial ties and find two categories: equity and non-equity agreements. The classification of the LAREA/CEREM group is based on the juridicial form of the agreements. Hagedoorn's (1990) is based on the organizational interdependence ('organizational and economic solidity') they entitle. Link and Bauer's (1987) is based on several other variables, such as the nature of the research conducted, the strategic character of the projects and the institutional nature of the partners – and in this case there is no more the idea of an ordered continuum. We use these last two – depicted in Tables 10.2 and 10.3 – as examples for further discussion.

These examples illustrate that we should be careful with the interchangeable use of the terms 'cooperative agreements', 'inter-firm cooperation' and 'strategic alliances' when referring to cooperation. The confusion has its origins in the fact that one of the most distinguishing features of the recent wave of cooperation in relation to what was observed before the 1970s is its inter-firm and strategic character (as opposed to neutral-competitive cooperation). The first example is restricted to inter-firm strategic agreements (the recent analysis of

Hagedoorn leaves aside even inter-firm agreements judged to be motivated by cost reduction) and the second one is not.

There is still another difference between the two classifications reproduced. Although both refer to technological cooperation, the first includes technological cooperation related to manufacturing, whereas the second refers only to joint research. This difference is compounded when still other kinds of agreements, such as marketing, or R&D and marketing, are taken into account.

It is thus very difficult to analyse, compare and use available data on organizational forms of cooperation – they are based on different inconvertible variables, referring to quite different kinds of relations. A theoretical taxonomy is lacking to give a common base for empirical approaches.

11. Informal networks in the origination of successful innovations

Fred Steward and Steve Conway

THE IMPORTANCE OF EXTERNAL SOURCES IN TECHNOLOGICAL INNOVATION

The sources of technological innovation have been a subject of interest in many studies since the late 1950s. Early concerns focused on the utility of basic science to technological innovation (e.g. Sherwin and Isenson, 1967; Illinois Institute of Technology, 1968; Battelle Memorial Institute, 1973; Gibbons and Johnston, 1974), and the importance of sources external to the innovative firm (e.g. Myers and Marquis, 1969; Achilladis et al., 1971, Langrish et al., 1972). However, while this research suggested that external sources were responsible for between 34 per cent (Gibbons and Johnston) and 65 per cent (Langrish et al.) of the inputs important to the innovation process, evidence of the utility of basic science to technological innovation was mixed.

A diverse range of external sources has been found to contribute to the development of successful innovation, including research organizations, suppliers, competitors, users, consumers and distributors. Studies have shown users in particular, but also suppliers and competitors, as playing an important role in the innovation process (Hippel, 1976, 1977a, 1977b, 1987, 1988; Allen et al., 1983; Shaw, 1985; Schrader, 1991; Vanderwerf, 1990). Research has also shown the continuing role of the independent inventor as a source of innovative ideas leading to successful innovation in larger firms (Jewkes et al., 1969; Udell, 1990; Whalley, 1991). However, cross-sector studies have suggested the more limited importance of academic institutions as a source of ideas (e.g. Langrish et al., 1972).

Variations in the range and importance of these external sources to the innovative firm have been identified along a number of dimensions. For example, between industrial sectors (Myers and Marquis, 1969; Easingwood, 1986), between product and process innovations (Baker et al., 1967), between large and small firms (Allen et al., 1983), between the idea-generation and problem-solving stages of the innovation process (Myers and Marquis, 1969; Utterback,

1971), and between *basic* or *radical* innovations, and major and minor improvements, or what is sometimes termed *re-innovation* (Von Hippel, 1976, 1977a, 1977b; Spital, 1979; Rothwell, 1986).

Contrary to expectations, research as early as the 1960s (FBI, 1961) revealed that external sources are as important to innovators with in-house R&D as to those without. That is, external sources are an important complementary source of scientific and technical information, rather than a substitute for indigenous R&D. Cohen and Levinthal (1989) argue 'that R&D not only generates new information ... [but] also develops the firm's ability to identify, assimilate, and exploit existing knowledge from the environment' (p. 569), what they term the *two faces* of R&D. This view receives support in the literature (Rosenberg, 1990; Freeman, 1991; Pavitt, 1991; Gambardella, 1992).

THE IMPORTANCE OF INFORMAL BOUNDARY-SPANNING ACTIVITY

Although Burns (1969) argues that 'technological transfer is still envisaged as the passage of disembodied ideas and methods, endowed with some quasi-independence ... from one state of existence, or from one milieu ... to another', (pp. 14–15), the innovation literature reveals a strong interest since the 1960s in the *mechanisms* or *channels* of idea and information transfer (Allen and Cohen, 1969; Allen, 1969, 1977; Myers and Marquis, 1969; Utterback, 1971; Langrish et al., 1972; Gibbons and Johnston, 1974).

These authors identify a number of mechanisms for the transference of ideas and information across the organizational boundary, including; the hiring of new staff (termed *boundary crossing* by Aldrich, 1979); the use of trade publications and scientific journals (termed *formal* literature by Allen, 1977), and in-house publications (termed *informal* literature by Allen, 1977); formally established meetings and conferences; field tests; and informal person-to-person modes of communication, such as telephone or corridor conversations, correspondence and visits.

A number of authors have argued that the only effective mechanism of technology transfer is through the movement of people between organizations (Burns, 1969; Price, 1969; Allen, 1977). Burns (1969), for example, contends that 'the mechanism of technological transfer is one of agents, not agencies', (p. 12), while Allen (1977) argues that 'ideas have no real existence outside of the minds of men ... Consequently, the best way to transfer information is to move a human carrier' (p. 43). This view has received some empirical support (Langrish et al., 1972; Roberts and Wainer, 1971).

However, a number of other studies have indicated the importance of informal or personal *boundary-spanning* contact to the innovation process (Myers and Marquis, 1969; Utterback, 1971; Allen et al., 1983; Von Hippel, 1987; Schrader, 1991; Kreiner and Schultz, 1991) and particularly in relation to the transfer of *tacit* knowledge (Senker, 1993; Senker and Faulkner, 1993). This view is also supported by Cunningham and Homse (1984) who argue that; 'Personal contacts are the life-blood of supplier–customer relationships. They are the vehicle of communication, not only of factual information but of ideas, impressions, attitudes, commitment, integrity, and sometimes of commercial and technical information provided only to the trusted and privileged' (p. 1). Research of manufacturer–user relations by Von Hippel (1976, 1977a, 1977b) and Shaw (1985), placed most emphasis on *multiple* and *continuous* interaction. The notions of personal contact and multiple and continuous interaction indicate the importance of informal exchange activity within personal relationships between individuals. Freeman (1991) goes further, contending that 'behind every formal network [of relationships], giving it the breath of life, are usually various informal networks' (p. 503). However, Hamel et al., (1989) argue that management may set the legal parameters for exchange behaviour, 'but what actually gets traded is determined by day-to-day interactions of engineers, marketers, and product developers' (p. 136). With these points in mind, Freeman (1991) argues that:

> Personal relationships of trust and confidence ... are important at both the formal and informal level ... For this reason cultural factors such as language, educational background, regional loyalties, shared ideologies and experiences, and even common leisure interests, continue to play an important part in networking. An appreciation of these sociological factors ... is a necessary complement to narrower *economic* explanations. (p. 503)

The importance of an appreciation of sociological factors in the understanding of personal boundary-spanning relationships is also recognized by others, including Macaulay (1963), Lundvall (1988), Bianchi and Bellini (1991), and Saxenian (1991). Laumann and Pappi (1976) argue that a social system may be differentiated in any number of ways, depending on the questions the analyst is interested in answering, but that certain bases of social differentiation are likely, in any empirical case, to be of special significance. Laumann and Pappi (1976) also contend '... that there exists a multiplicity of social structures in any complex social system that arises out of the many possible types of social relationships linking positions [actors] to one another' (p. 6).

The degree to which individuals are linked by multiple role relations, such as friend, social club member and work colleague for example, is termed *multiplexity*. It is contended that the greater the number of role relations (or strands) linking two actors, the stronger the linkage (Tichy et al., 1979). In addition, Boissevain (1974) argues that 'There is a tendency for single-stranded relations to become many-stranded if they persist over time, and for many-stranded relations to be stronger than single-stranded ones, in the sense that one strand role reinforces another' (p. 30).

NETWORKS OF INNOVATORS

In his review of the literature, Freeman (1991, p. 500) noted that empirical studies of innovation since the 1950s had demonstrated 'the importance of both formal and informal networks, even if the expression *network* was less frequently used', and that 'multiple sources of information and pluralistic patterns of collaboration were the rule rather than the exception'. Auster (1990) views networks as *portfolios* of dyadic relationships. However, this ignores the potential for networks to be greater than the sum of their parts. This potential for synergy is implied by DeBresson and Amesse (1991), who argue that 'because interactions between firms … are iterative and broad in content, time and space, what matters is the complete set of relationships' (p. 364).

Freeman (1991) also attempts to classify the various patterns of research collaboration, or what he terms *categories of network*, by the following:

1. Joint ventures and research corporations
2. Joint R&D agreements
3. Technology exchange agreements
4. Direct investment motivated by technology factors
5. Licensing and second-sourcing agreements
6. Sub-contracting, production sharing and supplier networks
7. Research associations
8. Government-sponsored joint research programmes
9. Computerized databanks and value-added networks for technical and scientific interchange
10. Other networks including informal networks. Informal or personal networks represent networks of individuals, as opposed to networks of organizations (as in categories 1–8) or artefacts (as in category 9).

With reference to a number of studies undertaken since the mid-1980s, concerning the changing patterns of collaboration in the last decade or so, Freeman (1991) argues that:

In quantitative terms there is abundant evidence of a strong upsurge of various forms of research collaboration [categories 1–5], especially in the new generic technologies … involving extensive international collaboration as well as national and regional networks. There is also ample evidence of a qualitative change in the nature of the older networking relationships [categories 6–8] ... in-depth studies of the experience of databanks and value-added networks [category 9] are still few and far between. (p. 507)

In relation to the last category, Freeman (1991) argues that 'although rarely measured systematically ... informal networks are extremely important, but very hard to classify and measure' (pp. 500–502).

Contemporary research has thus applied the network metaphor almost exclusively at the organizational level (e.g. Håkansson, 1989; Hagedoorn and Schakenraad, 1992), with a focus on the analysis of formal networks of innovating organizations within and between industries, regions and states (see DeBresson and Amesse, 1991, and Freeman, 1991, for a review).

THE HOMOPHILY PRINCIPLE AND THE STRENGTH OF WEAK TIES

A basic research question in past investigations of the communication between dyads has been the degree to which the similarity of two actors affects their interaction (Rogers and Kincaid, 1981). The degree to which interacting pairs of actors are similar in certain attributes such as beliefs, values, culture, education and social status, for example, is termed *homophily*. The term *heterophily* is employed to refer to the degree of dissimilarity between interacting pairs of individuals (Rogers and Shoemaker, 1972).

Studies in the 1970s suggested that whereas information exchange occurs most frequently between homophilous actors, information exchange *potential* or *uniqueness* is greatest during heterophilous interaction (Rogers and Bhowmik, 1971; Rogers and Shoemaker, 1972). Rogers and Bhowmik (1971) argue that 'homophily and effective communication breed each other' (p. 529). Thus one would expect strong and multiple links to build up between homophilous actors over time, and for this to lead to *isomorphism*. Isomorphism is a constraining process that forces one unit in a population to resemble other units (DiMaggio and Powell, 1991). This might involve the adoption of shared norms, beliefs and ideas, for example, that influence the way actors approach a task. Therefore the ideas or information that pass between *socially distant* heterophilous actors are likely to be *unique*, and thus valuable to the innovation process (Granovetter, 1973).

In reality, heterophilous communication is more likely to occur between actors who have at least some attributes in common, while remaining essentially sociometrically distant. This view is supported by Rogers and Kincaid (1981), who argue that 'for maximum communication effectiveness, a source and receiver should be homophilous on some certain variables and heterophilous on some variables relevant to the situation' (p. 128).

The idea that human communication typically entails a balance between similarity and dissimilarity, and between familiarity and novelty, is encapsulated by the concept of the *strength of weak ties* (Liu and Duff, 1972; Granovetter, 1973). The *strength* is informational, and refers to the information exchange potential of the relationship, while *weak ties* refers to the low degree of *proximity* between two actors. Proximity is the extent to which two interacting individuals have personal networks that overlap. Thus heterophilous actors are likely to have *weak* or *low-proximity* linkages, with little overlap in their personal networks. Granovetter (1973) argues that 'Weak-ties are more likely to link members of different small groups than are strong ones, which tend to be concentrated within particular groups ... all bridges are weak-ties ... though weak-ties are certainly not automatically bridges' (pp. 351–63).

Heterophilous or weak ties are thus important, if somewhat fragile, strategic links for innovative organizations. Indeed, this view is supported by Collins (1972) who argues that 'Weak sociometric links are likely to be more important than strong ones for the transmission of influences over long [sociometric] distances and between groups which are not densely connected' (p. 47). These weak ties provide the *bridges* (Granovetter, 1973) between what have been termed *loosely coupled systems* (Weick, 1976).

BRIDGES, BOUNDARY SPANNING AND GATEKEEPERS

The evolution of local languages and coding schemes within social systems aids local information processing. Such languages and coding systems reflect, for example, the interests, requirements, norms and values of the group (Lewis, 1948). However, Tushman and Katz (1980) argue that this can result in 'a lack of linguistic commonality' between social systems, where 'the greater the mismatch in language and cognitive orientation, the greater the difficulties of communicating' (p. 1072). Thus, while the information potential of socially distant groups is likely to be great, so too is the mismatch of language and cognitive orientation. Tushman and Katz (1980) argue that one way to overcome this paradox 'is through gatekeepers; individuals in the communication network who are capable of understanding and translating contrasting coding schemes. With the help of these key individuals, external information can flow into the system by means of a two-step process' (p. 1072).

It is these key individuals or *gatekeepers* that establish the bridges between socially distant groups. The literature (Allen, 1969, 1977; Allen and Cohen, 1969; Tushman, 1977; Tushman and Katz, 1980) also strongly suggests that gatekeepers have a significantly greater readership of professional and scientific publications, and maintain longer-term relations with experts in a broader, more diverse range of fields outside their immediate working environment, than the average researcher. Gatekeepers are therefore likely to account for the vast majority, though certainly not all, of the boundary-spanning activity in their organization.

Research by Tushman and Katz (1980) however, has found that the importance of the gatekeeper role is contingent upon the nature of the work of the organizational unit, such that 'Gatekeepers are most important in development projects; units whose task is locally defined yet where the technology employed is changing ... As research projects are unencumbered by external communication boundaries, direct peer contact seems to be the most effective way to access external professional information' (p. 1083).

THE RESEARCH PROBLEM

The existing innovation literature has therefore consistently demonstrated the importance of external sources in the development of successful innovation and highlighted the vital role of informal boundary-spanning interaction between individuals as a transfer mechanism. Research has also shifted from an essentially dyadic approach in the 1980s, back to the network perspective employed in the 1960s to mid-1970s, though today this is mainly at the organizational level. There is also a recognition that sociological factors are an important but neglected aspect in the analysis of formal and informal relationships and networks.

The research problem is thus to combine an approach that engages the 'multiple sources of information and pluralistic patterns of collaboration' (Freeman, 1991, p. 500) with one which reduces this complexity to a level of analytical manageability. Only in this way can a basis of more systematic understanding of informal networks be established. As has been stated, 'innovation networks need a typology' (DeBresson and Amesse, 1991, p. 371), but they are 'very hard to classify and measure' (Freeman, 1991, p. 502).

In order to address this issue, the social network literature was heavily drawn upon (e.g. Mitchell, 1969; Boissevain, 1974; Laumann and Pappi, 1976). This led to the adoption of the concept of *focal nets* as the framework for analysis. A focal net is the set of dyadic relationships with a nodal *actor*. In the case of this research, it was the set of external links through which ideas, know-how, information and technology entered the innovation process of the award-winning products that were studied. Such networks, defined by particular patterns of exchange, are termed *transactional* networks (Fombrun, 1982).

This framework allows for the study of both the individual dyads and the overall morphology of the transaction network.

There is one aspect of the focal net concept, however, which is of particular importance. This is the presence of *bridges* which connect the transaction-defined focal net with one or more *attribute* networks, where networks are defined by the attributes of those actors within the network, such as role relations and cultural factors.

One key methodological problem arising from the network approach outlined is ensuring that the individual respondents within each of the innovating firms provide the full and relevant information about linkages and so enable the focal net to be fully mapped out by the researcher. This is of particular importance since bridges are defined in network theory as weak ties (Granovetter, 1973). Thus the research problem is to avoid 'only tracing out strong links', when tracing formal links (Collins, 1982, p. 47). One must therefore be wary about traditional sociometric techniques that 'tend to discourage the naming of those weakly tied to the respondent, by sharply limiting the numbers of choices allowed' (Granovetter, 1973, p. 353). For 'those ties which are furthest from the forefront of a respondent's mind could for some innovating networks be the most important ... a lack of consciousness of a source of knowledge is not the same as a lack of importance' (Collins, 1982, pp. 47–60). Roster methods should therefore be used, along with attention to respondent accuracy (Rogers, 1987), in order to ensure that weak ties are properly identified. These issues influenced the method of interviewing adopted in the research process. The questions were also structured to identify the full range of sources and check the responses.

The sample was drawn from the 1991 and 1992 winners of either the Queen's Award for Technological Achievement or the British Design Council Award. These awards focus on innovation that is both technically and commercially successful. A total of 52 interviews was undertaken within 41 organizations. This represents approximately 40 per cent of the original sample of 106 organizations. Accounting for the fact that some of the organizations interviewed had jointly received the Queen's Award, a total of 37 innovations was investigated. Both the primary and the final interview sample provide a broad geographical and sectoral spread, and include a diverse range of innovative consumer and industrial products and processes.

Although some background information was obtained on the organization and the development of the innovation during these interviews, the main focus was on the following three areas:

- the identification of the key cognitive (information, know-how, ideas) and technology inputs in the innovation process;
- the identification of the source of these inputs;

- where these were external to the firm, a detailed review of the dyadic relationship that existed between the external source and the award winning organization was undertaken.

In building up a picture of these dyads, data were sought on a wide range of variables, including the origin and nature of the relationship, the nature of the input, and the frequency and intensity of contact, for example.

IDENTIFYING INFORMAL ATTRIBUTE NETWORK TYPES

Analysis of the research data indicates that the nodal innovator dominated the development process in 31 of the 37 innovations studied. In a further four instances, the process was dominated by the formalized collaborative effort of two nodal innovators. Of the two remaining cases, one could be said to be dominated by the user, the other by a range of external sources coordinated by the nodal innovator. However, such an analysis in the von Hippel tradition conceals the multiplicity of external inputs and relationships in the innovation process.

In a large number of the cases, external sources supplement and complement the resources of the nodal innovator, through a variety of formal and informal links and networks. In addition, support is found for the contention by Freeman (1991) that 'behind every formal network and often giving it the breath of life are usually one or more informal networks' (p. 503).

Analysis also revealed the strategic importance of certain of the transaction-defined relationships. These strategic relationships, or links, provided a bridge between the transaction-defined focal nets and other sociometrically distant networks. However, these sociometrically distant networks are better defined by some sociological attribute.

Five themes of *shared commonality* emerged: leisure activity, profession, scientific and technical speciality, user or potential user of the innovation, and friendship. These five themes of shared commonality, or network *attributes*, are the basis of the five informal *attribute* networks described and illustrated in the following pages.

Recreation Networks

The cohesion in this type of informal network results from the mutual sense of attachment to some recreational activity, such as sailing, mountaineering and rugby, where the feelings of challenge, achievement and comradeship through participation create and maintain personal bonds. Friendship is no doubt an important factor in this type of network, but it is not its *raison d'être*.

This type of network is illustrated by a development undertaken by a medium-sized company, which specializes in the manufacture of navigation equipment for the marine market. The innovation itself provides for the automatic plotting of positional data obtained from navigation equipment, on to conventional navigation charts.

The concept for the product was sparked off by the company chairman who, like a number of his employees, is an experienced yachtsman. Much of the early discussion took place informally at the pub, between the chairman, two members of R&D, and sometimes other yachtsmen whom they knew well. The initial idea was to use a digitizing table to locate the ships' position, and then accurately to plot this on to a chart clipped on above. However, the technology was considered prohibitively expensive. The idea was then put forward internally of placing mats below the charts, which were silk-screened with conductive inks to make them electronically active. This application of printing technology, implemented by a supplier, proved to be key to the innovation.

Informal input arose from two external sources, principally close yachting associates, but also boating journalists. The first prototype was tested aboard a multi-million-dollar yacht loaned by a fellow yachtsman, along with two professional navigators whom they did not know at the time. With the use of a portable computer aboard the yacht, the developers made modifications to the software as problems in usage arose at sea, and these were immediately implemented. This enabled the in-house software to be tested and refined interactively with professional users and in the context of a real environment. The second prototype was tested extensively by a network of yachtsmen they knew and trusted. This also provided direct and invaluable feedback on the features and functionality of the product, particularly in the design of the user interface. Useful feedback was also obtained from a number of boating journalists who reviewed the pre-production model of the innovation. This informal input was largely derived from the personal networks of those on the project team. While friendship was an important factor in individual relationships, it was love of yachting that gave coherence and form to the network.

Several other examples of personal networks have been uncovered from the fieldwork, based on this feeling of shared recreational interest providing informal input into the innovation process. A second example involves the development of a rucksack. In this case, the company formalized five or six of the informal personal links that existed between very experienced mountaineers and the chairman, by paying them a retainer to form a think tank. The primary role of this body was to generate product ideas. A test team was also set up, drawing a similar number of people from all walks of life, who were involved in a wide range of outdoor pursuits. This team was formed to provide independent formal feedback on prototypes. The product concept, many of the important and innovative product features, and feedback on early prototypes were thus derived from the experience of the members of the think tank and test team, and indirectly from the experience of their own personal networks of mountaineers and walkers, with whom they frequently interacted.

Profession Networks

This type of informal network comprises individuals within a given profession, such as medicine and education. The informal contribution of such a network to the innovation process is best explained by what has been termed by Freeman (1991) 'professional ethics of cooperation'. This type of informal network has been seen to be mobilized in a number of the innovations studied.

An example from this research involves a large well established company with a workforce of just over 500 and an annual turnover in excess of £50m. It has an international reputation as a leading manufacturer and supplier of science and technology teaching equipment, which accounts for roughly 40 per cent of its business. The company recently developed an innovative system for use within primary schools, for the measurement and logging of light, sound, pressure, humidity, temperature and rotation data, through the use of hand-held sensors. Following around two years of development, the product was launched in January 1990. By mid- 1992, the system had been installed in over 300 primary schools.

The product comprises three elements: the hand-held sensors, the interfacing unit (linking the sensors to the computer), and the software that operates on the computer to present the data from the sensors. The product concept was developed internally, as an attempt to capitalize on the increasing usage of computers in primary schools and changes in the national curriculum. The electronics for the sensors and the interfacing unit were also developed in-house. Formal links were established to undertake the software development, the instruction manual and the industrial design of the product.

The informal input into the development arose from within the education sector, and played an important role in defining the features and functionality of the product. The directors of the company, and the sales, marketing and R&D staff each have wide personal networks that provide bridges to different levels and specialisms within the British education system, from primary and secondary school teachers, to headmasters and school inspectors. These personal networks have developed over a number of years.

On a general level, these personal networks allowed the company to plug into the views and ideas of the education system in an informal way. More specifically, the company was able to mobilize these networks to provide ideas on the practical requirements and features of scientific equipment for use within primary schools. Since the company's experience lay largely in the secondary school market, gaining of this knowledge was crucial for the commercial success of the innovation. Primary schools tend not to have basic science equipment such as stands and clamps, which would be required to hold the sensors in experiments run over a period of time. Teachers suggested that the sensors could be held instead by Lego or Meccano, which were commonly found in primary schools. The product was subsequently altered to be compatible with both Lego and Meccano. In addition, teachers suggested that a number of the sensors should be made waterproof. This suggestion was also implemented. Informal input arose both from discussions with teachers early on in the development process and during the informal testing of the prototypes in the classroom.

Other examples of this type of informal network from the research include: doctors and physiotherapists in the development of a nerve stimulator for pain-relief; stoma-care nurses in the development of a WC-disposable colostomy bag; and clinicians in the development of an anti-cancer drug. The primary contribution of this type of network appears to be input into the features of the innovation and the choice of solution, though not the solution itself.

Scientific Networks

Individuals in this type of informal network are organized around scientific specialities, and have a distinctive set of technical and cognitive norms. This type of informal network is based on the *invisible college* of Price (1963). Such networks are created, built and nurtured on the strength of the desire of scientists and engineers to interact with others in their field, to show off their ideas, to hear about new ideas and to explore new areas of interest.

This type of network is exemplified by the case of the development of a superconducting magnet, that forms the core component of the magnetic resonance imaging (MRI) bodyscanner developed by one of its sister companies. The innovating firm is one of only a few small companies competing successfully with the giant multinationals in this research intensive field. It is part of a worldwide group of companies, whose general business is medical imaging and whose headquarters are based in Israel. The group itself is a relatively small manufacturer of MRI bodyscanners with sales of $40m, representing 20 per cent of the total group turnover. The high levels of technological innovation and quality embodied in the magnet have enabled the group to capture a niche at the top end of the MRI bodyscanner market.

There are basically three cross-linked parameters to control in the development of superconducting magnets for MRI scanners: the emission of stray magnetic fields, which cause serious interference to electronic equipment; the homogeneity of the magnetic field, which affects the clarity of the image; and the loss of liquid helium used to cool the magnets down from superconducting temperatures, which represents an expensive running cost.

In this particular project which began in 1988, the company was directed by the group marketing department to focus on the development of a homogeneous and well shielded magnet. While the innovation was designed and built in-house over a two-year period, external sources provided the critical technical know-how, ideas and background information to the development. This input was often at the level of particle physics, for example. The majority of this external input was derived informally by plugging into the international research community. With this in mind, the company had been strategically located at the centre of research activity into both superconductivity and magnet technology, with a number of international research centres of excellence close by. In addition, the analysis of patents and competitors' products also provided an input.

The R&D staff within the company each attend one or more international conference per annum, in their specialist areas, and over the years have developed wide personal networks. In the development of this innovation, such conferences have provided an invaluable forum for the informal discussion and transfer of ideas, know-how and information. The weaker ties, which form the greater part of these personal networks, tend only to be mobilized at conferences but nonetheless play a useful role in the development process. Stronger ties tend to be forged where research interests are similar and friendship is involved. These links were mobilized both within and outside the conference circuit, and although largely informal, there were occasions when the company paid consultancy fees where there was a very specific one-way flow of expertise.

Informal contributions from this type of network were seen in many of the cases investigated. Other examples include basic research input into the techniques employed in the development of software for the analysis of magnetic fields, and in the development of a diagnostic expert system for vibration analysis. The case below also provides a good illustration of a bridge providing a critical link between an innovating organization and a small scientific community. Input from this type of informal network has tended to be in the form of fundamental research, or ideas and feedback, that have provided the basis for a technical solution.

User Networks

Informal personal networks also evolve between end users of given products or technologies. This may originate from, or be reinforced by, the more formalized structure of user groups. These networks can act as mutual technical support mechanisms, as pressure groups to lobby manufacturers and innovators, and as diffusers of innovations and techniques. One would expect user groups to be more prominent among industrial users than among consumers, and this is partly reflected in the research data.

Another example from the research, involving a development by a medium-sized company which supplies a variety of services and products to the oil and petrochemical industry, serves to illustrate both informal user and scientific networks. The innovation itself provides for the online monitoring of large industrial motors, many of which are used in critical duties in oil production, petrochemicals, steel manufacture and mining. In these industries, any down-time of machinery for fault diagnosis is very expensive, but the sudden failure of these machines can have drastic repercussions. Software was thus developed to diagnose the potential failure of a motor, so that it could be fixed at the most appropriate time.

The fundamental research for this innovation was undertaken in the early 1980s by staff at a nearby university. The work was initially sponsored by a major oil company and a power-generating company. Research at the university showed that metal fractures within a motor altered the electrical current inside the machine, which was reflected back in the supply cables. It was also found that different machines and faults altered the electrical current in different ways. By monitoring the current in the supply cable, faults can thus be diagnosed while the machine is in operation.

The company became involved in 1984, following the chance meeting of one of its managers and staff at the local university, and the recognition of the wide potential application of the technique to industry. A number of external sources proved critical to the original commercialization of the product in 1987. These sources included the original developers of the technique at the university and a large American manufacturer.

The most important of these sources was the university. A close and informal relationship was formed between the academic staff and the manager of the project, who acted as a gatekeeper within the company. Through the informal cooperation of many of their existing customers, the company applied the technique to well over a thousand operational motors. Academic expertise was then drawn upon informally when anomalies arose. In this way an extensive knowledge base was built up. In 1986 a formal relationship was initiated with an American manufacturer of industrial data-collection equipment, who developed the software. Subsequent development was in-house.

The product has since been substantially enhanced. External contributions have arisen from a more formal relationship with the local university, but principally from its wide user base. Over the years, the software has been used with a vast variety of motors and combinations of motors, many of which were never envisaged by the company. This experience has been fed back informally by users and built into the product. In addition, strong informal links exist with the project team and individuals in a number of *lead users*. These users have tested beta-versions of the software and provided many product ideas. A personal network of these and other users has developed, providing informal mutual support. This network was facilitated by semi-social user group meetings organized by the company.

Other examples from the research include informal input via consumer user groups in the development of electrical tricycles for disabled and old people. This type of network was seen to be instrumental in providing informal input via the two principal product design engineers into the features of the innovation, often through feedback following extensive usage and testing of prototypes. The most important contributors appear to be *early adopters* and *lead users* (also noted by Von Hippel, 1988), and these tend to represent the most important links or bridges between the innovating organization and the user network.

Friendship Networks

This type of informal network simply refers to personal networks based on friendship. The friendship network of an individual will tend to overlay in part many of the dyadic and network relationships of that individual. The research data have revealed many instances of the mobilization of friendship networks in the innovation process. Many of the strategic links identified either evolved from friendship relations or became multi-stranded over time, as mutual friendship, trust and respect developed from more formal or causal interactions.

The illustration here is provided by a small electronics firm, founded in the mid-1970s by an intellectual property rights lawyer and an inventor. The two had initially met through their wives, who were friends, and had set up the firm to develop and commercialize the idea of using the rear-heated window of a car as a radio antenna. In 1991, some two million units were being manufactured and sold under licence. However, before the successful commercialization of the product, the company had undertaken the development work financed by small budgets, complemented by serendipity and help from informal contacts.

Early on in the project, informal advice was provided by a professor at a local university, a components supplier, and a major glass manufacturer, whom the lawyer knew had attempted something similar in the past and had contacts with from his previous job in the glass industry. Whilst the majority of the work was undertaken in-house, two external sources provided vital contributions to the technical and eventual commercial success of the innovation. The first of these was a university in Wales, which was involved in the development of the original product launched in the late 1970s. The second external source, a development engineer employed by a major international automobile manufacturer, was involved in the subsequent refinement of the device for volume production cars in the early 1980s.

The relationship with the Welsh university began informally, when a friend of one of the founders put them in contact with two professors at the university. The relationship became formalized and a contract was drawn up between the university and the company. The input to the project from these two academics was largely in the form of structuring and directing the rather haphazard but inspired work of the inventor. The academics also utilized expensive equipment within the university department to analyse the quality of the signals produced by various prototypes. Once the inventor had developed a working system, the professors were then instrumental in optimizing the design. The link with the automobile company was totally informal and friendship-based. The relationship began with a chance social meeting between a man and one of the founders. They became friends, and it transpired that he was working for a large international automobile company as a development engineer, and that he was fed up with the work he was doing. The man became interested in the work his friend was involved with concerning radio antennae and eventually persuaded his boss to cover for him while he worked on testing and fine-tuning the antenna for a new mass-market model of car. This work proved successful and the automobile company decided to adopt the product on the new model, which was launched in mid-1983.

IMPLICATIONS FOR THE MANAGEMENT OF INNOVATION

Informal networks have been shown to be a valuable mechanism through which *fresh* ideas and information filter into the innovation process, and as such, represent an important *intangible* organizational resource, which is difficult to replicate by competitors (Saxenian, 1991; Hall, 1992). However, their operation generates a number of concerns for the organization that need to be addressed. Indeed, Wolek and Griffith (1974) argue that 'this reliance is somewhat troublesome, for it is the *formal* channels which seem to be much more amenable to control and institutional *support*' and that informal channels are 'sometimes interpreted as a sign of both weakness and need for better formal systems' (pp. 411–12).

The first of these concerns involves the flow of information across the organizational boundary. Informal *boundary-spanning* networks not only provide for sourcing and acquisition of information and know-how, but also result in information *leakage*. Mansfield (1985), for example, argues that the rapid diffusion of technology via informal channels is one reason why many firms have difficulty in appropriating benefits from their innovations. Carter (1989) however, argues that 'exchangers of information do incur costs. The cost to the trader … is not the loss of the information itself, but rather the *competitive back-lash*' (p. 158).

The information transfer behaviour of an employee, therefore, can not necessarily be assumed to be in accordance with the economic interests of his or her employer. This is because the *trading* or *sharing* of information by employees, may be guided by purely personal objectives (Rogers, 1982) or even misguided, due to the insufficient availability of managerial information to enable well-informed decisions to be made (Schrader, 1991). While Hamel et al., (1989) suggest measures to restrain informal boundary-spanning activity, Schrader (1991) argues that an organization should employ mechanisms to induce desirable information transfer behaviour. This may include incentive schemes to motivate employees to act in the interests of the organization and mechanisms to diffuse information internally.

A second concern is the fragility of *bridges* between the organization and external information networks. But herein lies the paradox. Granovetter (1973) contends that bridges 'are the channels through which ideas, influences, or information socially distant from ego [a given nodal actor] may reach him' (pp. 357–8) but argues that 'all bridges are weak ties' (p. 351). Thus, by strengthening and multiplying the number of personal links between the organization and the external network, there is a danger that the *freshness* and *uniqueness* of the input from that external network will be diluted, as a result of *isomorphism*.

A third and final concern to be addressed here is the unpredictable nature of the interaction patterns within external informal networks. Carter (1989) argues that 'because know-how trading is informal and *off-the-books* such trading is difficult for the firm to evaluate and to manage' (p. 155). In addition, Kreiner and Schultz (1991), in their study of the Danish biotechnology sector, found that 'the norms governing the interaction seem to reside in the network itself rather than in any of the participating organisations' (p. 24). Two of the cases studied provide particularly interesting and novel attempts by the firm to overcome, in part, the problems of managing the behaviour of informal networks. The first of these was mentioned earlier, involving the development of an innovative rucksack. The creation of a think tank and a test team, made up of very experienced mountaineers and walkers, allowed the company to formalize and in a sense internalize part of the informal network. This set-up provided a 'bridgehead' within the network from which the organization could tap into the experience and ideas of others, informally and indirectly. A similar set-up was employed in the development of a high-speed tractor. Here a user panel was established from lead users and agricultural experts to provide the company with a blueprint for a new generation of tractor.

Allen et al., (1983) contend that 'the overwhelming dominance of personal contact in technology transfer has been replicated in study after study, yet it is consistently ignored by policy-makers' (p. 208). However, for policy makers to implement policies to encourage the informal transfer of information, they need first to have a clearer understanding of the mechanisms through which the process occurs. This research is intended to build upon our knowledge of the informal mechanisms through which ideas and information enter the innovation process. The importance of such understanding is articulated by Wolek and Griffith (1974), who argue that 'for policymakers to effect improvements and changes in the flow of information, they must have a firm understanding of the existing and desired relationships which bind groups of professionals into productive communities' (p. 420).

REFERENCES

Achilladis, B., Robertson, A. and Jervis, P. (1971), *Project SAPPHO: A Study of Success and Failure in Innovation*, 2 vols, University of Sussex: Science Policy Research Unit.

Aldrich, H. (1979), *Organisations and Environments*, Englewood Cliffs, N.J.: Prentice-Hall.

Allen, T. (1969), 'The Differential Performance of Information Channels in the Transfer of Technology', in W.H. Gruber and D.G. Marquis (eds), *Factors in the Transfer of Technology*, Mass.: MIT Press, 137–54.

Allen, T. (1977), *Managing the Flow of Technology: Technology Transfer and the Dissemination of Technological Information with the R&D Organisation*, Cambridge, Mass.: MIT Press.

Allen, T. and Cohen, S. (1969), 'Information Flow in Research and Development Laboratories', *Administrative Science Quarterly*, **14**, 199–211.

Allen, T., Hyman, D. and Pinckney, D. (1983), 'Transferring Technology to the Small Manufacturing Firm: A Study of Technology Transfer in Three Countries', *Research Policy*, **12**(2), 199–211.

Auster, E. (1990), 'The Interorganisational Environment: Network Theory, Tools and Applications', in F. Williams and D. Gibson (eds), *Technology Transfer: A Communication Perspective*, London: Sage, 63–89.

Baker, N., Siegman, J. and Rubenstein, A. (1967), 'The Effects of Perceived Needs and Means on the Generation of Ideas for Industrial Research and Development Projects', *IEEE Transactions on Engineering Management*, **EM-14**(4), 156–63.

Battelle Memorial Institute (1973), *Interactions of Science and Technology in the Innovation Process*, Final Report to the National Science Foundation, NSF-C667, Columbus, Ohio.

Bianchi, P. and Bellini, N. (1991), 'Public Policies for Local Networks of Innovators', *Research Policy*, **20**(5), 487–97.

Boissevain, J. (1974), *Friends of Friends: Networks, Manipulators and Coalitions*, Oxford: Basil Blackwell.

Burns, T. (1969), 'Models, Images and Myths' in W.H. Gruber and D.G. Marquis (eds), *Factors in the Transfer of Technology*, Cambridge, Mass.: MIT Press, 11–23.

Carter, A.P. (1989), 'Knowhow Trading as Economic Exchange', *Research Policy*, **18**, 155–63.

Cohen, W. and Levinthal, D. (1989), 'Innovation and Learning: The Two Faces of R&D', *The Economic Journal*, **99**, 569–96.

Collins, H.M. (1982), 'Tacit Knowledge and Scientific Networks' in B. Barnes and D. Edge (eds), *Science in Context: Readings in the Sociology of Science*, Cambridge, Mass.: MIT Press, 44–64.

Cunningham, M. and Homse, E. (1984), 'The Role of Personal Contacts in Supplier–Customer Relationships', Occasional Paper No. 8410, UMIST, Manchester.

DeBresson, C. and Amesse, F. (1991), 'Networks of Innovators: A Review and Introduction to the Issue', *Research Policy*, **20**, 363–79.

DiMaggio, P. and Powell, W. (1991), 'The Iron Cage Revisited: Institutional Isomorphism and Collective Rationality in Organisational Fields' in W. Powell and P. DiMaggio (eds), *The New Institutionalism in Organisational Analysis*, Chicago: University of Chicago Press, 63–82.

Easingwood, C. (1986), 'New Product Development for Service Companies', *Journal of Product Innovation Management*, **3**(4), 264–75.

Federation of British Industries (1961), *Industrial Research in Manufacturing Industry*, London: FBI and NIESR.

Fombrun, C. J. (1982), 'Strategies for Network Research in Organisations', *Academy of Management Review*, **7**(2), 280–91.

Freeman, C. (1991), 'Networks of Innovators: A Synthesis of Research Issues', *Research Policy*, **20**(5), 499–514.

Gambardella, A. (1992), 'Competitive Advantages from In-house Scientific Research: The US Pharmaceutical Industry in the 1980s', *Research Policy*, **21**(5), 391–407.

Gibbons, M. and Johnston, R. (1974), 'The Roles of Science in Technological Innovation', *Research Policy*, **3**(3), 220–42.

Granovetter, M. (1973), 'The Strength of Weak Ties', *American Journal of Sociology*, **78**, 1360–80.

Hagedoorn, J. and Schakenraad, J. (1992), 'Leading Companies and Networks of Strategic Alliances in Information Technologies', *Research Policy*, **21**(2), 163–90.

Håkansson, H. (1989), *Corporate Technological Behaviour: Co-operation and Networks*, London: Routledge.

Hall, R. (1992), 'The Strategic Analysis of Intangible Resources', *Strategic Management Journal*, **13**(2), 135–44.

Hamel, G., Doz, Y. and Prahalad, C. (1989), 'Collaborate with Your Competitors – and Win', *Harvard Business Review*, **67**(1), 133–9.

Illinois Institute of Technology (1968), *Technology in Retrospect and Critical Events in Science*, Report to the National Science Foundation, NSF-C235.

Jewkes, J., Sawers, D. and Stillerman, R. (1969), *The Sources of Invention*, 2nd edn, London: Macmillan.

Kreiner, K. and Schultz, M. (1991), *Crossing the Institutional Divide: Networking in Biotechnology*, Paper presented at the 10th International Conference 'Strategic Bridging to Meet the Challenge of the 1990s', Stockholm, September.

Langrish, J., Gibbons, M., Evans, W. and Jevons, F. (1972), *Wealth From Knowledge: A Study of Innovation in Industry*, London: Macmillan.

Laumann, E. and Pappi, F. (1976), *Networks of Collective Action*, London: Academic Press.

Lewis, M. (1948), *Language in Society: The Linguistic Revolution and Social Change*, New York: Social Science Publishers, cited by Tushman and Katz, (1980).

Liu, W. and Duff, R. (1972), 'The Strength in Weak-Ties', *Public Opinion Quarterly*, **36**(3), 361–6.

Lundvall, B.-A. (1988), 'Innovation as an Interactive Process: From User–Producer Interaction to the National System of Innovation' in G. Dosi et al., (eds), *Technical Change and Economic Theory*, London: Pinter.

Macaulay, S. (1963), 'Non-Contractual Relations in Business: A Preliminary Study', *American Sociological Review*, **28**, 55–67.

Mansfield, E. (1985), 'How Rapidly Does New Industrial Technology Leak Out?', *Journal of Industrial Economics*, **34**, 217–23.

Mitchell, J.C. (1969), 'The Concept and Use of Social Networks' in J.C. Mitchell (ed.), *Social Networks in Urban Situations*, Manchester: Manchester University Press, 31–50.

Myers, S. and Marquis, D. (1969), *Successful Commercial Innovations*, Washington D.C.: National Science Foundation.

Pavitt, K. (1991), 'What Makes Basic Research Economically Useful?', *Research Policy*, **20**, 109–19.

Price, D.J. De Solla (1963), *Little Science. Big Science*, New York: Columbia University Press.

Price, D.J. De Solla (1969), 'The Structures of Publication in Science and Technology' in W.H. Gruber and D.G. Marquis (eds), *Factors in the Transfer of Technology*, Cambridge, Mass.: MIT Press, 91–104.

Roberts, E. and Wainer, H. (1971), 'Some Characteristics of Technical Entrepreneurs', *IEEE Transactions on Engineering Management*, **EM-18**(3).

Rogers, E. (1982), 'Information Exchange and Technological Innovation' in D. Sahal, (ed.), *The Transfer and Utilisation of Technical Knowledge*, Lexington, Mass.: Lexington Books, 105–23.

Rogers, E. (1987), 'Progress. Problems and Prospects for Network Research: Investigating Relationships in the Age of Electronic Communication Technologies', Paper presented at the VII Sunbelt Social Networks Conference, Florida, February.

Rogers, E. and Bhowmik, D.K. (1971), 'Homophily-Heterophiiy: Relational Concepts for Communication Research', *Public Opinion Quarterly*, **34**, 523–38.

Rogers, E. and Kincaid, D.L. (1981), *Communication Networks*, New York: Free Press.

Rogers, E. and Shoemaker, R. (1972), *Communication of Innovations*, New York: Free Press.

Rosenberg, N. (1990), 'Why Do Firms Do Basic Research (With Their Own Money)?', *Research Policy*, **19**, 165–74.

Rothwell, R. (1986), 'Innovation and Re-Innovation: A Role for the User', *Journal of Marketing Management*, **2**(2), 109–23.

Rothwell, R., Freeman, C., Horsley, A., Jervis, P., Robertson, A., and Townsend, J. (1974), 'SAPPHO Updated – Project SAPPHO Phase II', *Research Policy*, **3**(3), 258–91.

Rothwell, R. and Dodgson, M. (1991), 'External Linkages and Innovation in Small and Medium-Sized Enterprises', *R&D Management*, **21**(2), 125–37.

Saxenian, A.L. (1991), 'The Origins and Dynamics of Production Networks in the Silicon Valley', *Research Policy*, **20**(5), 423–37.

Schrader, S. (1991), 'Informal Technology Transfer Between Firms: Co-operation Through Information Trading', *Research Policy*, **20**(2), 153–70.

Senker, J. (1993), 'The Contribution of Tacit Knowledge to Innovation', Paper presented at the 'Exploring Expertise' Workshop, University of Edinburgh, November.

Senker, J. and Faulkner, W. (1993), 'Networks. Tacit Knowledge and Innovation', Chapter 5, this volume.

Shaw, B. (1985), 'The Role of the Interaction Between the User and the Manufacturer in Medical Equipment Innovation', *R&D Management*, **15**(4), 283–92.

Sherwin, E. and Isenson, R. (1967), 'Project Hindsight', *Science*, **156**, 1571–7.

Smith, H., Dickson, K. and Smith, S. (1991), 'There are Two Sides to Every Story: Innovation and Collaboration within Networks of Large and Small Firms', *Research Policy*, **20**, 457–68.

Spital, F. (1979), 'An Analysis of the Role of Users in the Total R&D Portfolios of Scientific Instrument Firms', *Research Policy*, **8**(3), 284–96.

Tichy, N., Tushman, M. and Fombrun, C. (1979), 'Social Network Analysis For Organisations', *Academy of Management Review*, **4**(4), 507–19.

Tushman, M.L. (1977), 'Communication Across Organisational Boundaries: Special Boundary Roles in the Innovation Process', *Administrative Science Quarterly*, **22**, 587–605.

Tushman, M. and Katz, R. (1980), 'External Communication and Project Performance: An Investigation into the Role of Gatekeepers', *Management Science*, **26**(11), 1071–85.

Udell, G. (1990), 'It's Still Caveat, Inventor', *Journal of Product Innovation Management*, **7**(3), 220–43.

Utterback, J.M. (1971), 'The Process of Innovation: A Study of the Origination and Development of Ideas for Scientific Instruments', *IEEE Transactions on Engineering Management*, **EM-18**(4), 124–31.

Vanderwerf, P. (1990), 'Product Tying and Innovation in US Wire Preparation Equipment', *Research Policy*, **19**(1), 83–96.

Von Hippel, E. (1976), 'The Dominant Role of Users in the Scientific Instrument Innovation Process', *Research Policy*, 5(3), 212–39.

Von Hippel, E. (1977a), 'The Dominant Role of the User in Semi-Conductor and Electronic Sub-Assembly Process Innovation', *IEEE Transactions on Engineering Management*, **EM-24**(2), 60–71.

Von Hippel, E. (1977b) 'Transferring Process Equipment Innovations From User-Innovators to Equipment Manufacturing Firms', *R&D Management*, **8**(1), 13–22.

Von Hippel, E. (1987), 'Co-operation Between Rivals: Informal Know-how Trading', *Research Policy*, **16**(4), 291–302.

Von Hippel, E. (1988), 'The Sources of Innovation', New York: Oxford University Press.

Weick, K. (1976), 'Educational Organisations as Loosely Coupled Systems', *Administrative Science Quarterly*, **21**, 1–19.

Whalley, P. (1991), 'The Social Practice of Independent Inventing', *Science, Technology and Human Values*, **16**(2), 208–32.

Wolek, F. and Griffith, B. (1974), 'Policy and Informal Communications in Applied Science and Technology', *Science Studies*, **4**, 411–20.

Index